'This is interfaith dialogue at its best. Netla[...] standing of Buddhism, followed by a car[...] Buddhism, followed by a constructive summ[...] and Buddhism. They also succeed in establishing the plausibility of Christianity in the light of various possible Buddhist critiques. No reader, Christian or Buddhist, will be left unchallenged by this lucid exposition, critique, and proclamation.'

Gavin D'Costa, Professor of Christian Theology, Bristol University, UK

'This is a book which we have been waiting a long time to see. It is a well written, constructive, and thorough treatment of Buddhism which demonstrates Netland's and Yandell's extensive experience with both the teachings of Buddhism, as well as the popular, lived faith of Buddhists. It provides an excellent survey of the spread of Buddhism in the ancient East as well as in the contemporary West, always keeping in mind the philosophical nuances of Buddhism as well as the popular, folk practices of Buddhists in their global and ethnic diversity. In a day when the search for common ground has often eclipsed the real and striking differences between the living faith of Buddhists and Christians, this book clearly sets forth the distinctiveness of the Christian faith vis a vis Buddhim, but does it in a refreshingly irenic way. The authors highlight common ground where it exists, but they are equally clear about the differences in each faith's understanding of the religious ultimate, the human predicament and the ways to overcome this. This volume regularly inspires and informs the reader. It is a must-read for all people who are seriously interested in the Buddhist-Christian encounter. I highly recommend it!'

Timothy C. Tennent, Professor of World Missions and Indian Studies, Gordon-Conwell Theological Seminary, USA

'This book has two considerable virtues. The first is that it takes with respectful seriousness what Buddhists and Christians claim about the way the world is and how human beings are. Yandell and Netland are abundantly clear about the important agreements and differences between the two traditions. The second is that it is interested in whether these claims might be true, and with that in mind offers clear and interesting arguments about what they assume and imply. Either virtue suffices to make the book worth reading; the presence of both makes it essential.'

Paul J. Griffiths, Warren Chair of Catholic Theology, Duke Divinity School, USA

'At last we have a book that moves beyond the inaccurate, rather imprecise and sentimental level of so many books about Buddhism and the Christian-Buddhist encounter, and focuses on a serious consideration of Buddhist truth-claims. The opening chapters give an acceptable first survey of Buddhism, and include material on dimensions of Buddhism, such as the 'Personalist' school or the historical context for the introduction of some rather idiosyncratic forms of Japanese Zen into the West, that are often neglected in popular introductions. It gives enough detail on Buddhist doctrines for one new to the subject to understand what the issues are and engage in a critical yet respectful manner with them. At many points this clearly written and readable book corrects, from the point of view of Buddhism as it has existed in history and in its Asian context, common Western misperceptions of Buddhism. But the really exciting section of this book is the philosophical analysis of key Buddhist doctrines such as not-Self and momentariness. Netland and Yandell take Buddhist truth-claims seriously, as Buddhists ask us to do, and in their analysis of those claims they make a truly original contribution, pitched at an accessible yet refined level of philosophical sophistication and knowledge of Buddhist doctrines and debates. The book throws down a challenge to Buddhists to clarify what they mean when they make their claims, and to enter into debate in defence of their truth. This philosophical analysis is followed by an outline of some absolutely fundamental differences between Christianity and Buddhism, and Christ and the Buddha. Here we see the basis of a critical Christian theological engagement with Buddhism as a religion. The book challenges Christians to move beyond polite smalltalk, or minimalising of essential differences that demand choice and commitment, and engage with Buddhists in debating their mutually incompatible claims to (as the Buddhists put it) "see things the way they really are" regarding God, Jesus Christ, personhood and our meaning, purpose and destiny. This book shows us (to use another Buddhist expression) "analytical meditation" at its finest. It is an exciting book that I shall certainly use and recommend to my students. For those Christians and Buddhists who take truth seriously, and understand the significance of reasoning in making crucial choices, Netland and Yandell's book will contribute significantly to setting the agenda for serious dialogue between Christianity and Buddhism for some time to come.'

Paul Williams, Codirector, Centre for Buddhist Studies, University of Bristol, UK

'Yandell and Netland have produced a brilliant, clear, engaging introduction to Buddhism that is both sympathetic and critical, highlighting points of convergence and divergence from Christianity. Their book would be excellent in university courses in philosophy of religion or religious studies, but it would also reward general readers interested in finding both a reliable philosophical guide to Buddhism as well an exploration of Buddhist teaching in relation to Christian faith.'

Charles Taliaferro, Professor of Philosophy, St. Olaf College, USA

'Keith Yandell and Harold Netland accomplish several important things in this concise work: (1) they authoritatively summarize Buddhist history; (2) they systematically outline Buddhist teachings; and (3) they clearly compare and contrast Buddhism with Christianity. A unique resource for Christians interested in Buddhism and Buddhist-Christian relationships.'

Terry Muck, Professor of Missions and World Religions, Asbury Seminary, USA

'While in recent years Evangelicals have finally engaged the question of the theology of religions, there are very few Evangelicals equipped to do what Professor Netland, himself a leading theologian of religions, and Professor Yandell, a distinguished philosopher, have produced; namely an informed and incisive engagement of a particular religion from an Evangelical perspective. This book not only contains valuable lessons both from Buddhism as a religion and the Buddhist–Christian encounter but also serves as a paradigm for later works: a careful mapping out of the key ideas of a living faith and a sympathetic, yet unapologetic critique from a Christian perspective. For sure, I will include this book as a text in my courses in World Religions.'

Veli-Matti Kärkkäinen, Professor of Systematic Theology, Fuller Theological Seminary, USA and Docent of Ecumenics, University of Helsinki, Finland

'Yandell and Netland present an extraordinarily lucid and accessible account of Buddhist thought that simultaneously recognizes and preserves its nuanced complexity. The first half recounts the development of Buddhism from its birth in northern India to its modern day embracement by those in the West seeking an alternative spirituality. In the second part they carefully and critically examine the cogency of central Buddhist doctrines, particularly the view of the persons that underlies the Buddhist doctrines of suffering, karma and rebirth, and liberation to nirvana. Those who adopt the current mantra that all religions are ultimately alike, that Buddhism and Christianity do not differ, that the Buddha and Jesus were historically interchangeable, will be seriously challenged by the way the authors meticulously deconstruct the pluralist view.'

Bruce R. Reichenbach, Professor of Philosophy, Augsburg College, USA

Buddhism

A Christian Exploration and Appraisal

Keith Yandell *and* Harold Netland

IVP Academic
An imprint of InterVarsity Press
Downers Grove, Illinois

InterVarsity Press
P.O. Box 1400, Downers Grove, IL 60515-1426
Internet: www.ivpress.com
E-mail: email@ivpress.com

InterVarsity Press® is the book-publishing division of InterVarsity Christian Fellowship/USA®, a movement of students and faculty active on campus at hundreds of universities, colleges and schools of nursing in the United States of America, and a member movement of the International Fellowship of Evangelical Students. For information about local and regional activities, write Public Relations Dept., InterVarsity Christian Fellowship/USA, 6400 Schroeder Rd., P.O. Box 7895, Madison, WI 53707-7895, or visit the IVCF website at <www.intervarsity.org>.

All Scripture quotations, unless otherwise indicated, are taken from the Holy Bible, New International Version®. NIV®. Copyright ©1973, 1978, 1984 by International Bible Society. Used by permission of Hodder and Stoughton Ltd. All rights reserved. "NIV" is a registered trademark of International Bible Society. UK trademark number 1448790. Distributed in North America by permission of Zondervan Publishing House.

ISBN 978-0-8308-3855-4

Printed in the United States of America ∞

 InterVarsity Press is committed to protecting the environment and to the responsible use of natural resources. As a member of Green Press Initiative we use recycled paper whenever possible. To learn more about the Green Press Initiative, visit <www.greenpressinitiative.org>.

Library of Congress Cataloging-in-Publication Data

Netland, Harold A., 1955-
  Buddhism: a Christian exploration and appraisal / Harold Netland
  and Keith Yandell.
      p. cm.
  Includes bibliographical references and index.
  ISBN 978-0-8308-3855-4 (pbk.: alk. paper)
  1. Christianity and other religions—Buddhism. I. Yandell, Keith
E., 1938- II. Title.
  BR128.B8N38 2009
  261.2'43—dc22

                                                                2009011682

| P | 21 | 20 | 19 | 18 | 17 | 16 | 15 | 14 | 13 | 12 | 11 | 10 | 9 | 8 | 7 | 6 | 5 | 4 | 3 | 2 |
| Y | 21 | 20 | 21 | 20 | 21 | 20 | 21 | 20 | 19 | 18 | 17 | 16 | 15 | 14 | 13 | 12 | | | | |

Contents

Introduction   vii

1. Early Buddhism   1

   Background to Early Buddhism   1
   Gautama the Buddha   9
   Teachings of the Buddha   14
   The Four Noble Truths   15
   Impermanence and No-self   18
   Nirvana   22
   The Growth of Buddhism   26
   Theravada Buddhism   26

2. The Dharma Goes East   33

   Mahayana Buddhism   33
   Mahayana Literature   38
   The Bodhisattva Ideal   40
   Nagarjuna and Emptiness   42
   The Buddha Nature   47
   Pure Land Buddhism   49
   Zen Buddhism   56
   Vajrayana and Tibetan Buddhism   62
   Tibetan Buddhism   64

3. The Dharma Comes West   69

   The World's Parliament of Religions   72
   Buddhism in America   75

Orientalism   80
D.T. Suzuki and Zen   83
Masao Abe   95

4. Aspects of Buddhist Doctrine   105

Religious Exclusivism   106
Buddhist Doctrine and Truth   111
Rebirth and Karma   117
Impermanence, No-self and Dependent
    Co-origination   121
Appearances and Reality   128
Dependent Co-origination and Determination   131
Conscious States   136
Enlightenment and Nirvana   141

5. Some Buddhist Schools and Issues   145

Personalism   147
Action, Karma and Rebirth   150
Rebirth and Karma Fine-Tuned   151
Memory   152
Seeking and Finding Enlightenment   153
Interpretations of Madhyamaka: Nihilism   157
Interpretations of Madhyamaka: Absolutism   161
Interpretations of Madhyamaka: Ineffabilism   161
Buddhist Reductionism   166

6. The Dharma or the Gospel?   175

The Gospel and the Dharma   177
God   181
Jesus   192
Conclusion   211

Bibliography   213

Index   227

Introduction

A century ago it was not unusual to find social theorists who confidently claimed that the relentless drive of modernization – fueled by technology, science, and education – would eventually eliminate the need for religion. The various religions would simply wither away. Yet the world today remains highly religious, and it is religious in some surprising ways.

Whereas the twentieth century dawned with Christianity still culturally and religiously dominant in Europe, with the advent of the twenty-first century we see significant shifts in the religious demographics of the West. In 1800 Christians were found primarily in Europe, with newly formed Christian communities increasingly springing up in the Americas and Asia. The link between Christian identity, geography, and culture was so strong that, in the eyes of many, to be European was to be Christian. During the past century, however, much of Europe has experienced a decline in both the number of Christians and the social significance of Christianity. Much of Europe is now culturally and religiously 'post-Christian.'

The decline of Christianity in parts of the West has been accompanied by the dramatic growth of the Christian church in much of Africa, Asia, and Latin America. There are now far more Christians outside the West than in Europe and North America. Harvey Cox observes that 'Sometime around 1970 the demographic center of Christianity shifted. Since then the majority of the world's 2 billion Christians are no longer to be found in old European and North American precincts of Christendom but in Asia, Africa, and South America. It is startling to realize

that the two largest Christian countries in the world, after the
United States, are Brazil and Mexico (with Russia and China close
behind).'[1] Reflecting upon the surprising change in demographics
of Christianity worldwide, historian Philip Jenkins states, 'We are
currently living through one of the transforming moments in the
history of religion worldwide.'[2]

But the changes are not only to be found in Christianity.
Buddhism too is undergoing transformation as it moves from
its traditional homeland in Asia into European, Australian, and
North American contexts. In so doing, Buddhism is rapidly
establishing itself as a viable alternative to traditional religion
for many in the West. It is not accidental that the Western
fascination with Buddhism coincides with Christianity's loss
of its position of religious dominance in Europe.[3] While the
actual number of Buddhists in the United States remains
comparatively small – perhaps around 4 million Buddhists in
the US[4] – Buddhism exerts an influence disproportionate to the
number of adherents, as many American Buddhists are found in
culturally influential sectors such as education, entertainment,
and the media.

The growing attraction of Buddhism is both a product
of and a contributing factor to the wider social and cultural

----

[1] Harvey Cox, 'Christianity,' in *Global Religions: An Introduction*, ed. Mark
Juergensmeyer (New York: Oxford University Press, 2003), p. 17.

[2] Philip Jenkins, *The Next Christendom: The Coming of Global Christianity* (New
York: Oxford University Press, 2002), p. 1.

[3] See James William Coleman, *The New Buddhism: The Western Transformation
of an Ancient Tradition* (New York: Oxford University Press, 2001); *Buddhism
in the Modern World*, eds. Steven Heine and Charles S. Prebish (New York:
Oxford University Press, 2003); *Westward Dharma: Buddhism Beyond Asia*,
eds. Charles S. Prebish and Martin Baumann (Berkeley, CA: University of
California Press, 2002); Richard Hughes Seager, *Buddhism in America* (New
York: Columbia University Press, 1999); Charles S. Prebish, *Luminous Passage:
the Practice and Study of Buddhism in America* (Berkeley, CA: University of
California Press, 1999).

[4] See Seager, *Buddhism in America*, p. 11; and Robert Wuthnow and Wendy
Cage, 'Buddhists and Buddhism in the United States: The Scope and
Influence,' *Journal for the Scientific Study of Religion*, 43:3 (2004), pp. 363–80.

transformations of religion in the West. The past half-century has witnessed enormous changes, brought about in part by increased immigration from Asia resulting in growing religious diversity. Further changes stem from the increased secularization of much of Europe and Canada, which has resulted in a deep skepticism about traditional Christian claims, as well as a rejection of institutional religion in favor of personal experience and alternative religious traditions – as reflected in the move away from 'religion' and toward 'spirituality,' and so on.[5]

Richard Hughes Seager suggests that American Buddhism comprises three distinct groups – the Buddhism of nineteenth-century Chinese and Japanese immigrants, the Euro-American Buddhism of non-Asian converts to Buddhism, and the ethnic Buddhism of Asian immigrants who came after the 1965 immigration reform legislation.[6] For many immigrant communities Buddhism provides continuity with ethnic and cultural patterns in the old world; others in the West find in Buddhism an attractive alternative to established religious and cultural traditions.[7] The Buddha offers many a vision of inner peace and tranquillity in an age marked by high stress, rampant materialism, and consumerism. For many in the West, Buddhism seems to promise a spirituality and serenity that enables one to transcend the

---

[5] On the impact of such transformations on religion, and the increased openness to alternative religions such as Buddhism, see Amanda Porterfield, *The Transformation of American Religion: The Story of a Late Twentieth Century Awakening* (New York: Oxford University Press, 2001); Wade Clark Roof, *Spiritual Marketplace: Baby Boomers and the Remaking of American Religion* (Princeton, NJ: Princeton University Press, 1999); Robert Wuthnow, *After Heaven: Spirituality in America Since the 1950s* (Berkeley, CA: University of California Press, 1998) and *America and the Challenges of Religious Diversity* (Princeton, NJ: Princeton University Press, 2005); Diana Eck, *A New Religious America: How A 'Christian Country' Has Become the World's Most Religiously Diverse Nation* (New York: HarperCollins, 2001); Paul Heelas and Linda Woodhead et al., *The Spiritual Revolution: Why Religion is Giving Way to Spirituality* (Oxford: Blackwell, 2005).
[6] Richard Hughes Seager, 'American Buddhism in the Making,' in *Westward Dharma*, pp. 106–19. See also idem, *Buddhism in America*, chapter 1.
[7] See *Why Buddhism? Westerners in Search of Wisdom*, ed. Vicki Mackenzie (London: Element, 2002).

pressures of modern life, but without the ecclesiastical structures, dogma, and authoritarianism of traditional Western Christianity. In particular, since Buddhism does not teach the existence of an almighty creator God, it offers the prospect of deep spirituality without having to bother with God.

Part of the attraction of Buddhism is also due to the perception that the Buddha and Jesus were not all that different and that Christianity and Buddhism are just two complementary ways of approaching spiritual truth. Thus, it is said, one can remain firmly committed to one's own tradition while also borrowing extensively from the other – or, better yet, one can be both Christian and Buddhist simultaneously since there is no inherent incompatibility between these religious paths.[8]

To be sure, Christianity and Buddhism do have some similarities, and there is much to be gained by both Christians and Buddhists from listening carefully to the other. In a fragmented world in which – all too often – religion is used to sanction injustice and violence, it is crucial that we find ways to bridge differences and work for peace. Surely Jesus and the Buddha would expect no less from their followers. Nonetheless, a great deal of what Christianity and Buddhism share is rather abstract and can be expressed negatively. For example, Buddhism and Christianity share the following convictions:

- This life is not all that there is.
- Whatever can be lost is not of ultimate value.
- Not everything that exists is physical.
- Possession of great wealth and power is ultimately unfulfilling.

---

[8] On some of the issues here see, for example, John B. Cobb, Jr., 'Can a Christian Be a Buddhist, Too?' *Japanese Religions* 10 (December 1978), pp. 1–20; and *Beyond Dialogue: Toward a Mutual Transformation of Christianity and Buddhism* (Philadelphia, PA: Fortress Press, 1982); Paul O. Ingram, 'On the Practice of Faith: A Lutheran's Interior Dialogue With Buddhism,' *Buddhist-Christian Studies* 21 (2001), pp. 43–50; *Buddhist-Christian Dialogue: Mutual Renewal and Transformation*, eds. Paul O. Ingram and Frederick J. Streng (Honolulu, HI: University of Hawaii Press, 1986); and William Johnston, *Christian Zen* (New York: Harper Colophon, 1971).

- Always placing oneself above all others is wrong.
- It is bad to be a slave to one's passions.

Yet, although both Buddhism and Christianity call for denial of the self, 'denying the self' means something quite different in a Christian context than it does in a Buddhist context. Similarly, having one's religious illness cured requires very different things in the one tradition than it does in the other.

Thus, even as we acknowledge areas of common ground and the need for respectful cooperation, honesty demands that we recognize the basic differences between the two visions of reality and how we are to live. Christianity affirms the existence of an eternal, omnipotent creator God. Buddhism denies this. Christianity maintains that in Jesus of Nazareth the eternal God became incarnate, and thus that Jesus Christ is fully God and fully human. There is nothing like this in Buddhism. Christian metaphysics entails the reality of individual souls or selves. Buddhism has traditionally denied this. Buddhism locates the source of suffering and problems in our world in desire/craving and ignorance. Christian faith claims that it is not ignorance but rather sin against a holy and righteous God that is the root of all of our problems. And so on.

Religions and Belief

In highlighting some differences between Christianity and Buddhism above, we provided examples of differences in the two religions' *beliefs*. Some, however, will object that focusing upon beliefs in this manner is to misconstrue what religions are all about. Religions, we are told, are ways of life and should not be understood in terms of truth claims. Many of those in the West who are attracted to Buddhism are not primarily interested in its metaphysical claims but rather in the practical benefits that accompany meditation and a Buddhist way of life. Buddhism seems, for many, to be a form of spiritual therapy that can be embraced quite apart from accepting the particular doctrines Buddhism traditionally has advanced.[9]

There is, of course, much more to a given religion than simply beliefs or doctrines. Religions, as we experience them, are multidimensional and highly complex phenomena. Ninian Smart emphasized this, suggesting seven dimensions for understanding any given religion.[10] These include the *ritual* and the *mythological* or *narrative* dimensions. Narratives that shape the Christian understanding of God and his dealings with humankind are central to the Christian Bible. Similarly, the Buddhist writings contain many stories about the Buddha and his followers which have guided Buddhists throughout the centuries. Moreover, as we shall see in later chapters, Christianity and Buddhism both exemplify the significance of the *doctrinal* or *philosophical dimension*. Doctrines can be thought of as systematic attempts to clarify and integrate the central beliefs of a religious tradition. Both Christianity and Buddhism include the *ethical* dimension, with moral teachings that bear directly upon the manner in which the believer is to live his or her life. The *social* and *institutional dimension* reflects patterns and mores dictating desirable relationships among the believers in the religious community, as well as the institutions that provide necessary structure and organization to the tradition. The *experiential dimension* involves the participation of the religious believer in the various rites and patterns of the religious tradition (e.g. through worship, prayer, meditation, etc.). Finally, the *material dimension* refers to the many visible or material objects – religious art, icons, buildings, gardens, instruments to help in worship, etc. – which express religious meanings or otherwise facilitate the practice of religion.

It is also important to distinguish between what is often called formal or 'high' religion and 'folk' religion.[11] Formal religion

---

[9] This seems to be the position of Stephen Batchelor, *Buddhism Without Beliefs: A Contemporary Guide to Awakening* (New York: Riverhead Books, 1997).

[10] See Ninian Smart, *The World's Religions*, 2nd edn. (Cambridge: Cambridge University Press, 1998), pp. 11–22; and *Worldviews: Crosscultural Explorations of Human Beliefs*, 2nd edn. (Englewood Cliffs, NJ: Prentice Hall, 1995).

[11] See Paul G. Hiebert, R. Daniel Shaw, and Tite Tiénou, *Understanding Folk Religion* (Grand Rapids, MI: Baker, 1999).

refers to the official teachings and practices of a given religious tradition – the institutions, beliefs, and practices enjoined by the sacred scriptures and official authorities of the religion. Formal religions generally have carefully prescribed boundaries to protect the orthodoxy of the traditions, and considerable attention is given to interpreting implications of doctrine for proper living and for understanding the world around us.

Folk religion, by contrast, refers to the religious beliefs and practices of people not particularly interested in a systematic understanding of a religion. Folk religion is often animistic, acknowledging a complex realm of spirits and demons, and emphasizes the practical, existential concerns of everyday life (health, power, marriage, bountiful harvest, fear of death, the afterlife, the spirits, etc.). Folk practices are often at variance with the official teachings of high religion. A genuinely comprehensive understanding of any given religion will include appreciation of all seven dimensions as well as both high and folk religion.

While it is important to recognize the multi-dimensional nature of religion, we cannot minimize the central place of beliefs in religion – including Buddhism. For Buddhist communities (like all religious communities) characteristically teach their members to live in a certain way and to regard all of life from a particular perspective, which is rooted in particular beliefs about the cosmos and humankind's place within the cosmos.[12] It is true that each religious tradition demands from its adherents a particular religious 'way of life.' But sustaining this way of life are fundamental assumptions about the nature of the cosmos, the religious ultimate, the human predicament, and the possibility of deliverance from this predicament. Ninian Smart reminds us that 'the world religions owe some of their living power to their success in presenting a total picture of reality, through a coherent system of doctrines.'[13] These beliefs, particularly those concerning the religious ultimate and its relation to human beings, are what William Christian calls the *primary doctrines* of a religious

---

[12] See William A. Christian, Sr., *Doctrines of Religious Communities: A Philosophical Study* (New Haven, CT: Yale University Press, 1987), p. 5.
[13] Ninian Smart, *The Religious Experience of Mankind*, p. 8.

community.[14] We might also think of them as *defining beliefs* of a given religious tradition, in that they define the acceptable parameters of that tradition, and help to determine the nature of the other dimensions – ritual, ethical, experiential, etc. – of the tradition.

A religion proposes a diagnosis of a deep, crippling spiritual disease universal to non-divine sentience and offers a cure. A particular religion is true if its diagnosis is correct and its cure efficacious. The diagnosis and cure are embedded within a set of beliefs about reality which are accepted by the religious believers as true.[15] Religious communities typically expect their members to embrace the primary doctrines, and doing so involves, among other things, taking what is asserted by the doctrines as true. Thus, the fundamental assumptions about reality, which define the worldview of a given religious community are accepted – at least implicitly – by that community as true. In other words, while we can readily admit that there is much more to Buddhism than simply its beliefs or doctrines, it is important to recognize that the basic beliefs defining a Buddhist worldview have traditionally been accepted by Buddhists as true.

This book concerns some of the central teachings of Buddhism, as understood by the early Buddhist community and as they have developed in Asia over the course of two millennia. Buddhism makes significant claims about what is real, the nature of persons, life and death, and what is religiously ultimate. It is important for Westerners who are attracted to Buddhism to understand the nature of these assertions. Buddhist claims raise a host of interesting and controversial philosophical issues which deserve careful analysis and response. It is our contention that, whatever other merits Buddhism might have, some of its central beliefs are deeply problematic and should be rejected.

---

[14] William A. Christian, *Doctrines of Religious Communities*, pp. 1–2, 5–11.
[15] Keith Yandell, 'How to Sink in Cognitive Quicksand: Nuancing Religious Pluralism,' in *Contemporary Debates in Philosophy of Religion*, eds. Michael L. Peterson and Raymond J. VanArragon (Oxford: Blackwell Publishing, 2004), p. 191.

This book, then, is part of a genre sometimes known as inter-religious polemics or interreligious apologetics. In spite of the importance of religious beliefs, and the conflicting claims to truth put forward by various religions, interreligious polemics strikes many today as inappropriate. Many object that in a world torn apart by prejudice, hatred, and violence surely the religions should focus less upon what divides them and work together to address the many problems confronting humankind. There is some truth in this objection. There is far too much religious conflict in our world and religious leaders, along with others, have an obligation to promote mutual respect and appropriate forms of tolerance. All of this is readily accepted.

But none of this precludes a rigorous assessment of the basic claims of various religions.[16] Indeed, one might well argue that to engage the views of another religion in respectful but rigorous analysis is to take that religion more seriously than is the case when we ignore fundamental differences out of a desire not to cause offence. Religions deal with ultimate matters – questions of life and death, human origins and destiny, the nature of the human predicament, and the proper way to alleviate the problems of our world. To refuse to engage the central issues of sharp disagreement is actually to trivialize the religions.

Furthermore, there is no necessary connection between holding the beliefs of a particular group to be false or unjustified and treating members of that group inappropriately. Certainly one can consider the beliefs of another to be false and yet treat that person with dignity and respect. For to deny this is to suggest that we can only respect and treat properly those with whom we happen to agree. To the contrary, is it not rather a mark of maturity to be able to live peaceably and cooperate with, and act properly toward, those with whom we might profoundly disagree? Being tolerant of others in different religious traditions, then, does not entail simply accepting their beliefs uncritically, or even the refusal to make any judgment about the content of their basic beliefs. It

---

[16] On this and related issues Paul J. Griffiths, *An Apology for Apologetics: A Study in the Logic of Interreligious Dialogue* (Maryknoll, NY: Orbis Books, 1991).

is perfectly compatible with holding that at least some of their beliefs are false.

Some object that interreligious polemics, or the attempt to argue against the truth of other religious traditions and for the truth of one's own perspective, is simply a modern Western concern that is not shared by the great Asian traditions. Buddhism and Hinduism, in particular, are frequently thought of as highly inclusive and tolerant religions which do not reject other religious perspectives. But this is seriously misleading. Not only have there been vigorous, and at times vicious, debates among competing schools *within* Hinduism or Buddhism, but there is a long history of intellectual debate *between* various Asian religions – Hindus disputing with Buddhists or Jains, Daoists against Confucians, Buddhists against Daoists and Confucians, Shintoists against Buddhists, and so on. Richard Fox Young notes,

> Hindu apologists did not defend Hinduism as such, but proponents of the great *darsanas*, philosophical views or systems, endeavored to brace their own ideas or doctrines by exposing the fallacies of others. To cite only one instance, Sankara's commentary on the Brahmasutras refuted, in turn, each of the major theories, cosmological metaphysical, soteriological, etc., to which other Hindu thinkers, Buddhists, Jains, and materialists subscribed. Apologetics was so much a part of classical works on religion and philosophy that a text without at least an adumbration of the standard criticisms of its rivals would surely seem incomplete.[17]

As we shall see in subsequent chapters, correct belief was regarded as essential by many of the early Indian religious and philosophical traditions, for Brahmins, Buddhists, and Jains alike believed that achieving the soteriological goal – liberation or enlightenment – depended in part upon having a correct understanding of reality. Each tradition teaches that its understanding is correct and those of the others mistaken in essential respects.

---

[17] Richard Fox Young, *Resistant Hinduism: Sanskrit Sources on Anti-Christian Apologetics in Early Nineteenth Century India* (Vienna: Institut für Indologie der Universität Wien, 1981), p. 13.

Outline of the Book

This book provides an introduction to Buddhism and some of its central metaphysical claims. Although we write as Christians, the book is not intended as a refutation of Buddhism or even as an argument for the truth of Christian theism as opposed to Buddhism. The first three chapters trace the historical development of Buddhism, from its inception in India to its ongoing transformation as it moved into China, Japan, and then the West. Chapter 3 explores some of the ways in which Buddhism changed as it adapted to the very different contexts of the modern world and the West. Although the teachings of Buddhism are introduced in the early chapters, some of the core metaphysical doctrines are explored more fully in chapters 4 and 5. Special attention is given to the counter-intuitive Buddhist teaching on impermanence and no-self, as these are central to other beliefs and practices. Some of the problems confronting these Buddhist doctrines are noted.

The final chapter sets out in summary fashion the basic contrasts between the fundamental claims of Buddhism and Christian theism. If we are to take either religion seriously, we must give careful attention to what each says about the root problem afflicting humankind and how this can be overcome. Although we are convinced that the central claims of Christianity are true, it is not our purpose to demonstrate that in this book. Chapter 6 makes clear the differences in the two religions' respective understandings of the religious ultimate, the human predicament, and the way to overcome this predicament. It is our contention that, while both Christianity and Buddhism can be appreciated on a variety of grounds and adherents of both traditions should be treated with respect, the clear differences between the two religions on the most basic religious issues makes it impossible to treat them as somehow 'equally true' as religious worldviews. Moreover, as the early Christians and Buddhists would undoubtedly agree, the differences in claims between the religions have enormous consequences since both traditions admit that our spiritual well-being is directly related to our grasping which – if any – of these perspectives is in fact true.

1

Early Buddhism

What we today know as Buddhism is a large family of diverse religious and philosophical traditions, which have developed over the past 2,500 years in many cultures. Emerging originally in what is now the border region of India and Nepal, Buddhism quickly spread throughout the Indian subcontinent, moving into South-East Asia, Central Asia, then into China, Korea, and Japan. More recently Buddhism has become established in North America and Europe. As the teachings of the Buddha were embraced by people in different cultural and religious settings Buddhism itself changed in significant ways, resulting in an enormous variety in teachings and practices among contemporary Buddhists. But in spite of this diversity, all Buddhists trace their beliefs and practices in some sense back to the Enlightenment of Gautama the Buddha under the Bodhi Tree and the teachings deriving from this experience. To be a Buddhist is to take refuge in the Three Jewels – the Buddha, the Dharma (Teaching), and the Sangha (Community). To appreciate Buddhism in any of its forms, then, we must first grasp something of the life and teachings of Gautama the Buddha. But before turning to this we must have some awareness of the social and religious world of north India during the sixth century BC.

Background to Early Buddhism

Sometime during the middle of the second millennium BC a group of tribes, referring to themselves as Aryans, invaded and gradually established their dominance over the northern Indian subcontinent.[1] The Aryans brought with them a religious culture which was largely polytheistic, with some similarities to the religious practices of the ancient Greeks and Romans, as well as the Persians. Most of the gods of the Aryan pantheon were identified with forces of nature. These influences, combined with the indigenous practices and beliefs of the pre-Aryan Indus Valley civilizations, gave rise to some of the central themes that would dominate Indian religious and philosophical thought for centuries.

Between roughly 1500 and 800 BC the Vedas, a collection of sacred hymns and treatises concerned largely with sacrificial ritual, appeared. The term 'Vedas' is often used in a strict sense to refer to the four Samhita Vedas – the Rigveda Samhita, the Artharvaveda Samhita, the Samaveda Samhita, and the Yajurveda Samhita. But it can also be used more generally to refer to not only the Samhita Vedas but also to the Brahmanas (prose texts dealing with sacrificial ritual) as well as to the Upanishads (more philosophical sacred writings which date from roughly the eighth to the fourth centuries BC). In this sense the Vedas can be said to form the essential canon of sacred scriptures for orthodox Hindus.

Vedic religion, rooted in the authority of the Vedas, was characterized by polytheism, the identification of various deities with forces of nature, and carefully prescribed rituals of sacrifice. It was believed that by responding appropriately to the spiritual forces behind natural phenomena, one could secure health, wealth, fertility, long life, or victory in battle. As sacrifice played a central role in Vedic religion, the priestly or Brahmin caste,

---

[1] Helpful information on the philosophical, religious and social background of India in the fifth and sixth centuries BC can be found in David Kalupahana, *A History of Buddhist Philosophy: Continuities and Discontinuities* (Honolulu, HI: University of Hawaii Press, 1992), chapter 1; Richard King, *Indian Philosophy: An Introduction to Hindu and Buddhist Thought* (Washington, DC: Georgetown University Press, 1999), chapters 1–4; K.N. Jayatilleke, *The Message of the Buddha*, ed. Ninian Smart (New York: The Free Press, 1974), pp. 11–24, 53–64; and Luis Gomez, 'Buddhism in India,' in *The Religious Traditions of Asia*, ed. Joseph M. Kitagawa (New York: Macmillan, 1989), pp. 41–62.

which held the secrets necessary for effective sacrifice, occupied an increasingly prominent place in the social and religious life of the people. Although a variety of deities, such as Indra, Varuna, Vishnu, Rudra, etc., appear in the Vedas, there are also indications of a rudimentary monotheism in some of the Vedas. In a famous passage, for example, the Rigveda declares, 'They call it Indra, Mitra, Varuna, Agni, and it is the heavenly bird that flies. The wise speak of what is One in many ways; they call it Agni, Yama, Matarisvan.'[2] The notion of one infinite Being projecting himself in many different forms in our world, which is introduced in the Rigveda, becomes a prominent theme in the Upanishads and later Hindu thought.

The Upanishads appeared from roughly the eighth through fourth centuries BC. A central theme of the Upanishads is the idea that behind the changing phenomenal world of our experience is a timeless, unchanging, unifying Reality or Being. Thus, a recurring issue concerns the relation between the ultimate Reality, Brahman, and atman (the self).

Although Brahman had been introduced in the earlier Vedas as the sustaining power of the cosmos, it is in the Upanishads that we find serious concern with the nature of Brahman and its relation to the human person. Brahman was said to be the ultimate reality, the Supreme Being, the ground underlying all that is, and that upon which all else depends. 'Verily, this whole world is Brahman. Tranquil, let one worship It as that from which he came forth, as that into which he will be dissolved, as that in which he breathes.'[3] In a cryptic statement – in what is perhaps the most famous passage in the Upanishads – the atman or true self of the individual person is identified with the ultimate reality, Brahman: 'That thou art' (*tat tvam asi*).[4] Thus, according to

---

[2] Rig Veda, I, 164, 46; in *The Rig Veda: An Anthology*, ed. and trans. by Wendy Doniger O'Flaherty (Hammondsworth: Penguin Books, 1981), p. 80.

[3] Chandogya Upanishad, 3.14.1; in *A Source Book in Indian Philosophy*, ed. Sarvepalli Radhakrishnan and Charles A. Moore (Princeton, NJ: Princeton University Press, 1957), p. 65.

[4] Chandogya Upanishad, 6.9–13; in *Source Book in Indian Philosophy*, pp. 68–70.

a major Hindu tradition, the one eternal Reality underlying the phenomenal world is in actuality identical to one's true self. The problem is that humans mistakenly ascribe independent reality to individual selves (jiva) in the world, not realizing that they are but manifestations of Brahman.

Central to much Indian religious and philosophical thought are the notions of transmigration and karma. By the sixth century BC the process of transmigration and operation of the law of karma had been generally accepted as basic facts of existence.[5] Physical death was not regarded as the termination of life. Persons, and other living beings, are continually being reborn. Although the physical body may die, there is an indestructible element – the soul or atman – which passes on from one life to another. What regulates the endless cycle of deaths and rebirths is karma. The term 'karma' literally means 'deeds' or 'action;' but it came to denote

> the impersonal and transethical system under which one's current situation in the world is regarded as the fruit of seeds planted by one's behaviour and dispositions in the past, and the view that in all of one's present actions lie similar seeds that will have continuing and determinative effect on one's life as they bear fruit in the future.[6]

Birth leads inevitably to death. Death, in turn, inevitably results in rebirth in another body. It is karma which determines the conditions of each existence. Thus, one's present existence is determined by the cumulative effects of past actions and dispositions, and one's future states are determined by present (and past) actions and dispositions. Unless checked by counteractive measures, the influences of moral actions in the present will extend into subsequent lives. The Chandogya Upanishad, from the seventh or eighth century BC, states that

---

[5] Thomas J. Hopkins, *The Hindu Religious Tradition* (Belmont, CA: Dickenson Publishing Company, 1971), p. 50.
[6] William K. Mahoney, 'Karman: Hindu and Jain Concepts,' in *The Encyclopedia of Religion*, vol. 8, ed. Mircea Eliade (New York: Macmillan, 1987), p. 262.

Those who are of pleasant conduct here – the prospect is, indeed, that they will enter a pleasant womb, either the womb of a brahmin [priestly caste], or the womb of a ksatriya [warrior] or the womb of a vaisya [merchant]. But those who are of stinking conduct here – the prospect is, indeed, that they will enter a stinking womb, either the womb of a dog, or the womb of a swine, or the womb of an outcast.[7]

The entire repetitive process of birth, death, and rebirth, impersonally regulated by karma, came to be referred to as samsara (literally, 'to wander or pass through a series of states or conditions'). The Japanese Buddhist scholar Akira Hirakawa notes that assumptions about karma, rebirth, and samsara were being clarified and gaining general acceptance at the time of the Buddha. '[T]he concept of repeated cycles of birth and death was being given its classical formulation at the same time that Buddhism was being established. Once the concept of rebirth was established, people naturally began to speculate about whether some entity or soul might travel through the cycles of birth and death.'[8]

Samsara – repeated rebirth and death – was understood in negative terms, and the religious objective of the three major Indian religions (Hinduism, Jainism, and Buddhism) became release or liberation (moksha) from the bondage of samsara by rendering karma ineffective. While some, especially in the affluence and comfort of the twenty-first century West, might find the idea of rebirth attractive – a limitless series of different lives with all the opportunities for pleasure that this promises – the world in which Buddhism emerged finds it intolerable. An ancient Jain parable graphically depicts a perspective common to many Indian traditions, including Buddhism.

There was once a man who, oppressed by his poverty left home and set out for another country. But after a few days he lost his way, and

---

[7] Chandogya Upanishad 5.10.7; in *A Source Book in Indian Philosophy*, pp. 66–7.

[8] Akira Hirakawa, *A History of Indian Buddhism: From Sakyamuni to Early Mahayana*, trans. Paul Groner (Honolulu, HI: University of Hawaii Press, 1990), p. 18.

found himself wandering in a dense forest. There, he met a mad elephant which charged him with upraised trunk. Immediately as he turned to flee there appeared before him a terrible demonness with a sharp sword in her hand. In fear and trembling he looked about him in all directions for a way of escape until he saw a great tree and ran towards it. But he could not climb it, and afraid of death, he flung himself into an old well nearby. As he fell he managed to catch hold of a clump of reeds growing from the wall, and clung to them desperately. For below him he could see a mass of writhing snakes, enraged at the sound of his falling, and at the very bottom, identifiable from the hiss of its breath, a mighty black python with its mouth wide open to receive him. And even as he realized that his life could last only as long as the reed held fast, he looked up and saw two mice, one black and one white, gnawing at the roots. Meanwhile, the enraged elephant charged the tree and dislodged a honeycomb. It fell upon the man clinging so precariously. But even as the bees angrily stung his body, by chance a drop of honey fell on his brow, rolled down his face and reached his lips, to bring a moment's sweetness. And he longed for yet more drops, and so forgot the perils of his existence.

Now hear its interpretation. The man is the soul, his wandering in the forest is existence. The wild elephant is death, the demonness old age. The tree is salvation, where there is no fear of death, but which no sensual man can attain. The well is human life, the snakes are passions, and the python hell. The clump of reeds is man's allotted span, the black and white mice the dark and light halves of the month. The bees are diseases and troubles, while the drops of honey are but trivial pleasures. How can a wise man want them, in the midst of such peril and hardship?[9]

Similarly, an ancient Hindu text asks,

In this ill-smelling, unsubstantial body, which is a conglomerate of bone, skin, muscle, marrow, flesh, semen, blood, mucus, tears, rheum, feces, urine, wind, bile, and phlegm, what is the good of enjoyment of desires? In this body, which is afflicted with desire, anger, covetousness, delusion, fear, despondency, envy, separation

---

[9] *Eerdmans' Handbook to The World's Religions* (Grand Rapids, MI: Eerdmans, 1982), p. 210.

from the desirable, union with the undesirable, hunger, thirst, senility, death, disease, sorrow, and the like, what is the good of enjoyment of desires?

And we see that this whole world is decaying, as these gnats, mosquitoes, and the like, the grass, and the trees that arise and perish ...

In this sort of cycle of existence (samsara) what is the good of enjoyment of desires, when after a man has fed on them there is seen repeatedly his return here to earth? Be pleased to deliver me. In this cycle of existence I am like a frog in a waterless well.[10]

Religious movements in ancient India provided a variety of ways to achieve liberation from samsara. A major theme among Hindu traditions is that what breaks the cycle of rebirths is the liberating knowledge of the unchanging Brahman. For Advaita Vedanta, this required acceptance of one's essential identity with Brahman. The Advaitin religious goal, then, is to become one with the ultimate Reality, Brahman, or rather, to recognize that one's true self is already identical with Brahman, and through this knowledge to attain liberation from rebirth, or moksha. Other traditions emphasized proper performance of one's duty or loving devotion to a deity as more effective ways of liberation. They also wondered how Brahman could be confused concerning his own identity. But, despite these differences, the idea of release from the cycle of rebirths as the primary religious goal was common to the major Hindu traditions at the time of the Buddha.

The Indian sub-continent in the sixth century BC was characterized by social and religious change, with many new religious and intellectual movements emerging during the upheaval. Religious communities developed around wandering ascetics who lived in the forests, seeking liberation and peace. Donald W. Mitchell identifies four such communities at the time of the Buddha.[11] The Jains taught that all beings have a 'life principle' or jiva, which is bound by karma to rebirth in the material world.

---

[10] Maitri Upanishad I. 3–4, as cited in *A Sourcebook in Indian Philosophy*, pp. 93–4.

[11] Donald W. Mitchell, *Buddhism: Introducing the Buddhist Experience*, 2nd edn. (New York: Oxford University Press, 2008), p. 10.

Severe asceticism was said to be the only way to enlightenment experience and release from rebirth. The Ajivakas believed in rebirth, but rejected the notion of karma. One's life and rebirth were said to be determined by fate, and peace to come from accepting one's fate. The Materialists, by contrast, denied both karma and rebirth. Since there is nothing apart from matter, with death one's self is annihilated. The Skeptics, much like the ancient Greek skeptical tradition, maintained that questions about the afterlife simply cannot be answered. Peace of mind was said to come from suspension of judgment about these matters. Adherents of the different schools debated these questions vigorously.

Noble Ross Reat notes that early Hindus and Buddhists had similar perspectives on karma and rebirth.

> The Upanishads and Buddhism have basically identical ideas on rebirth: Beings are, by ignorance, desire, and will, entangled in an ongoing process of repeated birth and death conditioned by actions (karma) and operating in such a way that it is possible to link a given being to a chain of past existences. Both systems encourage release from the chronic trauma of birth and death through ethical conduct, wisdom, and meditation.[12]

But, as we shall see, early Buddhism differed radically from surrounding traditions in its view of what it is that is reborn, and the way to eliminate rebirth. Early Buddhism stood apart from the broader Hindu milieu in two respects: first, it denied outright the authority of the traditional scriptures, the Vedas and Upanishads;[13] and second, typically it denied the existence

---

[12] Noble Ross Reat, '*Karma* and Rebirth in the Upanishads and Buddhism,' *Numen* 24 (December 1977), p. 163.

[13] 'In the Sangarava Sutta, the Buddha states that there are three types of religious and philosophical teachers, considering the basis of their knowledge, who prescribe divergent ways of life. First there are the Revelationists (anussavika) who claim final knowledge on the basis of revelation, such as, for instance, the brahmins of the Vedic tradition. Secondly, there are the rational metaphysicians (takki vinamsi) who claim final knowledge on the basis of their faith in reason and speculation. Thirdly, there are those who claim final knowledge of things not found in the traditional revealed scriptures

of individual, enduring souls which transmigrate through the cycle of rebirths. Because of this, Buddhism was recognized as constituting a genuinely different religious tradition, and not merely another alternative school within Hinduism. Although modern Hindu scholars have tended to minimize the differences between early Buddhist teaching and Hindu assumptions, there is no question that the Buddha's teaching was regarded as heretical by the Hindu religious establishment. David Kalupahana observes that, whereas centuries after his death the Buddha was accepted by many Hindus as an 'incarnation' (avatar) of the Hindu deity Vishnu, 'one should not forget that in his own day the Buddha was considered a heretic of the worst kind by orthodox religious teachers.'[14] While Hinduism was remarkably tolerant of diversity, it did not allow for explicit rejection of the authority and teachings of the Vedas.[15]

Gautama the Buddha

It was into this world that Siddartha Gautama,[16] the Buddha, was born. Etymologically, the word 'buddha' means 'one who has awakened or been enlightened.' Although it was used by various religious traditions prior to the rise of Buddhism, it came to be used by Buddhists to refer to the historical Gautama, the founder of Buddhism.

(ananussutesu dhammesu), based on a personal understanding derived from their extra-sensory powers of perception. It is significant that the Buddha classifies himself as a member of the third group' (K.N. Jayatilleke, *The Message of the Buddha*, p. 53). For the Buddha's views on claims to revealed scriptures, see chapter four of *The Message of the Buddha*.

[14] David Kalupahana, *Buddhist Philosophy: A Historical Analysis* (Honolulu, HI: University of Hawaii Press, 1976), p. 9.

[15] Wendy Doniger O'Flaherty states, 'The contradiction of the Vedas remains the basic heresy in the Hindu viewpoint' (Wendy Doniger O'Flaherty, 'The Origin of Heresy in Hindu Mythology,' *History of Religions*, vol. 10, no. 4 (1971), p. 272).

[16] Siddartha (Sidhattha in Pali) is the personal name, and Gautama (Gotama in Pali) is the family name. Gautama Buddha was born into the Sakya tribe, and so he is also referred to as Sakyamuni, or 'sage of the Sakyas.'

Although there can be little question about the historicity of Gautama, there is uncertainty about details of his life and thought. Indeed, scholars are not agreed even about the century in which he lived. Dates of his birth range from 624 BC to 446 BC.[17] Western scholars traditionally adopt the dates 563–483 BC for the Buddha's life, and Hirakawa states that 'most modern scholars agree that the Buddha died within a few years of 480 BCE.'[18] Recently, however, many scholars have begun to place his life in the fifth century BC, with the Japanese scholars Hakuju Ui and Hajime Nakamura accepting the dates 466–386 BC. Our access to the historical Gautama is complicated by the fact that the earliest Buddhist scriptures were not put into writing until the first century BC.[19] Prior to this time the authoritative discourses were passed on orally by monks, from one generation to the next. Furthermore, the extant versions of the complete life of Gautama, which are widely recognized as containing legendary and mythological elements as well as historically reliable material, did not appear until much later. Richard Robinson and Willard Johnson observe that, 'The extant versions of the complete life of the Buddha were composed four hundred or more years after his death.'[20] For example, the influential Buddhacarita ['The Acts of the Buddha'], one of the first full length 'biographies' of the

---

[17] For discussion of the issues, see Donald W. Mitchell, *Buddhism*, p. 11; Hajime Nakamura, *Gotama Buddha* (Tokyo: Buddhist Books International, 1977), pp. 12–14; and *Gotama Buddha: A Biography Based Upon the Most Reliable Texts*, vol. 1, trans. Gaynor Sekimori (Tokyo: Kosei Publishing Company, 2000), pp. 68–72; Akira Hirakawa, *A History of Indian Buddhism*, pp. 20–24; and David Edward Shaner, 'Biographies of the Buddha,' *Philosophy East and West*, vol. XXXVII, no. 3 (July 1987), pp. 306–22.

[18] Akira Hirakawa, *A History of Indian Buddhism*, p. 22.

[19] 'The Pali canon is traditionally said to have been brought to Sri Lanka from northern India in the third century BCE, and was written down in the first century BCE. Scholars are skeptical that what we have today is the same as what was originally brought to Sri Lanka' (Donald W. Mitchell, *Buddhism*, p. 66).

[20] Richard H. Robinson and Willard L. Johnson, *The Buddhist Religion: A Historical Introduction*, 4th edn. (Belmont, CA: Wadsworth Publishing Company, 1997), p. 10.

Buddha, was written by Asvaghosa around the second century AD.[21]

There are, however, certain details about the life of Siddharta Gautama which are generally accepted as historically reliable. These include the facts that Gautama was born in what is today the borderland of India and Nepal, into the ksatriya (warrior) caste. His father was a noble or chieftain of the Sakya clan. Gautama was married and had a child, but against his father's wishes he rejected the comfortable lifestyle of his family and entered the ascetic life. After considerable ascetic discipline, he experienced what he called Enlightenment or Awakening, and he began to preach a message based upon this experience. His first attempts to share the insights of his Enlightenment met with failure, but he eventually attracted a large following of devoted adherents. He died in a remote place after eating a meal.

The accounts of his life in the later Buddhist scriptures contain, of course, much more fascinating material. For example, in the Buddhacarita young Gautama is portrayed as being brought up in a life of luxury, isolated from the cares and sorrows of the real world. Yet one day, as he ventured outside the palace confines, the young prince saw an old man – the first of the famous 'four sights.' Having never before been exposed to old age, young Gautama was perplexed and asked his charioteer the meaning of this strange sight. The charioteer replied that such was the fate of all persons. On later excursions he encountered a man with a diseased body and then a corpse. Confronted with the reality of death, Gautama was greatly dismayed and cried out, 'This is the end which has been fixed for all, and yet the world forgets its fears and takes no heed!... Turn back the chariot! This is no time or place for pleasure excursions. How could an intelligent person pay no heed at a time of disaster, when he knows of his impending destruction?'[22] On yet another occasion Gautama encountered a

---

[21] For discussion of the problem of sources for the historical Gautama, see Hajime Nakamura, *Gotama Buddha: A Biography Based Upon the Most Reliable Texts*, pp. 15–24.

[22] Buddhacarita 4, in *Buddhist Scriptures*, ed. and trans. by Edward Conze (New York: Penguin, 1959), p. 40.

wandering ascetic, who inspired in him the ideal of renouncing the life of comfort and pleasure he had known in order to discover the cause and cure of suffering.

Determined to discover the cure for suffering, young Gautama resolved to abandon his lifestyle in favor of that of a wandering ascetic. Taking one last look at his infant son and wife, he quietly slipped out of the palace one night, and from then on lived the life of a wandering recluse. He initially sat at the feet of various ascetics, or yogis. Mastering their techniques of meditation and self-mortification but failing to find ultimate satisfaction and release from samsara in their practices, he moved on. Rejecting extreme asceticism, the Buddha embraced the 'Middle Way,' steering clear of the excesses of both sensual pleasure and the mortification of the flesh.

Then, on a night of the full moon, Gautama passed through the four stages of dhyana (trance) and – fully enlightened – attained a state of complete spiritual insight into the nature of reality. From this point on he was a buddha (an 'awakened' or 'enlightened one'). The truth said to be discerned in the Enlightenment became the basis for the Buddha's preaching and teaching. Gautama is said to have been made aware of the fundamental causes of existence and suffering and how to make them cease. Something of the nature of the experience is captured in the following depiction.

I [Gautama] truly made effort and endeavor, my thought was firm and undistracted, my body was tranquil and passive, and my mind was concentrated. I was free of desires and unwholesome thoughts, and though I still had initial thought and discursive thought, I had arrived at the first meditation with the joy created by such a separation.... [Having attained the second, third, and fourth meditations], in this manner my mind became concentrated, purified, cleansed, without defilement, pliable, flexible, established and unmovable. I then directed my mind to wisdom raising the recollections of my past lives ... recalling numerous past lives along with each individual appearance and detailed conditions.... This was the first light of wisdom attained during the early part of the night.... I then directed my mind towards the knowledge of the birth and death of all living beings.... I observed living beings die and be born ... following the results of their karma.... This was the second light of wisdom attained during the middle of the night.... Then, I directed my mind towards the knowledge that eliminates ignorance. At that time, I realized [the truth about] the dissatisfactory condition of life [its nature, cause, cessation and the path to its cessation].... When I realized this, my mind was freed from the defilement of desire, my mind was freed from the defilement of ignorance, and as I became free, I realized that I was free.... This was the third wisdom attained at the end of the night.[23]

With the Enlightenment the Buddha believed that he experienced an initial foretaste of nirvana, and was liberated from the chain of causes resulting in rebirth. When Gautama eventually died he would not be reborn. Although tempted to remain in the state he had entered, out of compassion for all living beings the Buddha returned to his fellow ascetics and began to proclaim the new insight he had gained through his Enlightenment. At Benares he preached his famous First Sermon to five ascetics with whom he had formerly associated. They accepted his teaching and became the first of many followers comprising the sangha, or community of monks who accepted, practiced, and passed on the Buddha's teaching.

Over the next forty-five years the Buddha traveled widely and attracted many disciples including, it is said, his son and half-brother (who became monks). Gautama's cousin Ananda became a close companion of the Buddha and was instrumental in establishing the official teaching of the Buddha after his death. The Buddha rejected the caste system of the day as unjust, thus opening the sangha to persons of all castes. After initially limiting membership in the monastic community to men, the Buddha eventually accepted women as well. Tradition says that his wife and stepmother were among the first nuns.

At the age of eighty, the Buddha died after eating a meal and becoming ill. In the Mahaparinibbana Sutta, shortly before his death, the Buddha is depicted as saying to his cousin Ananda, 'It may be, Ananda, that in some of you the thought may arise, "The word of the master is ended, we have no teacher more! [*sic*]" But

---

[23] Majjhima-Nikaya, I, 21ff.; as cited in Mitchell, *Buddhism*, p. 19.

it is not thus, Ananda, that you should regard it. The truths, and the rules of the order, which I set forth and laid down for you all, let them, after I am gone, be the Teacher to you.'[24] The last words of the Buddha were, 'Behold now brethren, I exhort you, saying, "Decay is inherent in all component things! Work out your salvation with diligence!"'[25] The Buddha's death is known as the parinirvana, or the complete or final nirvana, since his existence in the phenomenal world ceased and he was not reborn.

Teachings of the Buddha

Tradition maintains that a few months after the death of the Buddha a special Council was held at Rajagaha to establish the authentic teaching of the Buddha. Donald W. Mitchell notes that, 'As a result of this council, what was recited by the community was said to have been memorized, establishing an oral tradition that was passed down for several centuries before being committed to writing.'[26] This oral tradition was divided into two general collections, or 'baskets' (pitakas), which provided the basis for the later written texts of early Buddhism. The Vinaya Pitaka (Basket of Discipline) includes the Buddha's rules for life within the monastic community, and the Sutta (Sutra in Sanskrit) Pitaka (Basket of Discourses) includes the teachings of the Buddha. A third collection of canonical teachings, the Abhidhamma Pitaka (Basket of Higher Teachings) is also traditionally said to have been recited at the First Council, although many scholars regard the material in this collection to be the later product of philosophical systematization of the Buddha's teachings.

> The Buddha's original teachings in the *Sutra Pitaka* were given in stories, illustrations, anecdotes, and so on, and were not an attempt to present a complete philosophical system. As the early

---

[24] Mahaparinibbana Sutta 6.1, in *Buddhist Suttas*, trans. by T.W. Rhys Davids (New York: Dover Publications, 1969), p. 112.

[25] Mahaparinibbana Sutta 6.10, in *Buddhist Suttas*, p. 114.

[26] Donald W. Mitchell, *Buddhism*, p. 65.

Buddhists explained and defended their views, there developed certain philosophical viewpoints that were more formally and systematically presented in the *Abhidharma Pitaka*. Centuries after the Buddha's passing, the emerging Buddhist sects added this later scriptural material, thereby producing the more fully developed 'Three Baskets' (*Tripitaka*; Pali: *Tipitaka*), which was the authoritative scripture for much of early Buddhism.[27]

The Tipitaka is preserved in the Pali language and it comprises the Pali Canon, which was put into writing during the first century BC.[28]

The Four Noble Truths

What was the truth which the Buddha is believed to have realized in his Enlightenment? The heart of the Buddha's new teaching is contained in what is often called the Four Noble Truths.[29] A concise expression of the Four Noble Truths is given in the traditional account of the Buddha's first sermon, as recorded in the Samyutta-Nikaya:

(1) Now this, O monks, is the noble truth of pain: birth is painful, old age is painful, sickness is painful, death is painful, sorrow, lamentation, dejection, and despair are painful. Contact with unpleasant things is painful, not getting what one wishes is painful. In short the five khandas[30] of grasping are painful. (2) Now this, O monks, is the noble truth of the cause of pain: that craving which

---

[27] Ibid., p. 66. On the formation of the canon, see also Richard H. Robinson and Willard L. Johnson, *The Buddhist Religion: A Historical Introduction*, pp. 51–5.

[28] Donald S. Lopez, *The Story of Buddhism: A Concise Guide to Its History and Teachings* (New York: HarperCollins, 2001), p. 106.

[29] For helpful discussions of the Four Noble Truths, see Walpola Rahula, *What the Buddha Taught*, 2nd edn. (New York: Grove Press, 1974), chapters 2–5; Michael Carrithers, *The Buddha* (New York: Oxford University Press, 1983), chapter 4; and Donald W. Mitchell, *Buddhism*, chapter 2.

[30] The five khandas, or Five Aggregates, are Matter, Sensations, Perceptions, Mental Formations, and Consciousness.

leads to rebirth, combined with pleasure and lust, finding pleasure here and there, namely, the craving for passion, the craving for existence, the craving for non-existence. (3) Now this, O monks, is the noble truth of the cessation of pain: the cessation without a remainder of that craving, abandonment, forsaking, release, non-attachment. (4) Now this, O monks, is the noble truth of the way that leads to the cessation of pain: this is the noble Eightfold Path, namely, right views, right intention, right speech, right action, right livelihood, right effort, right mindfulness, right concentration.[31]

The First Truth is the truth concerning dukkha. The Pali word 'dukkha' is often translated 'suffering' or, as in the above passage, 'pain.' But suffering here must be understood in a very broad sense to include not only physical pain and discomfort but also any lack of emotional or psychological well being. Walpola Rahula suggests that it includes the idea of a pervasive imperfection, impermanence, emptiness, or insubstantiality.[32] Michael Carrithers prefers to translate 'dukkha' as 'discomfort, dissatisfaction, or discontent.'[33] The First Noble Truth asserts that all of existence is characterized by dukkha; that is, dukkha is found in every aspect of existence.

The Second Noble Truth concerns the origin of dukkha, and holds that there are discernible causes of suffering and that the root cause of suffering is tanha (literally 'thirst,' but often translated 'craving' or 'desire'). It is not merely the wrong desires but rather desire or craving itself which results in dukkha. That is, it is the very condition of desiring, craving, or thirsting for anything at all – including non-existence – which causes suffering.

The Third Noble Truth affirms that the disease of dukkha is curable, and that when tanha ceases then dukkha ceases as well. The Fourth Noble Truth states that the cessation of dukkha is achieved through following the Noble Eightfold Path:

1. right views
2. right intention

---

[31] Samyutta-nikaya, v. 420; in *A Source Book in Indian Philosophy*, pp. 274–5.
[32] Walpola Rahula, *What the Buddha Taught*, p. 17.
[33] Michael Carrithers, *The Buddha*, p. 56.

3. right speech
4. right action
5. right livelihood
6. right effort
7. right mindfulness
8. right concentration.

The eight constituents fall into three general categories – moral self-discipline, meditation, and wisdom.

Although in the West Buddhism is often regarded as rejecting rationality, many Buddhists emphasize the highly rational nature of the Buddha's teaching. The Four Noble Truths, for example, exhibit a rational structure that proceeds logically from diagnosis of the problem to a prescription for cure of suffering. Rahula compares the Buddha to a 'wise and scientific doctor for the ills of the world.'[34] Moreover, many Buddhists emphasize that Buddhism is based solely upon reason and personal experience, not upon faith. Thus the Japanese Buddhist scholar Hajime Nakamura claims that, 'Gotama was described as one who reasoned according to the truth rather than on the basis of the authority of the Vedas or tradition. Theravada and Mahayana Buddhism have accepted two standards for the truth of a statement: it must be in accord with the [Buddhist] scriptures and must be proved true by reasoning. No Buddhist is expected to believe anything which does not meet these two tests.'[35] Similarly, the Sri Lankan Buddhist K.N. Jayatilleke, after arguing that the Buddha embraced the correspondence theory of truth, asserts that for the Buddha inconsistency is a criterion of falsehood.

> Although correspondence with fact is considered to be the essential characteristic of truth, consistency or coherence is also held to be a criterion. In contrast, inconsistency is a criterion of falsehood. In arguing with his opponents, the Buddha often shows that

---

[34] Walpola Rahula, *What the Buddha Taught*, p. 17.
[35] Hajime Nakamura, 'Unity and Diversity in Buddhism,' in *The Path of the Buddha: Buddhism Interpreted by Buddhists*, ed. Kenneth W. Morgan (New York: Ronald Press Company, 1956), p. 372.

their theories lead to inconsistencies or contradictions, thereby demonstrating that they are false, using what is known as the Socratic method.... This means that truth must be consistent. Therefore, when a number of theories with regard to the nature of man and his destiny in the universe contradict each other, they cannot all be true, though they could all be false if none of them correspond with fact.[36]

As we shall see in Chapter 2, however, this emphasis upon logical consistency is not adopted by some Mahayana traditions, especially Zen.

Impermanence and No-Self

We noted earlier that the concepts of samsara, karma, and rebirth already were current in the Indian subcontinent at the time of the Buddha.

> Although the various Hindu schools of thought disagreed about a number of issues, [they] all agreed that sentient beings were subject to an incessant cycle of rebirths, that this was largely an unsatisfactory state of affairs and that there was a way out – the attainment of liberation (moksha). This metaphysical scheme was also accepted by the various Buddhist (and Jaina) traditions and provided something of a canvas upon which intellectual debate could proceed. Another unifying factor within the Hindu brahmanical fold was the belief in an essential self (atman) – an immaterial entity which transmigrated from life to life.[37]

In the Buddhist tradition it is typically held that, as a result of his Enlightenment, the Buddha rejected the last of these beliefs, and revised that belief's traditional metaphysical content. The Buddha contended that all things constituting the world as we know it are marked by dukkha (suffering), anatta (absence of self), and anicca (impermanence).

---

[36] K.N. Jayatilleke, *The Message of the Buddha*, pp. 43–4.
[37] Richard King, *Indian Philosophy*, p. 78.

The doctrine of rebirth or transmigration current at the time of the Buddha was that there are eternal souls which transmigrate from one psychophysical organism to another in a succession of lives. However, the Buddha held that there is nothing permanent in the world; only nirvana is permanent. Everything else is in constant flux, an unending process of coming into being and passing out of existence. Donald W. Mitchell explains impermanence by saying that, 'all things are impermanent in two senses: They arise and pass away, and while existing they are in a state of constant change.'[38] Even the gods – if they exist – continually undergo change, eventually dying and being reborn in another state of existence.

But if there is *nothing* permanent in the world then there cannot be any permanent or enduring souls either. Thus, as Richard King observes, the Buddha clearly rejected an assumption widely accepted by his contemporaries: 'For the Buddhist there is no *atman* or essential self underlying the changing stream of events which constitute the mind-body complex. The Buddhist doctrine of no-abiding-self (Pali: *anatta*; Sanskrit: *anatman*) provided a stark philosophical contrast to brahmanical notions of a substantial self (*atman*).'[39] The Buddhist notion of no-self is a logical implication of the impermanence of everything that exists.

The Buddha always affirmed that persons have an empirical self-hood constituted by a body and a mind. But he also claimed that the various constituents of this conventional selfhood are characterized by impermanence and *dukkha*; they are always changing, and they ordinarily produce mental and physical processes that are experienced as ultimately dissatisfactory. The Buddha also taught that when one examines these constituents of conventional selfhood, one does not find any permanent substance. Impermanence is not just a characteristic of the phenomena of the external world; it applies to oneself.... It was also the Buddha's view that the belief in a permanent substantial self is not only false, but also leads to selfishness and egoism, which, in turn, make the world so dissatisfactory for everyone.[40]

---

[38] Donald W. Mitchell, *Buddhism*, p. 36.
[39] Richard King, *Indian Philosophy*, p. 78.
[40] Donald W. Mitchell, *Buddhism*, p. 37.

Thus, belief in something permanent and unchanging, especially belief in an enduring substantial person or soul, is not only mistaken; it is the root cause of the chain of events resulting in continual rebirth. 'For the Buddha, it was the belief in self, the belief that among the various constituents of mind and body there is something that lasts longer than an instant, that is the cause of all suffering.'[41]

What we think of as a person or a soul is really no more than an ever-changing combination of psychophysical forces which, according to Buddhism, can be divided into the 'Five Aggregates' – Matter, Sensations, Perceptions, Mental Formations, and Consciousness. Although we have experiences and there is consciousness, there is no enduring, substantial person or soul underlying these experiences. And it is the illusion of just such a permanent, enduring soul that produces dukkha. As the Buddha put it, 'In short these five aggregates of attachment are *dukkha*.'[42] The illusion of a permanent self merely fans the flames of desire or craving, resulting in further rebirth and thus more suffering.

The Buddha, then, did not accept the doctrine of the transmigration of souls. And yet he did accept the notion of samsara, the successive cycle of births and rebirths. But if there is no soul to pass on from one life to another, what sense can we make of the notion of repeated rebirths?[43] The answer to this question reveals one of the Buddha's innovations. What is passed on, it was claimed, is simply the cumulative effects of actions. Although the Buddha rejected the idea that there is an enduring, substantial person that passes from one life to another, he did accept the idea of karma and that the effects of actions continue beyond the

---

[41] Donald S. Lopez, Jr., *The Story of Buddhism*, p. 46.

[42] Cited in Rahula, *What the Buddha Taught*, p. 20.

[43] 'This tension between the notion of the person as an agent, capable of winning salvation, and the notion of the person as a fiction, indeed a dangerous fiction that is the source of all woe, would persist in one form or another throughout the developments of Buddhist thought in Asia. It would be stated perhaps most powerfully in the *Diamond Sutra*, where the buddha-to-be, called a bodhisattva, is said to vow to lead all beings into the final nirvana, knowing that there are no beings to be led to the final nirvana' (Donald S. Lopez, Jr., *The Story of Buddhism*, p. 48).

present life. This paradox is captured by the fifth-century monk Buddhaghosa in the Visuddhi-magga, a classic Theravada text:

Misery only doth exist, none miserable,
No doer is there; naught save the deed is found.
Nirvana is, but not the man who seeks it.
The Path exists, but not the traveler on it.[44]

Although there is no substantial self or soul who engages in the actions, merely the peculiar combination of forces known as the Five Aggregates, the effects of volitional action affect other aggregates in what we would call life after death, after the physical body dies.

For the Buddha, then, the human predicament is to be thought of in terms of bondage to samsara, the cycle of rebirths characterized by pervasive suffering or dissatisfaction. In early Buddhism rebirth is said to take place within an elaborate cosmology. The universe has no beginning and comprises three broad realms – the heavens, the world we inhabit, and hells – each of which in turn can be divided into sub-realms. Thus, beings are continually reborn into one of six realms based upon their karma. The highest realm is that of the gods, who inhabit several levels of heaven. The traditional gods of ancient India are located here. Although the gods live very long lives, eventually they too are reborn. The next realm is that of the demigods, deities less powerful than the gods but greater than humans. The third realm is that of humans. The lower three realms are regarded as the unfortunate places of rebirth. Immediately below humans is the realm of animals, and below them is the realm of ghosts, some of whom also inhabit the human world. Ghosts are invisible to all but the spiritually advanced, and they are continually suffering from hunger and thirst (hence, hungry ghosts), often depicted as wandering spirits. The lowest realm is that of 'an extensive and harrowing complex of hells.'[45]

---

[44] Cited in *A Sourcebook in Indian Philosophy*, p. 289.
[45] Donald Lopez, *The Story of Buddhism*, pp. 22–2. See also Akira Hirakawa, *A History of Indian Buddhism*, pp. 170–74.

If samsara is the disease, what then is the cure? How can one be free of dukkha and the chains of samsara? What is needed is not simply improvement of one's position within the endless cycle of birth and rebirth, but rather complete liberation from karma and samsara. This is possible, according to the Buddha, through the elimination of tanha – desire, thirsting, or craving. For this, strict adherence to the Noble Eightfold Path is necessary, and an essential element of this Path – right view – involves having a correct understanding of reality. In other words, the key to eliminating desire and craving, and thus release from the chains of samsara, lies in accepting and appropriating the Buddha's analysis of reality. One of the most important aspects of this correct understanding of reality is the denial of any enduring, substantial self. Some of the implications of this will be explored more fully in Chapters 4 and 5.

Nirvana

Nirvana (nibbana in Pali) is thus the spiritual goal of early Buddhism. But just what is nirvana? Two common misunderstandings should be avoided. First, nirvana is not simply another term for heaven or paradise.[46] The term 'nirvana' has become commonplace in the West as a synonym for 'paradise,' or a place of hedonistic bliss, but this is not the sense of the term in early Buddhism. It is true that nirvana is described as blissful. In the Pali text Milindapanho, for example, the monk Nagasena responds to King Milinda's questions by characterizing nirvana as follows:

---

[46] 'According to Buddhism, the final goal is not a paradise or a heavenly world. The central theme of Buddhism is that, by following the right Path, one can free oneself from the bondage of existence and come to the realization of the Supreme Truth. The attainment of Enlightenment is identical with Nirvana. All Buddhists agree that Enlightenment is their goal and that it is attained by following the right path' (Hajime Nakamura, 'Unity and Diversity in Buddhism,' p. 380). However, as we shall see in Chapter 2, some popular forms of Mahayana Buddhism in East Asia have embraced a kind of paradise as the soteriological goal.

There is this thing called nirvana, which is peaceful, blissful, and exalted, and that is what a person realizes through right practice, by means of understanding karmic constituents according to the teachings of the Buddha, and wisdom.... And how is nirvana to be recognized? It can be recognized through its safety, its freedom from mishap and danger, its tranquility, its peacefulness, its blissfulness, its pleasantness, its excellence, its purity, its coolness. Your majesty, it is like a man who is being burned by a fire, a great pile of flaming sticks of wood; when by means of a great effort he escapes from there, out into the open where there is no fire, he realizes utter bliss. Similarly, your majesty, through right practice and proper concentration one can realize the utter bliss of nirvana, in which the torment of the threefold fire of desire, hatred, and delusion has gone out.[47]

And yet nirvana cannot be identified with the ideas of paradise or heaven found in, for example, Christianity or Islam. For strictly speaking, one cannot speak of the Buddha (or anyone else for that matter) *entering* nirvana. It is not a place. Moreover, as noted above, there is no enduring soul or person to 'enter' nirvana.

This leads us to a second misunderstanding, which regards nirvana as simply annihilation or extinction. It is tempting to think of nirvana as the absence of existence, or sheer nothingness, since it is often described in negative terms as 'cessation,' 'absence of craving,' 'detachment,' 'the unborn,' or 'the unconditioned.'[48] Moreover, the term 'nirvana' literally means 'blowing out' or 'extinguishing' and was used to describe the cessation of a fire.[49] Buddhist teaching holds that the cessation of suffering is brought about by the elimination of the fires of craving or thirst. As Mitchell puts it, 'When craving ceases, its effect, namely *dukkha* [pain or suffering], ceases and the result is Nirvana.'[50] Thus, in the Samyutta-Nikaya, the Buddha says that nirvana is 'the complete cessation of craving (thirst), letting it go, renouncing it, being

---

[47] Milindapanho, in *The Experience of Buddhism: Sources and Interpretations*, ed. John S. Strong (Belmont, CA: Wadsworth Publishing, 1995), p. 108.

[48] As we shall see in the next chapter, this tendency becomes stronger with Mahayana Buddhism, as nirvana is identified with sunyata or emptiness.

[49] On the etymology of the term see Richard H. Robinson and Willard L. Johnson, *The Buddhist Religion*, p. 40.

[50] Donald W. Mitchell, *Buddhism*, p. 51.

free from it, detachment from it.'[51] One of the Buddha's disciples, Sariputta, said that 'The destruction of desire, the destruction of hatred, and the destruction of delusion – that, my friend, is what is called nirvana.'[52] Similarly, Donald Lopez speaks of Nirvana as 'the state of utter absence of suffering;' it is 'the absence of suffering in the present and the absence of any possibility of suffering in the future. All suffering has been destroyed because the causes of suffering, the afflictions, have been destroyed.'[53]

But nirvana is not sheer annihilationism, the negation of any reality whatsoever. To the contrary, it is what is most real. Only nirvana is unborn, unconditioned, deathless, and unchanging. In one text the Buddha states,

> There is, monks, an unborn, not become, not made, uncompounded, and were it not, monks, for this unborn, not become, not made, uncompounded, no escape could be shown here for what is born, has become, is made, is compounded. But, because there is, monks, an unborn, not become, not made, uncompounded, therefore an escape can be shown for what is born, has become, is made, is compounded.[54]

It is sometimes maintained that, although nirvana is real, it cannot be described because it is unlike anything with which we are familiar in this world. Responding to King Milinda, the monk Nagasena said, 'Your majesty, nirvana cannot be compared to anything. It is not possible to elucidate its form, makeup, age, or size by means of any simile, explanation, reason, or inference.'[55] Yet, clearly there are some positive claims about nirvana, as is evident in the passages quoted above.

Nirvana is often said to transcend all dualities or dichotomies. Referring to nirvana, the Buddha said, 'Here the four elements

---

[51] Samyutta-Nikaya, I. 36, as cited in Donald W. Mitchell, *Buddhism*, p. 61.

[52] From the Samyutta-Nikaya 4, as cited in John Strong, ed., *The Experience of Buddhism*, p. 105.

[53] Donald S. Lopez, Jr., *The Story of Buddhism*, p. 47.

[54] Udana 81, in *Buddhist Texts Through the Ages*, trans. and ed. by Edward Conze, I.B. Horner, David Snellgrove, and Arthur Waley (Oxford: Oneworld, 1995), p. 95.

[55] Milindapanho, in *The Experience of Buddhism*, p. 107.

of solidity, fluidity, heat and motion have no place; the notions of length and breadth, the subtle and the gross, good and evil, name and form are altogether destroyed; neither this world nor the other, nor coming, going or standing; neither death nor birth, nor sense-objects are to be found.'[56] Significantly, moral categories such as good and evil cannot be attributed to nirvana. Walpola Rahula is quite explicit on this point: 'Nirvana is beyond all terms of duality and relativity. It is therefore beyond our conceptions of good and evil, right and wrong, existence and non-existence.'[57] The 'beyond … existence and non-existence' comment is particularly striking and its conceptual content will be considered in Chapter 4.

Finally, two aspects of nirvana should be distinguished. First, a monk may attain what is sometimes called nirvana 'with remainder,' which is nirvana with the Five Aggregates. This means that the monk has, in this life, attained supreme insight into the nature of reality, and that, although he will continue to go on living in this world as before, upon death there will be no more rebirth. The Buddha himself is said to have lived this kind of nirvana for the last forty-five years of his life. Nirvana 'with remainder' is obviously describable. At death, however, the monk attains the second phase, or nirvana 'without remainder' or the 'final nirvana.'

According to the Buddha, then, there is a deathless, permanent, unconditioned realm – nirvana – which can be attained, and attainment of nirvana rules out rebirth in another life. Walpola Rahula summarizes the Buddha's teaching as follows:

> According to Buddhism, the Absolute Truth is that there is nothing absolute in the world; that everything is relative, conditioned and impermanent, and that there is no unchanging, everlasting, absolute substance like Self, Soul or Atman within or without. This is the Absolute Truth.... The realization of this Truth, i.e., to see things as they are without illusion or ignorance, is the extinction of craving, 'thirst,' and the cessation of *dukkha*, which is *Nirvana*.[58]

---

[56] Udana, as cited in Walpola Rahula, *What the Buddha Taught*, p. 37.
[57] Walpola Rahula, *What the Buddha Taught*, p. 43.
[58] Walpola Rahula, *What the Buddha Taught*, p. 40. It is worth observing that, despite the alleged ineffability of nirvana, these, too, are descriptions, this time of nirvana 'without remainder.'

The notion of nirvana, especially when combined with the Buddhist teaching on no-self, is, to say the least, paradoxical. Some of the implications of this will be explored further in chapters four and five.

The Growth of Buddhism

At the time of the Buddha's death, Buddhism had become established throughout central India. It quickly spread beyond India, however, as Buddhist teachings and practices were transmitted by merchants who came to India for business, converted to Buddhism and then returned to their homes preaching the dharma.[59] According to tradition, King Asoka, the great third-century BC Mauryan ruler who converted to Buddhism, sent proclaimers of the Buddhist message to rulers in Syria, Egypt, and Macedonia in the west, and to Sri Lanka and South-East Asia to the south.[60] Tradition maintains that around 250 BC King Asoka sent his own son and daughter to Sri Lanka and that through their efforts the entire country eventually was converted to Buddhism. From the Indian subcontinent, Buddhism moved north into China sometime during the first century AD, and then on into Korea in the fourth century. It was introduced into Japan in the sixth century, and into Tibet in the seventh century. The story of Buddhism in China, Tibet, and Japan will be continued in Chapter 2. We will conclude this chapter by looking briefly at the tradition which became dominant in South-East Asia.

Theravada Buddhism

According to Buddhist tradition, about a hundred years after the First Council a Second Council was held at Vaisali. The Second Council was convened to address disputes over the interpretation of certain rules for life in the monastic community in the Vinaya Pitaka (Basket of Discipline), part of the Pali Canon. The Second

---

[59] See Akira Hirakawa, *A History of Indian Buddhism*, pp. 76–7.
[60] Donald W. Mitchell, *Buddhism*, pp. 70–72.

Council resulted in a schism within the Buddhist community between those calling for more progressive approaches to Buddhist teachings and monastic rules and those insisting upon more traditional interpretations.[61] The mahasanghika, or 'great community,' advocated more liberal interpretations, whereas the sthaviras (Pali: theras), or 'the elders,' insisted upon strict, traditional interpretations. The more orthodox or strict monks were called the Sthaviravadins (Pali: Theravadins) or 'Adherents of the Teachings of the Elders,' and the term 'Theravadin' eventually became the designation for the older and more traditional forms of Buddhism. The more liberal or innovative groups became known as the Mahasanghikas, and they gave rise to several new schools, anticipating in some respects what later developed into the Mahayana traditions.

Around 250 BC King Asoka called a Third Council to clarify further proper interpretation of the Buddha's teachings. About this time one school within the Sthaviravada group became established in Sri Lanka, and adopted the term 'Theravada' for itself.[62] Theravada thus became the primary form of Buddhism in Sri Lanka and from there it spread throughout South-East Asia. It

---

[61] Whether the schism actually occurred at the time of the Council or came later is a matter of some dispute. Helpful discussions can be found in Paul Williams, *Mahayana Buddhism: The Doctrinal Foundations* (London: Routledge, 1989), pp. 16–26; and Richard H. Robinson and Willard L. Johnson, *The Buddhist Religion*, chapter 4.

[62] Scholars are divided over the question of the relation between the earlier Sthaviravada tradition and the later Theravada school in Sri Lanka. Theravada Buddhists characteristically regard Theravada Buddhism as original Buddhism, in direct continuity with the Sthaviravada community. Speaking of the Theravada teachings found today in the Buddhism of Burma, Sri Lanka, Thailand, Cambodia, and Laos, U. Thittila states, '[T]here is no doubt that these versions represent the true Teaching of the Buddha as he originally gave it' (U. Thittila, 'The Fundamental Principles of Theravada Buddhism,' in *The Path of the Buddha: Buddhism Interpreted by Buddhists*, p. 71). Many contemporary scholars, however, question the simple equation of Theravada Buddhism with the original teachings of the Buddha, although many would acknowledge that we are probably closer to the Buddha's actual teachings with Theravada rather than with later Mahayana teachings.

is today found largely in Sri Lanka, Burma, Thailand, Laos, and Kampuchea. The overview of Buddhist teaching in this chapter largely reflects the Theravada tradition. Five distinctives of Theravada Buddhism will be briefly mentioned.

First, Theravada Buddhism accepts the Pali Canon as faithfully conveying the teachings of Gautama the Buddha and thus as fully authoritative for Buddhist belief and practice.[63] Mahayana Buddhists, while acknowledging the authority of the Pali Canon also recognize many other sutras and commentaries as equally, and sometimes more, authoritative than the earlier Pali texts. With the later rise of the Vajrayana tradition, an additional set of texts came to be accepted as authoritative. Various schools within Mahayana and Vajrayana Buddhism adopted different scriptures as authoritative, or gave different weight to various texts, so that relatively few texts were accepted as fully authoritative by all traditions.

Second, Theravada has emphasized the doctrinal importance of the Four Noble Truths and the Path of Purification as leading to nirvana. While generally discouraging metaphysical speculation, the Theravada tradition has emphasized what it regards as the central truths of the Buddha's teachings – that there is no atman or self; the world is impermanent and all existence is characterized by suffering or sorrow; and that liberation from rebirth, or nirvana, is the goal.

The way to the goal of nirvana is through the Path of Purification, as outlined in the Noble Eightfold Path. The eight constituents of the Path are grouped into three divisions: morality (Right Speech, Right Action, Right Livelihood), concentration (Right Mindfulness, Right Effort, and Right Concentration) and wisdom (Right Understanding and Right Thought). The fifth-

---

[63] On the Pali Canon and Buddhist texts in general, see Lewis R. Lancaster, 'Buddhist Literature: Canonization,' in *The Encyclopedia of Religion*, vol. 2, ed. Mircea Eliade (New York: Macmillan, 1987), pp. 504–509; Reginald A. Ray, 'Buddhism: Sacred Text Written and Realized,' in *The Holy Book in Comparative Perspective*, eds. Frederick M. Denny and Rodney L. Taylor (Columbia, SC: University of South Carolina Press, 1985), pp. 148–80; and Akira Hirakawa, *A History of Indian Buddhism*, pp. 71–5.

century AD Theravada monk Buddhaghosa explained the path as follows:

> [One] should, having become well established in morality, develop the serenity and insight that are described as concentration and wisdom. This is how the Blessed One teaches the Path of Purification under the headings of morality, concentration and wisdom.... Here the training of higher virtue is shown by morality; the training of higher consciousness by concentration; and the training of higher understanding by wisdom. The system's goodness in the beginning is shown by morality.... Its goodness in the middle is shown by concentration.... Its goodness in the end is shown by wisdom.[64]

The one who follows the Path of Purification successfully is an Arahat ('Worthy One'), is free from all defilements, and will not be reborn. The arahat has attained in this life the condition of nirvana 'with remainder' and upon death realizes nirvana 'without remainder.'

> [The Arahat is] the perfected saint who completely annihilates the remaining five fetters of craving for existence in the world of form, craving for existence in the immaterial world, pride or conceit, restlessness, and ignorance. He then realizes that rebirth is exhausted, the Holy Life is fulfilled and what has to be done has been done. This is the highest, holiest peace and end of greed, hatred, and delusion. The Arahat stands on heights more than celestial, realizing the unutterable bliss of Nibbana. There is nothing in him to cause him to be born again or grow old again, or die again. There is nothing more for him to do, for he has shown that man can follow the Path of the Buddha to Nibbana.[65]

Third, the teachings of Theravada Buddhism typically are understood as being incompatible with belief in a Creator God

---

[64] Visuddhimagga, I. 8. 10, as cited in Donald W. Mitchell, *Buddhism*, p. 75.
[65] U. Thittila, 'The Fundamental Principles of Theravada Buddhism,' p. 111. Note that 'unutterable bliss,' like 'indescribably delicious,' in fact describes a sort or degree of bliss. It ranks the bliss (or deliciousness) as superb, highest degree of, or best sort of, bliss. This is actually very descriptive.

or a Supreme Being. The Burmese Buddhist scholar U. Thittila states,

> In Buddhism, there is no such thing as belief in a body of dogmas which have to be taken on faith, such as belief in a Supreme Being, a creator of the universe, the reality of an immortal soul, a personal savior, or archangels who are supposed to carry out the will of the Supreme Deity. It is true that there are different types of devas or spiritual beings mentioned in Buddhism, but they are beings like ourselves, subject to the same laws of cause and effect. They are not immortal, nor do they control the destiny of mankind. The Buddha does not ask us to accept belief in any supernatural agency or anything that cannot be tested by experience.[66]

Similarly, Walpola Rahula claims, 'According to Buddhism, our ideas of God and Soul are false and empty.'[67] And Jayatilleke observes that if by 'God' we mean a Supreme Being, creator of everything else apart from God, then 'the Buddha is an atheist and Buddhism in both its Theravada and Mahayana forms is atheistic.... In denying that the universe is a product of a Personal God, who creates it in time and plans a consummation at the end of time, Buddhism is a form of atheism.'[68]

Fourth, Theravada Buddhism emphasizes that the human individual is responsible for his or her own liberation or enlightenment. There is no God to whom one can turn for salvation. True, the Buddha himself did proclaim the dharma, the teaching resulting in liberation if properly embraced, and in this way he can be said to assist all sentient beings. But it is up to the individual to grasp the truth, to appropriate it, and thereby to attain nirvana. The Buddha said, 'One is one's own refuge, who else could be the refuge?'[69] Rahula states,

---

[66] Ibid., p. 71. Buddhist perspectives on the existence of God will be considered further in Chapter 6.

[67] Walpola Rahula, *What the Buddha Taught*, p. 52.

[68] K.N. Jayatilleke, *The Message of the Buddha*, p. 105.

[69] Dhammapadatthakatha, XII. 4, as cited in Rahula, *What the Buddha Taught*, p. 1.

[The Buddha] taught, encouraged and stimulated each person to develop himself and to work out his own emancipation, for man has the power to liberate himself from all bondage through his own personal effort and intelligence. The Buddha says, 'You should do your work, for the Tathagatas only teach the way.' If the Buddha is to be called a 'savior' at all, it is only in the sense that he discovered and showed the Path to Liberation, *Nirvana*. But we must tread the Path ourselves.[70]

Later, Mahayana Buddhism in China and Japan, in contrast to a strictly 'do-it-yourself' approach, distinguished between those Buddhist traditions which teach that liberation or salvation is available only through one's own efforts (Japanese: jiriki) and those schools which teach that it is available only through the merit or power of another (tariki), as in the Pure Land traditions. But Theravada Buddhism clearly embraces self-effort.

All the teachings of the Buddha can be summed up in one word: Dhamma.... It means truth, that which really is. It also means law, the law which exists in a man's own heart and mind. It is the principle of righteousness.... If a man will live by Dhamma, he will escape misery and come to Nibbana, the final release from all suffering. It is not by any kind of prayer, nor by any ceremonies, nor by any appeal to a deity or a God that a man will discover the Dhamma which will lead him to his goal. He will discover it in only one way – by developing his own character.[71]

Finally, Theravada Buddhism is also distinctive in its emphasis upon the humanity of the Buddha. Walpola Rahula claims,

Among the founders of religions the Buddha (if we are permitted to call him the founder of a religion in the popular sense of the term) was the only teacher who did not claim to be other than a human

---

[70] Ibid., pp. 1–2. A Tathagata is 'one who has come to the Truth' or 'enlightened one,' a Buddha. The quotation from the Buddha is from the Digha-Nikaya, II.

[71] U. Thittila, 'The Fundamental Principles of Theravada Buddhism,' pp. 67–68.

being, pure and simple, ... The Buddha claimed no inspiration from any god or external power either. He attributed all his realization, attainments and achievements to human endeavor and human intelligence. A man and only a man can become a Buddha.[72]

When compared with the elaborate metaphysical understanding of the Buddha's nature which developed in Mahayana, the Theravada tradition is rather modest in its emphasis upon the humanity of Gautama. And yet even within Theravada Buddhism Gautama is regarded as something more than just another respectable human teacher. Jayatilleke notes,

> The idea that the Buddha was a 'mere human being' is also mistaken. For when the Buddha was asked whether he was a human being, a Brahma (God) or Mara (Satan), he denied that he was any of them and claimed that he was Buddha, i.e., an Enlightened Being who had attained the Transcendent. This does not, however, make the Buddha unique for it is a status that any human being can aspire to attain.[73]

Although the Theravada tradition does regard Gautama as something more than merely a human being, as we shall see, Mahayana Buddhism developed an elaborate metaphysical understanding of the supramundane Buddha quite different from earlier traditions. The story of some of these transformations introduced by Mahayana, as Buddhism spread from India and south Asia throughout north and east Asia, continues in the next chapter.

---

[72] Walpola Rahula, *What the Buddha Taught*, p. 1.
[73] K.N. Jayatilleke, *The Message of the Buddha*, p. 53.

2

The Dharma Goes East

Buddhism today is a genuinely global religion, with adherents not only throughout Asia but also increasingly in Europe and North America.[1] As it encountered different cultures and religious traditions, Buddhism itself underwent significant changes, resulting in an astonishing variety of schools and traditions. Thus today there is enormous diversity within the Buddhist family. It has become customary to group Buddhist traditions into three general categories – the Theravada, Mahayana, and Vajrayana traditions. Theravada Buddhism was introduced in Chapter 1; here we will consider primarily Mahayana and, very briefly, Vajrayana Buddhism. A comprehensive survey of the many Mahayana traditions is impossible. We will introduce some major themes of Mahayana and then focus briefly upon two Mahayana schools that are especially prominent today.

Mahayana Buddhism

From roughly 100 BC to 100 AD the Indian sub-continent went through significant social and cultural changes that affected

---

[1] See *Buddhist Missionaries in the Era of Globalization*, ed. Linda Learman (Honolulu, HI: University of Hawaii Press, 2005). On the encounter between missionary Buddhism and local cultures in Asia, see Jerry H. Bentley, *Old World Encounters: Cross-Cultural Contacts and Exchanges in Pre-Modern Times* (New York: Oxford University Press, 1993), especially chapter 3.

Buddhism.[2] For example, theistic and devotional movements became more prominent in popular Hinduism, as Indian culture and religion encountered various Hellenistic and Zoroastrian traditions which spread into northwestern India. Eventually, a widespread Buddhist movement emerged which self-consciously identified itself as the Mahayana, or Great Vehicle, in contrast with what it somewhat pejoratively referred to as the Hinayana, or Lesser Vehicle. Modern Theravada Buddhism can be seen as a continuation of the earlier Hinayana tradition. Mahayana Buddhism is today the dominant form of Buddhism in China, Korea, Vietnam, and Japan. Like Theravada, Mahayana Buddhism claims to represent the original and most mature teaching of the Buddha. While there are clear similarities between Theravada and Mahayana Buddhist traditions, the differences between them are also unmistakable, and at times are so great that one wonders whether we are still dealing with the same religion.

The emergence of Mahayana was gradual, occurring within a number of already established Buddhist schools.

> The earliest use of the word 'Mahayana' in Indian inscriptions dates from the sixth century CE, although other terms with an exclusive reference to Mahayana monks and lay followers had been used from about the fourth century.... This is a very long time after the earliest Mahayana literature, and indicates that while doctrinally there may have been a growing idea of the Mahayana as an alternative aspiration and spiritual path from, say, the first century BCE, nevertheless the notion of a clear separate group identity among Mahayana followers, represented by their using a separate name for themselves, took centuries to develop.[3]

Mahayana, in its early development, was not so much a new school of Buddhism as it was a broad movement affecting many schools, attracting adherents and exerting influence within already

---

[2] Richard H. Robinson and Willard L. Johnson, *The Buddhist Religion: An Historical Introduction*, 4th edn. (Belmont, CA: Wadsworth, 1997), pp. 8ff.
[3] Paul Williams, *Mahayana Buddhism: The Doctrinal Foundations* (London: Routledge, 1989), p. 28.

existing traditions. It promised a more generous, liberal, and creative approach than the traditionalists offered.

As Buddhism spread throughout Asia it encountered cultures and religious traditions very different from those of the Indian subcontinent. Mahayana Buddhism has been remarkably flexible in adapting to new environments. This is evident, for example, in Buddhism's encounter with indigenous Chinese culture and religion, which were quite different from those of India and Sri Lanka. Buddhism entered China in the first century AD as a foreign religion and initially met resistance. Nevertheless, there were factors which encouraged eventual Chinese acceptance of Buddhism. For example, Buddhism brought with it certain social and religious advantages previously unavailable.

> These included a full-time religious vocation for both men and women in an organization largely independent of family and state, a clear promise of life after death at various levels, and developed conceptions of paradise and purgatory, connected to life through the results of intentional actions (*karman*). In addition, Buddhism offered the worship of heroic saviors in image form, supported by scriptures that told of their wisdom and compassion. For ordinary folk there were egalitarian moral principles, promises of healing and protection from harmful forces, and simple means of devotion; for intellectuals there were sophisticated philosophy and the challenge of attaining new states of consciousness in meditation, all of this expounded by a relatively educated clergy who recruited, organized, translated, and preached.[4]

Nonetheless, the different social, religious, and philosophical contexts of China raised new challenges for Buddhism. When Buddhism entered China, Confucianism and Daoism were already well established. The social and ethical framework of the Chinese, shaped by Confucianism, was based upon the family, not the individual, and emphasized the virtue of filial piety (hsiao). Given the emphasis upon filial piety and the ancestral cult, the individualism of Indian Buddhism, exemplified in the

---

[4] Daniel L. Overmyer, 'Chinese Religion,' in *The Religious Traditions of Asia*, ed. Joseph M. Kitagawa (New York: Macmillan, 1989), p. 276.

ideal of the arahat and celibacy of the monk, made Buddhism seem suspect.

> Buddhism as a religion in India aimed at individual salvation in nirvana, a goal attainable by leaving the household life, to use the familiar phrase in Buddhist literature, and entering the houseless stage, which means the life of celibacy and mendicancy. Upon assuming the monastic robe, the Buddhist monk terminated his ties with family and society, so that his wife became a widow; his children orphans. When this religion was introduced into China, where filial piety and family life were the dominant features of society, the conflict was joined.[5]

Thus, from the beginning Buddhism was attacked by Confucianists for being unfilial and socially subversive. Buddhists responded by trying to show that there was nothing in Buddhist teaching or practice that undermined filial piety or social cohesion, and that, to the contrary, filial piety itself is implicit in the Buddhist sutras. As it adapted to the Chinese context, the ancient practices of the ancestral cult were eventually incorporated into Buddhism.

Moreover, the notions of samsara and karma, so central to Indian religious and philosophical thought, were lacking in the Chinese context. Release from samsara was thus not the burning issue for Chinese that it had been for Indians. The Chinese had a much more positive view of life, nature, and society. Consequently, one finds in the Mahayana tradition as it developed in China, Korea, and Japan a decreasing emphasis upon the notion of nirvana as release from samsara, and greater stress upon the much more positive notion of enlightenment in this life. 'Mahayanists were generally more interested in the truth to which enlightenment was an awakening than the pain from which it was a release. This emphasis on the positive aspect of enlightenment also caused to be diminished the importance of *nirvana* as the release from rebirth.'[6]

---

[5] Kenneth K.S. Ch'en, *The Chinese Transformation of Buddhism* (Princeton, NJ: Princeton University Press, 1973), p. 15.
[6] Thomas Kasulis, 'Nirvana,' in *The Encyclopedia of Religion*, vol. 10, ed. Mircea Eliade (New York: Macmillan, 1987), p. 450.

The concept of nirvana as release came to be replaced with that of enlightenment as 'awakening' (wu in Chinese, satori in Japanese). The ideal became not so much release from samsara but rather harmony within the social and cosmic order, which is achieved through a penetrating and liberating insight into the true nature of reality. This shift in emphasis is particularly evident in the Chinese schools of T'ien-t'ai (Tendai in Japan), Hua-yen (Kegon), and Ch'an (Zen) Buddhism.

Mahayana Buddhism in China and Japan was significantly affected by its encounter with Daoism. Daniel Overmyer points out that, 'Chinese intellectuals first attempted to understand Buddhism through its apparent similarities to certain beliefs and practices of Taoism and the immortality cult. Thus, bodhisattvas and Buddhas were correlated with sages and immortals, meditation with circulation of the vital fluids, and nirvana with *wu-wei*, spontaneous and purposeless action.'[7] Daoist terms were used to translate key Buddhist concepts into Chinese – e.g. the Buddhist term 'dharma' (teaching, law, truth) was translated as 'Dao' ('Way'); 'wu-wei' was used for 'nirvana.' Moreover, like Daoism, some of later Buddhism taught that ultimate reality transcends conceptual and linguistic categories and is ineffable. Daoist influence was especially significant in the development of what came to be known as Ch'an in China and Zen in Japan.

As it spread throughout East Asia, Buddhism did not reject the popular indigenous religious cults and practices, rather it absorbed them. Buddhism adopted the ancient ancestor veneration practices, common in China and Japan, and popular local deities were included in the Buddhist pantheon as Buddhas or bodhisattvas. When it entered Japan in the sixth century, Buddhism encountered the indigenous Japanese religion of Shinto, with its worship of the ubiquitous kami (deities). Early Shinto was largely hostile to the foreign religion, but eventually Buddhism and Shinto achieved a remarkable rapprochement, in which the original nature of the Shinto kami was said to be Buddha and the many kami were seen as the Buddha's manifestations in

---

[7] Daniel Overmyer, 'Chinese Religion,' p. 276.

Japan.[8] While relations between Buddhism and Shinto over the centuries have been uneasy at best, in popular consciousness the two religions are accepted as complementary. Popular Buddhism in Japan thus includes worship of a vast pantheon of deities and higher beings, adapted from Shinto and folk religion. Throughout East Asia, then, the interaction between Buddhism and the many indigenous traditions has resulted in the rich variety within Mahayana Buddhism.

Mahayana Literature

It is sometimes said that the hallmark of Mahayana is its vastly expanded sacred literature, and not any particular doctrine or practice.[9] Although all Buddhists accept the authority of the Pali Canon, Mahayanists also accept many other sutras as authoritative, texts which are largely rejected by the Theravadins. There is no clearly defined Mahayana canon. Instead, Mahayana schools recognize a variety of sutras written in Sanskrit and then translated into Chinese and Tibetan, as well as original texts composed in China and Japan. The new sutras began appearing about the first century AD and claimed to convey the more advanced teaching of the Buddha, which was only hinted at in the Pali texts. Thus the later Mahayana texts are said to represent the final, mature doctrine of the Buddha, which was revealed only to his most astute followers.[10]

---

[8] See Joseph Kitagawa, *On Understanding Japanese Religion* (Princeton, NJ: Princeton University Press, 1987); and Ian Reader, *Religion in Contemporary Japan* (London: Macmillan, 1991), pp. 38–40.

[9] Richard H. Robinson and Willard L. Johnson, *The Buddhist Religion*, p. 84.

[10] Since the new Mahayana texts appeared after the Pali texts, Mahayanists had to defend their claim that the later texts actually contain the original teachings of Gautama. Mahayanists did this in two ways. First, they minimized the significance of the historical Gautama, and emphasized the importance of the ongoing presence and teaching of the 'transcendent Buddha,' and second, they developed a sophisticated hermeneutic allowing for the continued transmission of the 'Buddha-vacana' (word of the Buddha) through the transcendent Buddha and other enlightened beings. See

Among the more influential Mahayana texts are the Perfection of Wisdom Sutras (Prajnaparamita Sutras), written roughly from the first century through the eighth century, which include the popular Diamond Sutra and Heart Sutra.[11] In these texts we find dominant Mahayana themes such as the importance of cultivating wisdom (prajna), or the correct understanding of the way things really are; 'emptiness' (sunyata) as characteristic of all constituents of existence; and the bodhisattva path of compassion. Also significant are the Sutra Expounded by Vimalakirti (Vimalakirti-Nirdesa-Sutra), composed around the first century AD, which presents the doctrine of the 'emptiness' or 'suchness' (*tathata*) of all things, and the Sutra on the Descent into Lanka (Lankavatara Sutra), composed around the fourth century AD. The Lankavatara Sutra provides a subtle explanation of consciousness, how the mind mistakenly creates a false duality between what we take to be the self and the world, and how this deception can be overcome. One of the most popular and revered Mahayana texts is the Lotus Sutra (Saddharmapundarika-Sutra), written around 200 AD. The Lotus Sutra touches upon many key Mahayana themes, including the nature of the Buddha as a sublime being with supernatural powers; the use of 'skillful means' (upaya-kausala) in Buddhist teaching; the many buddhas and compassionate bodhisattvas who appear for the betterment of human beings; and the ideal of the bodhisattva path with its emphasis upon the welfare of others. The Larger and Smaller Sukhavati-Vyuha-Sutras (Land of Bliss/Happiness Sutras), composed around the second century AD, form the basis for the Pure Land traditions, one of the most popular Mahayana movements.

Reginald Ray, 'Buddhism: Sacred Text Written and Realized,' in *The Holy Book in Comparative Perspective*, eds. Frederick M. Denny and Rodney L. Taylor (Columbia, SC: University of South Carolina Press, 1985), pp. 150–51. On the relation of the historical Gautama to Mahayana Buddhism, see Whalen Lai, 'The Search for the Historical Sakyamuni in Light of the Historical Jesus,' in *Buddhist Christian Studies*, vol. 2 (1982), pp. 77–91.

[11] On the Mahayana texts, see Paul Williams, *Mahayana Buddhism*, especially pp. 29–54; and Donald W. Mitchell, *Buddhism: Introducing the Buddhist Experience*, 2nd edn. (New York: Oxford University Press, 2008), pp. 103–19.

Reflection upon the teachings of the many new sutras resulted in both new doctrines and fresh interpretations of older doctrines. Mahayana schools developed subtle and sophisticated metaphysical systems, which often include what seem to others to be paradoxical or counter-intuitive theses. We will highlight briefly here some key themes in Mahayana thought, and then return to explore some implications of these doctrines in greater depth in Chapters 4 and 5.

The Bodhisattva Ideal

Whereas Theravada Buddhism emphasized individual effort in attaining nirvana, in effect restricting the path to Arahatship to the few who could master the requisite disciplines within a monastic community, Mahayana opened the way to salvation to many, offering a vast multitude of spiritual guides and saviors to assist in deliverance from suffering. Chief among these benevolent beings are the bodhisattvas.

The bodhisattva, understood as a being who successfully undertakes the quest for enlightenment, is found in the early strands of Buddhism. Theravada texts, however, recognize only two such beings, Gautama before his enlightenment and Maitreya, the anticipated Buddha to come in the future. But with Mahayana the bodhisattvas comprise an innumerable company of supernatural beings who become the object of popular devotion and prayer, and who, out of deep compassion come to the aid of sentient beings caught in samsara. Bodhisattvas are beings who have experienced enlightenment but who have taken a special vow to continue being reborn into samsara, rather than enter nirvana, in order to assist others in their enlightenment. In fulfilling their vows over many lifetimes, bodhisattvas amass enormous amounts of merit which can be transferred to others, assisting them on the path to liberation. The bodhisattva thus came to represent the ideal of compassion, and they became objects of meditation, reverence, supplication, and even worship on the part of believers. As a Mahayana text put it,

The *bodhisattva* is endowed with wisdom of a kind whereby he looks on all beings as though victims going to the slaughter. And immense compassion grips him. His divine eye sees ... innumerable beings, and he is filled with great distress at what he sees, for many bear the burden of past deeds which will be punished in purgatory, others will have unfortunate rebirths which will divide them from the Buddha and his teachings, others must soon be slain, others are caught in the net of false doctrine, others cannot find the path [of salvation], while others have gained a favorable rebirth only to lose it again. So he pours out his love and compassion upon all those beings, and attends to them, thinking, 'I shall become the savior of all beings, and set them free from their sufferings.'[12]

The bodhisattva has infinite compassion for others:

A Bodhisattva resolves: I take upon myself the burden of all suffering. I am resolved to do so, I will endure it.... And why? At all costs I must bear the burdens of all beings.... I have made the vow to save all beings. All beings I must set free. The whole world of living beings I must rescue from the terrors of birth, of old age, of sickness, of death and rebirth, of all kinds of moral offence, of all states of woe, of the whole cycle of birth-and-death, of the jungle of false views, of the loss of wholesome dharmas, of the concomitants of ignorance, – from all these terrors I must rescue all beings.... I walk so that the kingdom of unsurpassed cognition is built up for all beings. My endeavors do not merely aim at my own deliverance. For with the help of the boat of the thought of all-knowledge, I must rescue all these beings from the stream of Samsara, which is so difficult to cross, I must pull them back from the great precipice, I must free them from all calamities, I must ferry them across the stream of Samsara. I myself must grapple with the whole mass of suffering of all beings.[13]

The path of the bodhisattva became a positive alternative to the earlier ideal of the arahat in Theravada Buddhism. Mahayanists

---

[12] From Astasahasrika Prajnaparamita 22.402–03; in *The Buddhist Tradition*, ed. William Theodore DeBary (New York: Random House, 1969), pp. 81–2.
[13] From the Vajradhvaja Sutra, Sikshasamuccaya, 280–81; in *Buddhist Texts Through the Ages*, trans. and ed. by Edward Conze, I.B. Horner, David Snellgrove, and Arthur Waley (Oxford: Oneworld Publications, 1995), p. 131.

charged that the way of the arahat was limited to the few and was selfish because it focused upon the individual monk's own liberation from samsara. The bodhisattva path, on the other hand, is open to the masses, providing a way for large numbers to pass beyond nirvana to attain full Buddhahood.

While on the level of popular folk religion the bodhisattvas often function as actual deities who respond to human entreaties, Buddhist doctrine has situated the bodhisattva within the classic teachings on impermanence and no-self. Thus, in endeavoring to rescue all sentient beings the enlightened bodhisattva realizes that in reality there are no beings to save. The Diamond Sutra portrays the bodhisattva thinking as follows:

> 'As many beings as there are in the universe of beings, comprehended under the term "beings"... all these I must lead to Nirvana, into that Realm of Nirvana which leaves nothing behind. And yet, although innumerable beings have thus been led to Nirvana, in fact no being at all has been led to Nirvana.' And why? If in a Bodhisattva the notion of a 'being' should take place, he could not be called a 'Bodhi-being.' And why? He is not to be called a Bodhi-being, in whom the notion of a self or of a being should take place, or the notion of a living soul or a person.[14]

Elaborating upon this paradoxical notion, Paul Williams says, 'The Bodhisattva's deeds and attitude are all sealed with the perfection of *prajna* [wisdom] – the Bodhisattva does not, in carrying out his infinite great and compassionate deeds, consider that there is any ultimately, inherently existing being who is helped. This is final, true, and total selflessness.'[15]

Nagarjuna and Emptiness

The 'emptiness' of all things is a prominent theme in Mahayana thought. Although it is present in the Perfection of Wisdom sutras,

---

[14] As cited in John M. Koller and Patricia Koller, *A Sourcebook in Asian Philosophy* (New York: Macmillan, 1991), p. 258.
[15] Paul Williams, *Mahayana Buddhism*, p. 50.

it is Nagarjuna (c. 150–250 AD) and the Madhyamaka tradition of Indian Buddhism that especially emphasized emptiness (sunyata) and had such an influence on Mahayana thought. Nagarjuna's views are set forth in the Mulamadhyamakakarika, his major work.[16]

Nagarjuna argued that all things are empty in the sense that they have no 'inherent existence' or essence. For an entity to have inherent existence is for it to exist in its own right, apart from other things. Inherent existence, then, is existence independent of the imputing or conceptualizing activity of the mind.[17] Nagarjuna thus rejects an earlier view from the Abhidharma philosophical traditions which maintained an ontological distinction between fundamental entities (or primary existents) and conceptual constructs (or secondary existents).[18] According to the Abhidharma perspective, things such as forests, tables, or persons appear to be independently existing, substantial realities whereas they are actually just conceptual constructs made up of other primary existents or dharmas. But these primary existents themselves were held to be products of causes and radically impermanent. Things such as tables or forests are 'empty' in that ultimately there are no such independently existing things; they are conceptual constructs from the dharmas and thus have only a provisional or conventional reality. But in Abhidharma thought, the basic dharmas do have 'inherent existence' or 'own existence,' even though they are impermanent.

---

[16] See *The Fundamental Wisdom of the Middle Way: Nagarjuna's Mulamadhyamakakarika*, trans. and commentary by Jay L. Garfield (New York: Oxford University Press, 1995). For somewhat different interpretations of Nagarjuna, see David J. Kalapuhana, *Nagarjuna: The Philosophy of the Middle Way* (Albany, NY: The State University of New York Press, 1986) and Frederick J. Streng, *Emptiness: A Study in Religious Meaning* (Nashville, TN: Abingdon Press, 1967).

[17] Paul Williams, *Mahayana Buddhism*, pp. 60–62.

[18] On the distinction and Nagarjuna's rejection of it, see Paul Williams, *Mahayana Buddhism*, pp. 60–63; and Richard King, *Indian Philosophy: An Introduction to Hindu and Buddhist Thought* (Washington, DC: Georgetown University Press, 1999), pp. 119–27.

Nagarjuna, by contrast, insists that *all* things without exception, including the primary existents or dharmas, are empty
and devoid of 'own existence.' He is not, of course, denying the
provisional or conventional reality of tables or forests; he fully
acknowledges that in our ordinary experience they do take on a
kind of reality.

> When the Madhyamaka speaks of all *dharmas* as empty (*sunya*)
> it means specifically that all *dharmas* (and therefore all things)
> are empty of inherent existence. They have no essence. They are
> only relative. It is inherent existence which is opposed by the
> Madhyamaka, not tables and chairs as such, but tables and chairs
> conceived as inherently existing and therefore, in the Buddhist
> context, as permanent and fully satisfying.[19]

The reason even the dharmas are empty is because all things arise
through 'dependent origination.' Nagarjuna states, 'Whatever
is dependently co-arisen [*pratityasamutpada*] that is explained to
be emptiness [*sunyata*].'[20] Williams explains that, '[I]t is because
entities originate in dependence on causes and conditions that
they lack inherent existence, they are empty.'[21] Three implications
of Nagarjuna's notion of the emptiness of all things should be
mentioned.

First, Nagarjuna's views on emptiness should not be taken as
either an extreme nihilism which rejects the existence or reality
of anything whatsoever, or as an implicit acknowledgement of
an ultimate Absolute or Supreme Being. Emptiness is neither the
sheer absence of anything nor is it an Absolute Reality.

> Emptiness is not, for example, an absolute that is separate from the
> world of ordinary experience. In fact, emptiness does not refer to a
> thing; it refers to the way all things actually are, namely, empty of
> the way they ordinarily seem to exist. To make emptiness into an
> entity about which one can have a view is to make the fundamental

[19] Paul Williams, *Mahayana Buddhism*, p. 61.
[20] *The Fundamental Wisdom of the Middle Way: Nagarjuna's Mulamadhyamakakarika*, XXIV.18, p. 69.
[21] Paul Williams, *Mahayana Buddhism*, p. 61.

mistake Nargajuna was trying to expose, namely, seeing anything as having a substantial identity.[22]

Emptiness here is not a 'something' that underlies all of the transitory phenomena of our experience. Rather, as Mitchell puts it, 'the myriad forms of existence are emptiness – they are empty of own-being.'[23]

Second, emptiness and the interrelatedness of all things have implications for how we understand samsara, the cycle of rebirth, and nirvana. Nagarjuna states,

There is not the slightest difference
Between cyclic existence [*samsara*] and nirvana.
There is not the slightest difference
Between nirvana and cyclic existence [*samsara*].[24]

True wisdom reveals that even nirvana is empty and is not an independent state distinct from the ordinary phenomenal world of samsara. 'Nirvana' and 'samsara' do not denote two separate realities; there is only the vast stream of emptiness which is experienced through ignorance as samsara or through wisdom as nirvana. One should not be attached to either samsara or nirvana. 'With wisdom's penetration into the ultimate truth of emptiness, one is detached from both the world and Nirvana, so that one can freely turn with compassion to address the needs of all living beings.'[25] There remains the question how 'one' and 'all living beings' are to be understood here.

Third, Nagarjuna distinguishes two levels of truth or reality, a distinction that is basic to much of Mahayana thought.

The Buddha's teaching of the Dharma
Is based on two truths:

---

[22] Donald W. Mitchell, *Buddhism*, p. 143.
[23] Ibid., p. 108.
[24] *The Fundamental Wisdom of the Middle Way: Nagarjuna's Mulamadhyakakarika*, XXV.19, p. 75.
[25] Donald W. Mitchell, *Buddhism*, p. 143.

A truth of worldly convention
And an ultimate truth.

Those who do not understand
The distinction drawn between these two truths
Do not understand
The Buddha's profound truth.[26]

The distinction is that between conventional truth and ultimate truth. Conventional truth applies to the ordinary world of experience. It is supposed to be a kind of truth – to be not simple falsity. But it describes a world which lacks inherent existence and thus cannot be what is truly ultimate. Jay Garfield explains the relation between the two truths:

> The term translated here as 'truth of worldly convention' (Tib: *kun-rdzob bden-pa*, Skt: *samvrti-satya*) denotes a truth dependent upon tacit agreement, an everyday truth, a truth about things as they appear to accurate ordinary investigation, as judged by appropriate human standards. The term 'ultimate truth' (Tib: *dam-pa'i don gyi bden-pa*, Skt: *paramartha-satya*) denotes the way things are independent of convention, or to put it another way, the way things turn out to be when we subject them to analysis with the intention of discovering the nature they have from their own side, as opposed to the characteristics we impute to them.[27]

Although the ultimate truth is said not to deny conventional truth, it reveals the true nature of what is 'known' on the conventional level. The goal is liberation from suffering, but this liberation comes only from deep insight into the actual nature of reality, an understanding of things as they actually are. This is the insight into the emptiness of all things and their interrelatedness through dependent origination. Only with this ultimate insight can one 'gain freedom within the dynamic of existence, Nirvana in *samsara*.'[28]

---

[26] *The Fundamental Wisdom of the Middle Way: Nagarjuna's Mulamadhyakakarika*, XXIV.8–9; p. 68.
[27] *The Fundamental Wisdom of the Middle Way: Nagarjuna's Mulamadhyakakarika*, pp. 297–8.
[28] Donald W. Mitchell, *Buddhism*, p. 144.

The Buddha Nat...

The increased prominence of the bodhisattva, and the growing attraction of the path of the bodhisattva leading to full Buddhahood, instead of the more restricted way of the arahat, were related to other developments in Mahayana thinking about the historical Gautama and the Buddha nature. Williams observes that, 'As Buddhahood became supreme over Arahatship, so attaining Buddhahood, and therefore becoming a Bodhisattva, became the new religious goal advocated for all Buddhist practitioners. This, if anything, characterizes the Mahayana.'[29]

Consideration of the nature of Buddhahood led to a reinterpretation of the Buddha. The Mahayana understanding of Buddhahood was given sophisticated expression in the doctrine of the Three Bodies of Buddha (Trikaya), three distinguishable, but closely related, levels or dimensions of the Buddha essence.[30] According to this doctrine, the historical Gautama Buddha was a human manifestation of an underlying, all-inclusive Buddha essence. This ultimate, all-inclusive Buddha essence was said to be the Dharmakaya, or Law Body. As the highest level of Buddha essence, the Dharmakaya is free from all the multiplicity, duality, and variability which characterize our phenomenal world, lacking all qualities and relations. This Buddha essence was later called by Mahayanists the Void, or Suchness, or Emptiness.

On a second level, however, the Buddha essence is manifest as the Body of Bliss, or Sambhogakaya, and it is on this level that bodhisattvas and Buddhas (those who have attained enlightenment) apprehend and enjoy the Buddha essence. Finally, there is the Transformation Body of the Buddha essence, or the Nirmanakaya, in accord with which the historical Gautama can be regarded as a concrete, historical manifestation of the one eternal

---

[29] Paul Williams, *Mahayana Buddhism*, p. 25.
[30] See Donald W. Mitchell, *Buddhism*, pp. 130–32; Paul Williams, *Mahayana Buddhism*, chapter eight; and Paul J. Griffiths, *On Being Buddha: The Classical Doctrine of Buddhahood* (Albany, NY: State University of New York Press, 1994).

Buddha essence. This raises, o̍   ̍ion of how such
talk of 'levels' is to be underst̍   ̍vels of what? The
Void is said to lack all qualities aṇ   ̍ṭons, and so cannot be
identical to bodhisattvas or anything historical and concrete. So
the levels cannot be levels of kinds of existents. But if the levels
are degrees of clarity or adequacy of knowledge of what is, only
the Void is the way things really are, and it can contain no subjects
of knowledge and nothing that is known, as this would require
qualities and relations. These, and related issues, will be explored
further in Chapters 4 and 5.

The doctrine of the Buddha's Bodies is also related to another
prominent Mahayana theme, the Tathagata-garba or 'womb or
embryo of the Buddha.' A number of Mahayana sutras written
between 200 and 350 AD, including the Tathagata Sutra, spoke
of the 'womb' or 'embryo' of the Buddha. All living beings are
said to possess or participate in the Tathagata-garba, which is
the universal Buddha nature. Because of this, all beings have the
potential to become Buddhas.

> Ultimately the *Tathagata-garba* is said to be identical with the Dharma-
> body (*Dharmakaya*) of the Buddha, the very essence of Buddhahood.
> Therefore, its condition is always nirvanic, and it responds to the
> teaching of the Dharma by generating from itself the thought or
> aspiration to attain awakening for the benefit of others (*bodhicitta*). It
> was taught that all living beings already possess this innate essence
> of Buddhahood; they just do not realize this fact.[31]

The idea that all living beings are potential Buddhas because of
their participation in the universal Buddha nature was to be a
prominent – and controversial[32] – theme in Chinese and Japanese
Mahayana schools. Much of East Asian Mahayana Buddhism has
embraced the universalistic teaching that all things share in the

---

[31] Donald W. Mitchell, *Buddhism*, p. 148.
[32] See the essays in *Pruning the Buddha Tree: The Storm Over Critical Buddhism*,
eds. Jamie Hubbard and Paul L. Swanson (Honolulu, HI: University of Hawaii
Press, 1997) for an overview of the contemporary debate among Japanese
Buddhists over whether the Tathagata-garba doctrine is authentically
Buddhist.

Buddha nature and have 'inherent' or 'original' enlightenment (Japanese: hongaku shiso). This theme became especially influential in the Shingon, Tendai, and Zen traditions of Japanese Buddhism.

It is impossible to include here discussion of all of the many Mahayana schools in China, Korea, and Japan. We will, however, give brief attention to two significant schools which emerged in China and were then transmitted to Japan – the Pure Land and Zen traditions. The Pure Land and Zen traditions are strikingly different and illustrate nicely the enormous variety within Mahayana Buddhism. People in the West are somewhat familiar with Zen, due to its increased popularity in the West since the 1960s. But the Pure Land tradition is less well known, despite the fact that it is one of the most popular forms of Buddhism in Japan and Taiwan.

Pure Land Buddhism

Many in the West are surprised when they first hear about Pure Land Buddhism, for it appears so different from either Theravada Buddhism or Zen, with which they are more familiar.[33] Moreover, at least at first glance, it bears some remarkable similarities to Protestant Christianity. Pure Land Buddhism has many more adherents in contemporary Japan than any other form of Buddhism, and yet it has received much less attention from Western scholars than other forms of Buddhism. Galen Amstutz suggests that, paradoxically, the similarity of Pure Land Buddhism to Protestant Christianity has actually resulted

---

[33] On Pure Land Buddhism, see Alfred Bloom, *Shinran's Gospel of Pure Grace* (Tucson, AZ: University of Arizona Press, 1965); James C. Dobbins, *Jodo Shinshu: Shin Buddhism in Medieval Japan* (Bloomington, IN: Indiana University Press, 1989); Galen Amstutz, *Interpreting Amida: History and Orientalism in the Study of Pure Land Buddhism* (Abany, NY: State University of New York Press, 1997); Esben Andreasen, *Popular Buddhism in Japan: Shin Buddhist Religion and Culture* (Honolulu, HI: University of Hawaii Press, 1998); and *Approaching the Land of Bliss: Religious Praxis in the Cult of Amitabha*, eds. Richard K. Payne and Kenneth K. Tanaka Honolulu, HI: University of Hawaii Press, 2004).

in reduced interest among Western scholars, as they have been attracted to what is different and exotic.[34] Similarly, Jan Van Bragt claims that 'the West is mainly interested in Buddhism as its antipode, partly in mistrust of its own religious tradition. It is therefore most attracted to these forms of Buddhism wherein that antipodal character appears most clearly – Theravada, Zen, Tibetan Buddhism. The Pure Land school, on the other hand, is perceived as very close to Christianity and far removed from the mainstream of Buddhism.'[35]

The textual basis for the Pure Land tradition is primarily in the Larger and Shorter Sukhavati-Vyuha [Land of Bliss] sutras, written probably in the second century AD.[36] These sutras speak of the Buddha Amitabha (Japanese: Amida), or Amitayus, who was earlier known as the bodhisattva Dharmakara. Under the guidance of a Buddha, Dharmakara meditated upon the many myriads of Buddha lands, contemplating the virtues of each one. He decided to integrate all the perfections of the various Buddha lands into one land of supreme purity and bliss, the Pure Land. Dharmakara then made a series of vows, stipulating that unless 48 conditions governing the Pure Land and the conditions for all sentient beings entering it were fulfilled, he would not become a fully enlightened Buddha in nirvana. The 18th Vow became central to the Pure Land traditions:

> If, after my attaining Buddhahood, all beings in the ten quarters should not desire in sincerity and trustfulness to be born in my country, and if they should not be born by only thinking of me ten times, except those who have committed the five grave offences and those who are abusive of the true *Dharma*, may I not attain the Highest Enlightenment.[37]

---

[34] See Galen Amstutz, *Interpreting Amida*.

[35] Jan Van Bragt, 'Buddhism – Jodo Shinshu – Christianity: Does Jodo Shinshu Form a Bridge Between Buddhism and Christianity?,' *Japanese Religions* 18 (January 1993), p. 47.

[36] Donald W. Mitchell, *Buddhism*, p. 117. Japanese scholars claim that the Shorter Sukhavati-Vyuha Sutra is the older of the two, possibly written in the first century BC. See Paul Williams, *Mahayana Buddhism*, p. 252.

[37] As cited in Alfred Bloom, *Shinran's Gospel of Pure Grace*, pp. 2–3.

It is held that over an enormous period of time Dharmakara devoted himself to the practice of good deeds in order to accumulate enough merit to fulfill his vows and save all sentient beings. Long ago Dharmakara became the Buddha Amitabha, and he now resides in the Pure Land, or Western Paradise. Because of his vast store of merit, Amitabha is able to assist others to gain rebirth in the Pure Land.

The Larger Sukhavati-Vyuha Sutra was translated into Chinese in the second century and by the sixth century there was a growing Amitabha cult in China. The Pure Land tradition developed in China through influential patriarchs such as T'an-luan (476–542 AD), Tao-ch'o (562–645 AD), and Shan-tao (613–681 AD).[38] T'an-luan made a critical distinction between 'self-power' and 'other power' in attaining salvation, opting for the 'other power' salvation of reliance upon the merit of Amitabha. He held that, whereas in earlier times it was possible to attain enlightenment through one's own efforts, the world had now entered such a degenerate stage that this was virtually impossible. By relying upon the 'other power' of Amitabha, however, one can be reborn into the Pure Land and will certainly achieve enlightenment there. The key to such rebirth is proper recitation of the name of Amitabha. 'To repeat constantly the name of Amitabha with a unified mind is to purify the mind of all its sins, and to ensure rebirth in the Pure Land, which is ultimately enlightenment itself.'[39]

Tao-ch'o further clarified the two ways of salvation – the Holy Path (Japanese: Shodomon) and the Gate of the Pure Land (Jodomon). The Holy Path is the way of the sages, the difficult path which relies upon self-power, and is open only to a very few. The Gate of the Pure Land is the easier path, open to all beings, and assures salvation through reliance upon the merit of Amitabha Buddha. Shan-tao, regarded by some Japanese Pure Land traditions as an incarnation of Amitabha, emphasized evil and suffering as endemic to human existence. Shan-tao acknowledged

---

[38] On the Pure Land tradition in China, see Kenneth Ch'en, *Buddhism in China: A Historical Survey* (Princeton, NJ: Princeton University Press, 1964), pp. 338–50.

[39] Paul Williams, *Mahayana Buddhism*, p. 259.

his own moral bankruptcy and inability to save himself, stating, 'I am actually an ordinary sinful being who has been, from time immemorial, sunken in and carried down by the current of birth-and-death. Any hope to be helped out of this current has been wholly denied to me.'[40]

The Pure Land traditions became established in Japan through the monk Honen (1133–1212) and his remarkable disciple Shinran (1173–1262), who lived at a time of significant social upheaval – civil war, famine, disease, and rampant corruption among the Buddhist hierarchy. Honen became the founder of the Jodo Shu (Pure Land) and Shinran the founder of Jodo Shinshu (True Pure Land) or Shin Buddhism. Both schools continue to flourish in Japan today.

Honen studied initially at the great Tendai Buddhist center at Mount Hiei, outside Kyoto, but he became disillusioned with the established Buddhist schools and left to study under a master of the Pure Land tradition. He became convinced that Japan had entered the 'latter days of the Law' – a period when Buddhist teachings become so degenerate that attaining salvation through one's own efforts is all but impossible. In 1175, while reading Shan-tao's commentary on a Pure Land text, Honen had an experience that led him to believe that the only path to salvation was to declare one's absolute faith in Amida's vow to save all sentient beings, and to engage in 'single-practice nembutsu' (recitation of the name of Amida: 'Namu Amida Butsu'). This meant placing sole reliance upon invocation of Amida's name as a means for salvation. Honen further held that one should recite the nembutsu repeatedly throughout life. Constant repetition of the nembutsu ensures continual purification of the mind and body, removes all doubt, can lead to enlightenment (satori) in this life, and results in rebirth in the Pure Land.

Although Honen maintained that nothing else was needed for salvation apart from proper recitation of the nembutsu, his teaching was ambiguous or inconsistent at points. For example, the nature of the recitation itself still seems to determine the efficacy of reciting the nembutsu. Honen states,

---

[40] As cited in Williams, *Mahayana Buddhism*, p. 261.

Even though through the days and years of life, you have piled up much merit by the practice of the *Nembutsu*, if at the time of death you come under the spell of some evil, and at the end give way to an evil heart, and lose the power of faith in the practice of the *Nembutsu*, it means that you lose that birth into the Pure Land immediately after death.... Sometimes a man dies from being choked when taking a meal. Now I say, call upon the sacred name every time you chew your food and swallow it.[41]

Bloom observes that, '[W]hatever efficacy the recitation of the name has it is neither permanent, nor necessarily cumulative and lasting. The problem of an untimely death or the possibility that one might not be in the possession of his right mind at the moment of death was a problem for Pure Land teachers.'[42] Thus, in spite of his explicit rejection of self-power (jiriki) in attaining salvation, and his call for complete reliance upon faith in the other power of Amida, it seems that implicit in Honen's teaching is a kind of self-effort in salvation. How one performs the nembutsu, and when it is recited, directly affect its efficacy.

The ambiguity between 'self power' and 'other power' was clarified by Honen's remarkable disciple Shinran. Both Honen and Shinran were persecuted by the Buddhist establishment – in part because of the perceived antinomian implications of Pure Land teachings – and Shinran was exiled for a time to northern Japan. There he adopted the life of a lay believer, married and raised a family, and became an enormously popular religious leader. The Amida cult spread rapidly among the masses, as Shinran emphasized that it is within the context of ordinary everyday activities, not by retiring to a monastery, that one must seek salvation. Rebirth in the Pure Land was now said to be open to people of all classes and not to depend upon rigorous self-discipline, meditation, or study.

Although Shinran followed Honen in most respects, he had a more penetrating understanding of human limitations and of the

---

[41] As cited in Bloom, *Shinran's Gospel of Pure Grace*, p. 21.
[42] Ibid.

all-sufficiency of Amida's grace.[43] Shinran had an acute sense of human sin and evil, and the radical inability of humankind to save itself. Human evil and helplessness magnify the compassionate action of Amida on our behalf. Whereas many would assume that the chances of a 'good person' being reborn into the Pure Land are greater than those of an 'evil person,' Shinran rejects this. In a famous passage Shinran claims,

> Even a good person can attain birth in the Pure Land, so it goes without saying that an evil person will. Though such is the truth, people commonly say, 'Even an evil person attains birth, so naturally a good person will.' This statement may seem well-founded at first, but it runs counter to the meaning of Other Power established through the Primal Vow. For a person who relies on the good he does through his self-power fails to entrust himself wholeheartedly to Other Power and therefore is not in accord with Amida's Primal Vow. But when he abandons his attachment to self-power and entrusts himself wholly to Other Power, he will realize birth in the Pure Land. It is impossible for us, filled as we are with blind passions, to free ourselves from birth-and-death through any practice whatever. Sorrowing at this, Amida made the Vow, the essential intent of which is the attainment of Buddhahood by the person who is evil. Hence the evil person who entrusts himself to Other Power is precisely the one who possesses the true cause for rebirth.[44]

Moreover, Shinran, unlike Honen, clearly rejected the idea that there is anything meritorious in the recitation of the nembutsu. It is not the act of reciting the nembutsu, but the faith – shinjin, arising from sincere trust in Amida – in accordance with which the nembutsu is recited, that produces rebirth in the Pure Land. But even having faith in Amida is not itself anything meritorious since it is actually the Amida Buddha who enables the 'arising of faith' within the individual in the first place. Here Shinran's thought reflects the East Asian Mahayana emphasis upon the universal Buddha nature inherent within all beings.

---

[43] See especially, Bloom, *Shinran's Gospel of Pure Grace*, chapter 3.
[44] As cited in Esben Andreasen, *Popular Buddhism in Japan*, p. 27.

[F]aith is not a volitional belief in something, but an articulation of our Buddha-nature. This is crucial, and places Shinran's thought squarely within the development of East Asian Buddhist theory. We can become enlightened because we are already enlightened – as Dogen said, only Buddhas become Buddhas. We cannot enlighten ourselves, for the ego cannot bring about egolessness. Only Other Power can help us. This is because within us all, at our very core, is Other Power itself, or the Buddha-nature which is Amitabha.... We can only have faith because faith is a shining forth of our innate Buddha-nature, which is Amitabha himself. All can be saved through faith, for all have the Buddha-nature, and all that is required is to stop striving and allow the Buddha-nature to radiate faith.[45]

Thus, it is the universal Buddha nature within us which produces shinjin, the arising of faith resulting in recitation of the nembutsu. Recitation of the nembutsu, then, is not something one does in order to attain salvation but is rather an act of worship or gratitude to Amida for the salvation already realized. Not surprisingly, Shinran has been compared to the Christian Protestant Reformer Martin Luther, who similarly emphasized salvation by faith alone. However, the similarities should not be exaggerated. For although there are some fascinating parallels between Shinran and Luther, the overall framework within which each speaks about evil, grace, faith and salvation is very different. Luther embraced a clear monotheism and regarded salvation as rooted in the historic event of the Incarnation, comprising the life, death, and resurrection of Jesus of Nazareth. Although Amida seems to function within Pure Land Buddhism in a way similar to God in Christianity, Amida should not be thought of as an eternal creator God who brings the universe into existence from nothing – that is, without any preexisting materials.[46] In Pure Land thought

---

[45] Paul Williams, *Mahayana Buddhism*, p. 272.
[46] The Protestant theologian Karl Barth was fascinated by the Pure Land tradition, but maintained that in spite of clear parallels with Protestant Christianity it lacked the one thing that is truly critical: 'That one thing is the name of Jesus Christ.' See Karl Barth, *Church Dogmatics: Volume 1:2, The Doctrine of the Word of God*, trans. by G.T. Thomson and Harold Knight (Edinburgh: T&T Clark, 1956) section 17, p. 343. See also Jan van Bragt,

Amida is identified with the Sambhoga-kaya (Body of Bliss) and
Nirmana-kaya (Transformation Body) of the Trikaya or threefold
Buddha essence. Moreover, in Christianity there is not the notion
of a 'Christ nature' that is our core or essence, as the Buddha
essence is for Pure Land Buddhism.

Zen Buddhism

When many in the West think of Buddhism what comes to
mind is Zen – or, more accurately, a particular image of Zen
popularized in the 1950s and 1960s. The Western conception of
Zen, however, does not always fit the actual Chinese and Japanese
historical tradition. We will consider the transmission of Zen to
the West more fully in Chapter 3, but here we will look briefly
at its roots in India, China, and Japan. Although Zen emerges
as a distinctive school in China, it draws upon earlier traditions
in Indian Buddhism. Heinrich Dumoulin observes that the
Indian roots of Zen are evident in two respects: Zen's connection
with the historical Gautama and its adoption and adaptation of
the ancient Indian meditative tradition of Yoga.[47] Zen maintains
that the core of what the Buddha realized in his enlightenment was transmitted directly and non-verbally from Gautama
to one of his disciples and has been passed on successively

'Buddhism – Jodo Shinshu – Christianity: Does Jodo Shinshu Form a Bridge
Between Buddhism and Christianity?;' Gerhard Schepers, 'Shinran's View of
the Human Predicament and the Christian Concept of Sin,' *Japanese Religions*
15 (July 1988), pp. 1–17; and John Ishihara, 'Luther and Shinran: SIMUL
IUSTUS ET PECCATOR and NISHU JINSHIN,' *Japanese Religions* 14 (July
1987), pp. 31–54.
[47] Heinrich Dumoulin, *Zen Enlightenment: Origin and Meaning* (New York:
Weatherhill, 1979), chapter 2. Dumoulin states, 'No other school of Mahayana
Buddhism venerates the historical Buddha Shakyamuni as strongly as Zen
has from its beginnings in China' (p. 17). For the historical development of
Zen, see Heinrich Dumoulin, *Zen Buddhism: A History, Volume 1: India and
China*, trans. by James W. Heisig and Paul Knitter (New York: Macmillan,
1988), and Heinrich Dumoulin, *Zen Buddhism: A History. Volume 2: Japan*,
trans. by James W. Heisig and Paul Knitter (New York: Macmillan, 1990).

from master to disciple ever since. According to a famous Zen tradition,

> Once when the World Honored One [Gautama the Buddha] was staying on the Mount of the Vulture, he held up a flower before the assembled ones. All fell silent. Only the venerable Kasyapa broke into a smile. The Honored One then spoke: 'The eye of the true Dharma, the wonderful Mind of Nirvana, the true formless Form, the mysterious Gate of the Dharma, which rests not upon words and letters, and a special transmission … outside the scriptures; this I hand over to the great Kasyapa.'[48]

In other words, the mature and complete teaching of Gautama is not what has been taught traditionally within the Theravada school but is actually something far deeper, something inexpressible in human words and categories. The Japanese Zen Buddhist D.T. Suzuki, for example, states that contrary to what the Theravada claim 'The Fourfold Noble Truth was not the content of Enlightenment, nor was the Twelvefold Chain of Causation, nor the Eightfold Righteous Path. The truth flashed through the Buddha's consciousness [at his Enlightenment] was not such a thought capable of discursive unfolding.'[49] Whether there can be such a thought is itself controversial, and so is whether, were it to occur, it could be believed or carried out in practice. What is unspoken need not be unspeakable.

Nevertheless, the tradition claims that the 'wonderful Mind of Nirvana' was then transmitted non-verbally through twenty-eight Indian patriarchs, the last of whom was the legendary Bodhidharma (c. 470–543 AD), said to have brought the 'lamp of enlightenment' to China. There is considerable controversy whether he was a historical person, but tradition attributes to Bodhidharma the formulation of the famous four line stanza said to express the heart of Zen:

---

[48] From the Mumonkan, as cited in Dumoulin, *Zen Enlightenment*, p. 16.
[49] D.T. Suzuki, *Essays in Zen: First Series* (New York: Weidenfeld, 1961 [1949]), p. 66.

A special transmission outside the scriptures,
Not founded upon words and letters;
By pointing directly to [one's] mind
It lets one see into [one's own true] nature and [thus] attain
    Buddhahood.[50]

In China this tradition became known as Ch'an Buddhism.[51] Ch'an Buddhism drew upon the Mahayana Prajnaparamita Sutras (Perfection of Wisdom Sutras), the Vimalakirti Sutra, and the Lankavatara Sutra, and adopted the ancient Yogic meditation techniques of disciplined sitting, breathing and concentration. Ch'an also embraced the Madhamaka's emphasis upon sunyata or emptiness. Kenneth Ch'en provides a succinct description of Ch'an Buddhism:

Ch'an has been described as an intuitive method of spiritual training aimed at the discovery of a reality in the innermost recesses of the soul, a reality that is the fundamental unity which pervades all the differences and particulars of the world. This reality is called the mind, or the Buddha-nature that is present in all sentient beings. In common with other Mahayana systems Ch'an teaches that this reality is *sunya*, empty or void, inexpressible in words and inconceivable in thought. To illustrate this the Ch'an masters often resorted to silence or negation to express the truth. Being inexpressible and inconceivable, this reality or the Buddha-nature can only be apprehended by intuition directly, completely, and instantly. Intellectual analysis can only divide and describe and scratch the surface but cannot apprehend the fundamental reality. In order to apprehend it one must calm the mind and have no conscious thought. In any conscious thought there is the ego at work, making for the distinction between subject and object. Conscious thought also begets karma, which ties one down to the

---

[50] As cited in Heinrich Dumoulin, *Zen Buddhism: A History. Volume 1: India and China*, p. 85. Most scholars think this formulation actually came much later than the time of Bodhidharma. Pages 85–94 in *Zen Buddhism* contain a helpful overview of issues relating to Bodhidharma and his relation to Zen. See also Kenneth Ch'en, *Buddhism in China*, pp. 350–53.
[51] 'Ch'an' is a Chinese rendering of the Sanskrit term 'Dhyana' (meditation); 'Zen' is the Japanese adaptation of 'Ch'an.'

endless cycle of birth and death and breeds attachment to external objects.... Instead, one should allow the mind to operate freely, spontaneously, and naturally.[52]

This, of course, raises the question of what free, spontaneous, neutral, *non-conscious* thought ought to be.

Ch'an Buddhism was shaped in part by its encounter with traditional Chinese Daoism. Both Ch'an and Daoism had a deep suspicion of words and concepts, maintaining that ultimate reality is inexpressible. For example, the Daoist classic the Dao de Jing begins with these enigmatic words:

The way [Dao] that can be spoken of
Is not the constant way;
The name that can be named
Is not the constant name.
The nameless was the beginning of heaven and earth;
The named was the mother of the myriad creatures.[53]

The Dao is said to be 'forever nameless' (XXXII.72). The Daoist sage 'practices the teaching that uses no words' (II.6). 'One who knows does not speak; one who speaks does not know' (LVI. 128).[54] It is not surprising, then, that Ch'an Buddhists found in Daoism a kindred spirit. The following narrative from a Mahayana text, summarized by Dumoulin, could just as well be speaking of a Daoist sage:

The *Vimalakirti Sutra* expresses the typical manner of Zen more concretely than any other Mahayana sutra. This sutra tells of the Bodhisattva of Wisdom (Manjusri), who is especially emulated in Zen. After several other Bodhisattvas had expressed themselves in well-chosen words about overcoming all oppositions in an all-embracing unity, the Bodhisattva of wisdom turned to the lay disciple Vimalakirti, to hear his answer to the essence of reality. But,

---

[52] Kenneth Ch'en, *Buddhism in China*, pp. 357–8.
[53] *Lao Tzu: Tao Te Ching*, I. 1–2. trans. by D.C. Lau (Harmondsworth: Penguin Books, 1963), p. 57.
[54] Ibid., pp. 91, 58, 117.

as the sutra has it, Vimalakirti said not a word, and was showered with praise. His answer of silence revealed supreme enlightenment, bound to no office and no monastic order. Vimalakirti, the lay disciple and housekeeper, proclaimed his perfect enlightenment without saying a word.[55]

Enlightenment was said to be a direct, intuitive insight into the true nature of reality, an understanding that transcends conceptualization and verbalization. This experience of awakening or enlightenment forms the heart of Zen.

In time, rival schools of Ch'an Buddhism developed, with disagreements over, among other things, whether enlightenment was a sudden, dramatic experience or the culmination of a longer, gradual process. Hui-neng (638–713), eventually acknowledged as the sixth patriarch of Ch'an, claimed that enlightenment comes suddenly from the Buddha-nature within one, and that it can happen anytime. This perspective was championed by the Lin-chi school of Ch'an, named after its founder Lin-chi (d. 867). Lin-chi was later taken to Japan by the monk Eisai (1145–1215) where it became known as Rinzai Zen. A contrasting view maintains that enlightenment comes gradually and is fostered over time through silent sitting meditation. In China this tradition was known as the Ts'ao-tung school, named after its two ninth-century founders Ts'ao-shan and Tung-shan. This school was introduced to Japan by Dogen (1200–53) and is known as Soto Zen. Although numerically much smaller than the Soto school, Rinzai Zen is better known in the West. Although in terms of adherents Zen is not among the larger Buddhist traditions in Japan today, it has had an influence upon Japanese culture disproportionate to its relatively small numbers.[56]

---

[55] Heinrich Dumoulin, *Zen Enlightenment*, p. 27. Without, however, the assumption that ultimate reality is ineffable – qualityless, relationless, completely inexpressible – the silence referred to in the quotation can just as well be understood as total ignorance. Moreover how can what is literally ineffable be characterized by detachment, peace, bliss, and fulfillment?

[56] See D.T. Suzuki, *Zen and Japanese Culture* (Princeton, NJ: Princeton University Press, 1959).

Enlightenment or satori is defined as the experience of awakening to the true nature of reality and the realization of the Buddha nature or the Buddha mind. Satori is said to be a direct, unmediated awareness of the ultimate nature of reality, a direct perception into the true nature of things. It is the awakening to one's own true nature. The Rinzai tradition of Japanese Zen, especially as interpreted by D.T. Suzuki, employs a variety of techniques in addition to meditation in order to prompt one to break through the confines of ordinary thinking into satori. These include spontaneous shouting (Ho!), the master occasionally striking the disciple, and especially the use the koan (riddle) or mondo (puzzling dialogue). Examples of famous koans include: 'What is the sound of one hand clapping?;' and the question, 'Does a dog also have a Buddha nature?' followed by 'Mu! [not, or nothing].'[57] Meditation upon such puzzles is said to help the mind to break free of the constraints of ordinary rational thought.

Enlightenment, especially in Rinzai Zen, is said to transcend the limitations of rational thought. The Japanese Buddhist D.T. Suzuki has been especially influential in popularizing Zen in the West, and we will conclude this section by quoting some of his depictions of satori. 'Satori may be defined as an intuitive looking into the nature of things in contradistinction to the analytical or logical understanding of it.'[58] The experience of enlightenment releases one from the limitations of logical and rational thought. Suzuki states, 'Zen has its own way of pointing to the nature of one's own being, and ... when this is done one attains to Buddhahood, in which all the contradictions and disturbances caused by the intellect are entirely harmonized in a unity of higher order.' He admits that, 'Logically considered, Zen may be full of contradictions and repetitions.'[59] Or again, 'From this it is apparent that Zen is one thing and logic another. When we fail to make this distinction and expect Zen to give us something

---

[57] On the koan, see Heinrich Dumoulin, *Zen Buddhism in the Twentieth Century*, trans. by Joseph S. O'Leary (New York: Weatherhill, 1992), pp. 121–30.

[58] D.T. Suzuki, *Essays in Zen*, p. 230.

[59] Ibid., p. 20.

logically consistent and intellectually illuminating, we altogether misinterpret the signification of Zen.'[60]

Those who attain satori transcend the limitations of dualism, including the distinction between good and evil. 'They were living in a realm beyond good and evil, and as long as they were there, no acts of theirs could be classified and judged according to the ordinary measure of ethics; they were neither moral nor immoral. These relative terms had no application in a kingdom governed by free spirits which soared above the relative world of differences and oppositions.'[61] Some, including some Christian mystics, suggest that what is encountered in satori is actually a divine being, God. But Suzuki rules this out.

> Satori is not seeing God as he is, as may be considered by some Christian mystics. Zen has from the very beginning made clear its principal thesis, which is to see into the work of creation and not interview the creator himself…. With the God of mysticism there is the grasping of a definite object, and when you have God, what is not God is excluded. This is self-limiting. Zen wants absolute freedom, even from God.[62]

Suzuki's characterization of satori and Zen is not accepted by all Buddhists. In the next chapter we will note how, as the ancient traditions of Zen were transmitted to the modern West, largely through Suzuki, they were interpreted and presented in particular ways.

Vajrayana and Tibetan Buddhism

Roughly five centuries after the emergence of Mahayana, yet another movement within Indian Buddhism appeared. This

---

[60] Ibid., p. 30. It is worth pointing out that, having proposed to forsake logic, the Zen master who claims to be enlightened cannot object if someone else proclaims him a deluded fool, for – on his view – the one does not preclude the other.

[61] Ibid., p. 77. It is not clear how there can be free spirits in such a distinctionless realm.

[62] Ibid., p. 263.

tradition came to be known as the Vajrayana ('Thunderbolt' or 'Diamond Vehicle'), and is sometimes referred to as Buddhist Tantra. The term 'tantra' refers to Buddhist texts concerned with rituals or instructions which open the door to esoteric Buddhist teachings and practices.[63] With Buddhist monastics increasingly preoccupied with sophisticated discussions of logic, epistemology, and metaphysics, lay Buddhists began to look elsewhere for resources to meet daily needs and to assist in the path toward Awakening. The practices associated with ancient Indian Tantra were one such resource.

Indian Tantrism provided Buddhists with a way in which the long path to Buddhahood could be completed more quickly, and in which one gains access to supernormal or magical powers along the way. Mitchell describes Indian tantra as emphasizing

> the power of ritual, meditative visualization, and esoteric practices to unite male and female energies in a way that is spiritually liberating. At the time Tantra began to influence the Buddhist community in India, perhaps sometime just prior to the sixth century CE, it was well established in certain Saivite sects of Hinduism. In that Saivite setting, Tantra included physical postures of body and hands called *mudras*, the use of magical phrases called *mantras*, the invoking and visualization of deities, breathing exercises, the movement of subtle forms of energy through psychic channels in the body, the cultivation of sensual bliss through sexual rituals.[64]

The Tantric practices were believed to open up certain psycho-physical pathways which had become 'blocked,' thereby enhancing one's spiritual energies and knowledge. In Buddhism, these esoteric practices were said not only to provide extraordinary powers in this life but also to aid in the pursuit of nirvana and Buddhahood. Buddhist traditions which adopted Tantra became known as Vajrayana Buddhism. Although Tantric Buddhism spread into China, Korea, and Japan, the only major East Asian school of

---

[63] Donald S. Lopez, Jr., *The Story of Buddhism*, p. 213; and Donald W. Mitchell, *Buddhism*, pp. 153–8.
[64] Donald W. Mitchell, *Buddhism*, pp. 154–6.

Tantric Buddhism today is the Shingon School in Japan. But the Tantra tradition remains an integral part of Tibetan Buddhism.

Tibetan Buddhism

Buddhism was introduced into Tibet in the seventh century AD. Prior to the arrival of Buddhism, Tibetan religion had been shamanistic and animistic, involving sacrificial rituals, a priesthood, magicians/diviners, and worship of various deities.[65] The king was central to the indigenous cult. From the tenth or eleventh century onward, Buddhism coexisted with the Bon religion. Although Bon is sometimes referred to as the indigenous religion of Tibet, the degree to which what we know today as Bon actually corresponds to the pre-Buddhist indigenous traditions is unclear. Although initially the Buddhists ridiculed and discredited Bon religion as simple animism, eventually aspects of Bon religion were absorbed by Buddhists, thereby shaping Tibetan Buddhism.

Legend has it that Buddhism entered Tibet through the Chinese and Nepalese wives of King Songsten Gampo (c. 609–650).[66] The first Tibetan king to truly embrace Buddhism and push it systematically was Trisong Detsen (c. 740–798) – the Tibetan 'King Asoka.' However, under his rule, the Tibetan Empire was severely cut back and a reaction against Buddhism set in. King Langdarma (c. 803–842) then severely persecuted Buddhism, but he was assassinated by a Buddhist monk and the country lapsed into 200 years of anarchy.

In the eleventh century Buddhism made a reappearance, as monks who had earlier fled to the east now returned to central Tibet and built a monastery. Indian sutras were translated and read, and the great Indian scholar Atisa (982–1054) arrived in Tibet in 1042. Atisa 'spent many years in Tibet teaching, translating, and establishing a form of Buddhism firmly based upon scholarship, morality, and a strict monastic tradition within which Tantric

---

[65] See Per Kvaerne, 'The Religions of Tibet,' in *The Religious Traditions of Asia,* ed. Joseph Kitagawa (New York: 1989), pp. 196–8.
[66] See Paul Williams, *Mahayana Buddhism,* p. 187.

practice nevertheless had a legitimate place.[67] Several distinct schools of Buddhism which drew upon a synthesis of Abhidharma, Mahayana, and Tantric Buddhism developed in Tibet over the next 900 years.

Over time four major schools of Tibetan Buddhism developed – the Geluk, Sakya, Kagyu, and Nyingma schools.[68] The various schools are united in their acceptance of a common Tibetan Buddhist canon and their common ancestry in Indian Mahayana and Vajrayana Buddhism. Moreover, each absorbed Tantric practices and teachings, with its emphasis upon visualization and cultivation of techniques for removing obstacles to the realization of Buddhahood. Although we cannot consider each of the schools here, given its prominence in the West, some distinctives of the Geluk tradition should be noted. The Geluk tradition is traced back to one of the great religious leaders of Tibet, Tsong Khapa (1357–1419), author of *The Great Graduated Path*, the major text of the Geluk school. Tsong Khapa founded the Riwo Ganden ('Joyous Mountain') monastery in 1409, and soon other monasteries were constructed throughout the country. The Geluk ('Order of Virtue') school associated with Tsong Khapa became famous for its strict standards of discipline and scholarship. It maintains a rigorous educational system for its monks, with carefully prescribed study in ritual, meditation, grammar, logic, debate, and epistemology, followed by rigorous exams.

Tibetan Buddhism is well known for its teaching of tulku reincarnation, according to which some lamas (Tibetan for 'guru') who have already attained lamahood in a previous life are said to reincarnate. Gendun Druba (1391–1474), third successor to Tsong Khapa as head of the Geluk school, was said to have predicted his own rebirth and then to be reincarnated as Gendun Gyatso (1475–1542). Gendun Gyatso then reincarnated as Sonam Gyatso (1542–88) and was given the title Dalai Lama ('Ocean of Wisdom') by the Mongol ruler Altan Khan. As Gendun Gyatso was the reincarnation of his two predecessors, he became known as the Third Dalai Lama.

---

[67] Ibid., p. 191.
[68] On the schools of Tibetan Buddhism, see David Snellgrove, 'The Schools of Tibetan Buddhism,' in *The Religious Traditions of Asia*, pp. 207–15.

He and every succeeding Dalai Lama have served as the spiritual head of the Geluk School. Under the Fifth Dalai Lama, Ngawang Losang Gyatso (1617–82), political power of a newly unified Tibet, as well as spiritual authority, was consolidated under the office of the Dalai Lama. The current Dalai Lama, Tenzin Gyatso (b. 1935), is the fourteenth Dalai Lama and is regarded in Tibetan Buddhism as not only a reincarnation of the previous Dalai Lamas but also an incarnation of the Buddha Avalokitesvara.[69] Speaking of this belief, the current Dalai Lama states,

> Now in my own case, I am held to be the reincarnation of each of the previous thirteen Dalai Lamas of Tibet.... who are in turn considered to be manifestations of Avalokiteshvara, or Chenrezig, Bodhisattva of Compassion, holder of the White Lotus. Thus I am believed also to be a manifestation of Chenrezig, in fact the seventy-fourth in a lineage that can be traced back to a Brahmin boy who lived in the time of Buddha Shakyamuni. I am often asked whether I truly believe this. The answer is not simple to give. But as a fifty-six year old, when I consider my experiences during this present life, and given my Buddhist beliefs, I have no difficulty accepting that I am spiritually connected both to the thirteen previous Dalai Lamas, to Chenrezig and to the Buddha himself.[70]

The Dalai Lama came to worldwide prominence after the Chinese invasion of Tibet in 1950, driving the Dalai Lama and thousands of Tibetans into exile. In 1950 there were over 6,000 Buddhist monasteries, but by 1959 virtually all were destroyed and most of the Buddhist monks exiled or killed. An estimated 1.2 million

---

[69] Although for most Mahayana Buddhists Avalokitesvara is a bodhisattva especially known for compassion, in Tibetan Buddhism he is a Buddha. 'For Tibetans, Avalokitesvara is not a bodhisattva, but a Buddha who attained Buddhahood in a previous world era and vowed to appear in the eras of future Buddhas to help bring the Dharma to the people. The Dalai Lamas are believed to be emanation-bodies of this Buddha, who, it is said, leads the Tibetan people both spiritually and politically' (Donald W. Mitchell, *Buddhism*, p. 169).
[70] Tenzin Gyatso, The Fourteenth Dalai Lama, *Freedom in Exile: The Autobiography of the Dalai Lama* (New York: HarperCollins, 1990), p. 11.

Tibetans, out of a total of 6 million, died at the hands of the Chinese.[71] The Dalai Lama, now based in Dharamsala, India, has traveled extensively throughout the West, promoting the cause of the Tibetan people as well as serving as the most visible spokesman for Buddhism in the West today.

---

[71] Donald W. Mitchell, *Buddhism*, pp. 185–6.

3

The Dharma Comes West

For over two millennia Buddhism was found exclusively in Asia. But Buddhism, like Islam and Christianity, is an example of what Mark Juergensmeyer calls transnational religions, or religions of expansion. A central element of transnational religions is 'the notion that their religion is greater than any local group and cannot be confined to the cultural boundaries of any particular region. These are religious traditions with universal pretensions and global ambitions. It is a hallmark of Muslims, Christians, and Buddhists that they believe that their religious ideas are universally applicable.'[1] That Christianity and Islam have 'universal pretensions and global ambitions' is hardly news. But Buddhism? Can this quaint and exotic religion of meditating monks and serene gardens have global ambitions?

In fact, Buddhism has always been a missionary religion, moving intentionally beyond its land of origin into very different cultures and societies. The Japanese Buddhist scholar Hajime Nakamura observes that, 'Soon after the founding of the Order, the Buddha sent out his followers on missionary journeys to spread the Dharma with the command, "Fare ye forth, brethren, on the mission that is for the good of the many, for the happiness of the many; to take compassion to the world; to work for the profit and good and happiness of gods and men. Go singly; go

---

[1] Mark Juergensmeyer, 'Thinking Globally About Religion,' in *Global Religions: An Introduction*, ed. Mark Juergensmeyer (New York: Oxford University Press, 2003), p. 7.

not in pairs.'"[2] In the previous chapter we saw how Buddhism moved from its home in India into Sri Lanka and South-East Asia, then north and east into China, Korea, Japan, and Tibet. In the nineteenth century Buddhism was transmitted to Hawaii, and in the twentieth century it became established in North America and Europe.[3] While the actual number of Buddhists in Europe and North America remains small, the religious and cultural impact of Buddhism in the West has been far greater than the numbers alone would indicate. In this chapter we will consider how Buddhism was introduced to the West, focusing especially upon the transmission of Zen Buddhism to the United States in the late nineteenth and early twentieth centuries and the role of D.T. Suzuki in this process. We will conclude by looking at Masao Abe, another prominent emissary of Buddhism to the West, considering especially his views on moral judgments from the perspective of Zen.

Although widespread exposure to Buddhism did not come until later, fascination with Buddhist thought by Western intellectuals is evident already in the early nineteenth century. Explorers and traders brought back fragmentary – and often distorted – information on Buddhism and Hinduism. The exotic and mysterious East had a powerful appeal. Martin Baumann

---

[2] Hajime Nakamura, 'Unity and Diversity in Buddhism,' in *The Path of the Buddha: Buddhism Interpreted by Buddhists*, ed. Kenneth W. Morgan (New York: Ronald Press, 1956), p. 367. For a helpful study of the missionary nature of twentieth century Buddhism, see *Buddhist Missionaries in the Era of Globalization*, ed. Linda Learman (Honolulu, HI: University of Hawaii Press, 2005).

[3] There are many helpful works on Buddhism in the West, including James William Coleman, *The New Buddhism: The Western Transformation of an Ancient Tradition* (New York: Oxford University Press, 2001); Charles S. Prebish, *Luminous Passage: The Practice and Study of Buddhism in America* (Berkeley, CA: University of California Press, 1999); *Westward Dharma: Buddhism Beyond Asia*, eds. Charles S. Prebish and Martin Baumann (Berkeley, CA: University of California Press, 2002); *The Faces of Buddhism in America*, eds. Charles S. Prebish and Kenneth K. Tanaka (Berkeley, CA: University of California Press, 1998); Richard Hughes Seager, *Buddhism in America* (New York: Columbia University Press, 1999); and Rick Fields, *How the Swans Came to the Lake: A Narrative History of Buddhism in America*, 3rd edn. (Boston, MA: Shambhala, 1992).

observes that, 'Around 1800, as texts and descriptions about Indian religions became known in literate and academic circles in Europe, a glorifying enthusiasm for the East took hold.'[4] Intellectuals such as Friederich Schlegel (1772–1829) and Arthur Schopenhaur (1788–1860) stimulated interest in Buddhist thought by making use of Buddhist themes in their writings. In 1881 Thomas W. Rhys Davids (1843–1922) established the Pali Text Society, which was devoted to the translation and publication of Pali Buddhist scriptures, in England. At the time of Rhys Davids' death it had published ninety-four volumes (26,000 pages) of Buddhist scriptures.[5] But undoubtedly the person most responsible for the translation, publication, and study of the scriptures of Asian religions was the Oxford professor Friedrich Max Müller (1823–1900). Müller edited the *Sacred Books of the East*, a monumental project of translating the sacred scriptures of the major Asian religions into English. In Great Britain and Germany, intellectuals took up the study of Pali texts and Theravada Buddhist thought. Baumann describes the image of a Buddhist which began to take hold among European intellectuals: 'Since the 1880s, the texts of the Pali Canon and the Theravada monk as ideal and model had dominated the European adoption of Buddhism. Philosophical, ethical, and cognitive interests stood out clearly. The norm of a Buddhist in Europe was conceived of as a rational, detached person who intellectually purifies himself (seldom herself) from the root defilements of ignorance, hatred, and lustfulness.'[6]

Across the Atlantic, from about the 1840s on, Americans also came into contact with Buddhism both through increased immigration of Asians (primarily Chinese) and from reports from merchants, missionaries, and explorers. Some Europeans and Americans began converting to Buddhism. The attraction

---

[4] Martin Baumann, 'Buddhism in Europe: Past, Present, Prospects,' in *Westward Dharma*, p. 86.
[5] J.J. Clarke, *Oriental Enlightenment: the Encounter Between Asian and Western Thought* (London: Routledge, 1997), p. 75.
[6] Martin Baumann, 'Buddhism in Europe,' p. 91. On the British encounter with Buddhism, see Philip C. Almond, *The British Discovery of Buddhism* (Cambridge: Cambridge University Press, 1988).

of Buddhism is evident in the remarkable reception that greeted the 1879 publication of Sir Edwin Arnold's epic poem on the life of the Buddha, *The Light of Asia*.[7] According to Carl Jackson, it is estimated that *The Light of Asia* 'went through sixty English and eighty American editions and that between five hundred thousand and one million copies were sold in Great Britain and the United States. Enthusiastically reviewed and widely quoted, hotly attacked and passionately defended, perhaps no work on Buddhism has ever approached its popular success. Certainly, no event in the late nineteenth century did more to rivet attention on Buddhism.'[8]

The World's Parliament of Religions

American awareness of Buddhism goes back at least to the Transcendentalists and other intellectuals in the 1840s. In a quite different context, Chinese and Japanese immigrants brought Buddhism with them when they settled on the West Coast in the mid-nineteenth century. But no single event was as significant for the American reception of Buddhism as the World's Parliament of Religions, held in Chicago September 11–27, 1893, in conjunction with the World's Columbian Exposition. This extravagant event, given widespread and positive coverage by the press, provided legitimation of Asian religions in the West and a prominent platform for Hindu and Buddhist spokesmen to address Western audiences.[9] A variety of Buddhist traditions

[7] Edwin Arnold, *The Light of Asia, or The Great Renunciation* (New York: A.L. Burt, 1879).

[8] Carl T. Jackson, *The Oriental Religions and American Thought: Nineteenth Century Explorations* (Westport, CT: Greenwood Press, 1981), p. 143.

[9] On the 1893 World's Parliament of Religions, see *The Dawn of Religious Pluralism: Voices From the World's Parliament of Religions, 1893*, ed. Richard Hughes Seager (La Salle, IL: Open Court, 1993); *A Museum of Faiths: Histories and Legacies of the 1893 World's Parliament of Religions*, ed. Eric J. Ziolkowski (Atlanta, GA: Scholars, 1993); and Joseph M. Kitagawa, 'The 1893 World's Parliament of Religions and Its Legacy,' in *The History of Religions: Understanding Human Experience* (Atlanta, GA: Scholars, 1987).

were represented, with Asian Buddhist participants including the Theravada monk Anagarika Dharmapala from Ceylon and the Japanese Rinzai Zen monk Shaku Soen. The Parliament was of enormous social and religious significance as America entered the twentieth century, not least in its contribution to the modern interreligious dialogue movement. But as Richard Hughes Seager observes, 'Above all else, however, the Parliament is a historical landmark because it set in motion the first Buddhist missions to the United States.'[10]

The story of Buddhism's introduction to the West can be seen as a fascinating case study of how an ancient religious and philosophical system adapts to a modern and culturally different context. The Buddhism D.T. Suzuki presented to the West had been shaped by historical circumstances both in Japan and in America, and reflected Suzuki's own particular spiritual and intellectual concerns. This, of course, is not unusual in cases of missionary religions; any transmission of a religious message to those who are culturally other will be influenced to some extent by contemporary social and cultural factors. But it is instructive to see how this worked with Suzuki and the Buddhist mission to the West.

The 1893 Parliament occurred at a critical point in the history of both the United States and Japan. While the United States was establishing itself as a modern industrial nation and global power, Japan was emerging from two centuries of self-imposed isolation from the rest of the world and embarking upon an ambitious path of rapid modernization. The Japanese delegation to the 1893 Parliament was deeply influenced by the social and political crises of late nineteenth-century Japan, and the effort by progressives to produce a 'new Buddhism' (shin bukkyo) appropriate to the modern state and fully equal to the intellectual and religious traditions of the West.[11] The mission of the delegation was 'to convince intellectuals that Japanese Buddhism was the equal of

---

[10] Richard Hughes Seager, *Buddhism in America*, p. 37.
[11] Judith Snodgrass, *Presenting Japanese Buddhism to the West: Orientalism, Occidentalism, and the Columbian Exposition* (Chapel Hill, NC: The University of North Carolina Press, 2003).

Western philosophy, superior to Western religion and completely in accord with Western science.'[12] The attempt to demonstrate a form of Buddhism fully compatible with modern science and superior to Western religious traditions, while remaining rooted firmly in ancient Japanese cultural distinctives, had an enormous effect upon subsequent perceptions of Buddhism in America.

The Japanese delegation, led by the Zen monk Shaku Soen, returned to Japan convinced that the materialistic and hedonistic culture of America was hungering for Eastern spirituality. Notto Thelle observes that

> The Japanese Buddhists did not hesitate to proclaim that the parliament was a unique breakthrough for Buddhist mission. The Buddhist presence was characterized as 'an epoch-making, unprecedented happening, unheard-of in history.' It was felt that the situation was ripe for 'Buddhism in Japan in the Far East to turn the wheel of Dharma in America in the Far West.' At the dawn of the twentieth century Buddhism was appearing at the scene of world culture spreading the unfathomable light and compassion of the Buddha. A representative Buddhist journal concluded that the parliament was 'the most brilliant fact in the history of Buddhism.'[13]

After the Parliament, Dharmapala and Shaku Soen made several tours in America promoting Buddhism.[14] But of even greater significance was Soen's encouragement for three of his friends – Sokei-an, Nyogen Senzaki, and D.T. Suzuki – to become transmitters of the dharma in America. 'Their work in the first decades of [the twentieth] century effectively laid the foundations for American Zen Buddhism.'[15]

---

[12] Ibid., p. 9.
[13] Notto Thelle, *Buddhism and Christianity in Japan: From Conflict to Dialogue, 1854–1899* (Honolulu, HI: University of Hawaii Press, 1987), pp. 221–2.
[14] A collection of talks given by Shaku Soen during his 1905–06 stay in the USA is found in Soyen Shaku, *Zen for Americans*, translated and edited by Daisetz Teitaro Suzuki (New York: Dorset Press, 1906).
[15] Richard Hughes Seager, *Buddhism in America*, p. 37.

Buddhism in America

Much, of course, has changed since the 1893 World's Parliament on Religions. Although hard numbers are difficult to come by, Martin Baumann estimated in 1997 that there were between 3 to 4 million Buddhists in the United States, the most in any Western country.[16] Robert Wuthnow and Wendy Cage suggest that 'Credible estimates of the numbers of Buddhists in the United States at the start of the 21st century range from 1.4 – 4 million.'[17] Most Buddhists in the USA and Europe are immigrants, with non-Asian converts to Buddhism comprising a significant minority.[18] Part of the difficulty in counting Buddhists is determining what constitutes 'being Buddhist.' Self-identified adherents are one thing, but both in Europe and the US there are many who, while not identifying themselves as Buddhist, nevertheless are sympathetic to Buddhism or have been influenced by Buddhist ideas.[19] If we include what Thomas Tweed calls 'night-stand Buddhists,' or those who are somewhat sympathetic to Buddhist themes without making a full commitment to Buddhism, then clearly the numbers are much higher.[20]

Richard Seager helpfully suggests that we think of American Buddhism as comprising three groups – old-line Asian-American Buddhism, Euro-American Buddhism, and the ethnic

---

[16] As cited in Richard Hughes Seager, *Buddhism in America*, p. 11.

[17] Robert Wuthnow and Wendy Cage, 'Buddhists and Buddhism in the United States: The Scope and Influence,' *Journal for the Scientific Study of Religion* 43:3 (2004), p. 364.

[18] Richard Hughes Seager, 'American Buddhism in the Making,' in *Westward Dharma*, p. 114; Martin Baumann, 'Buddhism in Europe,' p. 95.

[19] Wuthnow and Cage report that studies conducted in 2002 indicate that 'people who do not consider themselves Buddhists may nevertheless be influenced by some of its teachings and practices.' They conclude that, '[A] sizable number of Americans – as many as 25–30 million – believe they have had some contact with Buddhists or with Buddhist teachings and thus have had the opportunity to be influenced by Buddhism.' Robert Wuthnow and Wendy Cage, 'Buddhists and Buddhism in the United States,' pp. 364–65.

[20] Thomas Tweed, 'Who Is a Buddhist?,' in *Westward Dharma*, pp. 20–21.

Buddhism of newer immigrants.[21] Buddhism first came to the
USA in significant numbers with the Chinese who arrived on
the West Coast, attracted by the gold rush of 1848. Temples
were built in San Francisco. Japanese Pure Land Buddhism
arrived in 1899 with the Japanese Buddhist missionaries Shuye
Sonoda and Kauryo Nishijima, who established the Buddhist
Mission of North America and worked among Japanese
immigrants. Discrimination against Chinese and Japanese, such
as the Oriental Exclusion Act of 1924, strengthened the sense of
Buddhist identity among immigrant communities. In 1944 the
name of the Buddhist Mission of North America was changed
to Buddhist Churches of America (BCA) and ties with Japanese
Buddhism were either cut or redefined. After the Second World
War the BCA emerged as an ethnically distinct form of American
Buddhism, dominated by the Pure Land traditions of Japanese
Buddhism.

What Seager calls Euro-American or convert Buddhism is
primarily a post-Second World War phenomenon.[22] By the
1950s Buddhism was becoming more visible and influential in
the West, and was attracting significant numbers of non-Asian
Americans. The 1960s were a time of tremendous social, cultural,
and religious ferment, as traditional Western institutions and
assumptions were challenged and often rejected. Confidence in
traditional Western assumptions and institutions were undermined by the cumulative effects of two devastating world wars,
culminating in the terrors of the atomic bomb and the Cold War;
violent anti-colonialist movements of nationalism throughout
Africa, Asia, and Latin America; disillusionment with the
rampant consumerism and materialism of Western societies; the
perception of institutional Christianity as an irrelevant vestige of
a bygone era; and a deepening disenchantment with science and
technology. Eastern spirituality was welcomed as the antidote to
Western decadence and bankruptcy. Many looked to the East for

---

[21] Richard Hughes Seager, 'American Buddhism in the Making,' pp. 106–19.
See also Seager, *Buddhism in America*, chapter 1.
[22] Richard Hughes Seager, 'American Buddhism in the Making,' pp. 109–
14.

fresh ways of tapping into spiritual resources no longer available in the West.[23]

Disillusionment with traditional society gained widespread attention in the 1950s with the Beat existentialists and exploded into angry protest during the tumultuous 1960s. Buddhist themes and symbolism were prominent in Beat poet Jack Kerouac's 'Dharma Bums' (1958) and Gary Snyder's 'Smokey the Bear Sutra' (1969).[24] By the 1960s large numbers of Westerners were traveling to India and Japan to study with Eastern masters. An influential group of Western thinkers, having made the obligatory pilgrimage to the East, promoted the gospel of Eastern spirituality. Alan Watts, an Anglican priest who became disillusioned with traditional Christianity, was one of the most influential popularizers of Eastern spirituality in the 1950s and 1960s. Among his twenty-six books is the influential *The Way of Zen*.[25] Ever eclectic, Watts described his own spiritual orientation as 'between Mahayana Buddhism and Taoism, with a certain leaning towards Vedanta and Catholicism, or rather the Orthodox Church of Eastern Europe.'[26] This eclecticism, freely mixing elements from various traditions, characterized much of the Western appropriation of Eastern religions, including the popular fascination with Zen. By the 1990s, Buddhism, especially Tibetan Buddhism, was chic within the entertainment industry, as celebrities such as Richard Gere, Tina Turner, Adam Yauch of the Beastie Boys, Herbie

---

[23] See, for example, Robert S. Ellwood, *The Sixties Spiritual Awakening: American Religion Moving From Modern to Postmodern* (New Brunswick, NJ: Rutgers University Press, 1994), and *Alternative Altars: Unconventional and Eastern Spirituality in America* (Chicago, IL: University of Chicago Press, 1979); Harvey Cox, *Turning East: The Promises and Perils of the New Orientalism* (New York: Simon & Schuster, 1977); and Amanda Porterfield, *The Transformation of American Religion: The Story of a Late Twentieth Century Awakening* (New York: Oxford University Press, 2001), pp. 125–62.

[24] See *Asian Religions in America: A Documentary History*, eds. Thomas A. Tweed and Stephen Prothero (New York: Oxford University Press, 1999), pp. 196–200, 342–5.

[25] Alan W. Watts, *The Way of Zen* (New York: Pantheon Books, 1957).

[26] As quoted in 'Alan Watts: "Beginning a Counterculture" (1972),' in *Asian Religions in America*, p. 229.

Hancock, and Steven Seagal publicly embraced it.[27] Two major films on the Dalai Lama and Tibetan Buddhism, *Seven Years in Tibet* and *Kundun*, premiered in 1997. Increasing numbers of Americans claimed to be Buddhists. Seager observes that convert Buddhism in the USA comprises at least four distinct communities – Zen, Tibetan Buddhism, the Theravada Buddhism-inspired Insight Meditation Movement, and Soka Gakkai International.[28] Mention should also be made of what has come to be known as Engaged Buddhism, a term associated especially with the Vietnamese Zen monk Thich Nhat Hanh. Engaged Buddhists attempt to bring together traditional Buddhist commitments with distinctively modern concerns for liberty, equality, and justice, working to encourage justice on both local and global levels.[29]

The third group of American Buddhists identified by Seager includes the new immigrants or ethnic Buddhists who entered the USA after the 1965 immigration reform legislation.[30] Asian immigrants from South and East Asia – Chinese, Korean, Vietnamese, Cambodian, Laotian, Thai, and Sri Lankan – brought with them a wide variety of Theravada and Mahayana traditions. Whereas these distinct forms of Buddhism often were isolated from each other in Asia, they inevitably encounter each other today – as well as fresh Euro-American convert communities – in the fluid mix of American society, resulting in the blurring of distinctions between some older traditions.

We saw in the last chapter that Buddhism changed as it moved from South-East Asia into North and East Asia, sometimes

---

[27] See 'Buddhism in America,' in *Time* (October 13, 1997), pp. 72–84. On the popularity of Tibetan Buddhism in the West, see Amy Lavine, 'Tibetan Buddhism in America: The Development of American Vajrayana,' in *The Faces of Buddhism in America*, pp. 100–15; and Orville Schell, *Virtual Tibet: Searching for Shangri-La From the Himalayas to Hollywood* (New York: Metropolitan Books, 2000).
[28] Richard Hughes Seager, 'American Buddhism in the Making,' p. 110.
[29] See *Engaged Buddhism: Buddhist Liberation Movements in Asia*, eds. Christopher S. Queen and Sallie B. King (Albany, NY: State University of New York: 1996); and Sallie B. King, *Being Benevolence: The Social Ethics of Engaged Buddhism* (Honolulu, HI: University of Hawaii Press, 2005).
[30] Richard Hughes Seager, 'American Buddhism in the Making,' pp. 114–15.

producing new movements that seem to have little in common with the earlier Buddhism of India and Sri Lanka. Similarly, as Buddhism comes West it is undergoing yet further transformations as it adapts to modern Western cultural and intellectual contexts. G. Victor Sogen Hori notes that, 'Zen in America, as a historical entity, has been shaped as much by its present American context as by its Asian history.'[31] Thus, American Zen has developed new practices and institutions not seen in Japan (for example, residential communities, farms, Zen businesses, hospices, more egalitarian structures and relationships) and has downplayed some aspects of Japanese Zen (the authoritarian nature of the Zen master).

To some extent, this is inevitable, for every religion changes to some extent as it establishes itself in fresh social and cultural contexts. But the extent and nature of the changes in Western Buddhism cause some to question whether this is still Buddhism. There is no need for us to try to determine just what constitutes 'authentic Buddhism.' In any event, this is a question for Buddhists themselves to settle. But it is instructive to consider how Buddhism has been somewhat transformed as it encountered American culture. We will look briefly at two very effective promoters of Zen Buddhism in the West – D.T. Suzuki and Masao Abe – and how they transmitted a particular understanding of not only Zen but also of Buddhism and 'Eastern spirituality' in general which has been enormously influential. Many in the West today assume that Zen captures the 'essence' of Buddhism – indeed that it is the 'heart' of Eastern Spirituality itself – without realizing that this perception is largely the result of a carefully nurtured program to elevate a particular Buddhist tradition and to reinterpret it in light of concerns of Meiji Era Japanese nationalism. But first it will be helpful to consider briefly the recent discussion on 'Orientalism' and its relation to twentieth-century perspectives on Zen and Eastern spirituality.

---

[31] G. Victor Sogen Hori, 'Japanese Zen in America: Americanizing the Face in the Mirror,' in *The Faces of Buddhism in America*, p. 52.

Orientalism

Although the term 'orientalist' had been in use since the mid-nineteenth century to refer to Western scholars of the East, the 1978 publication of Edward Said's *Orientalism*[32] introduced the term with the particular connotation of signifying 'the complicity between Western academic accounts of the nature of "the Orient" and the hegemonic political agendas of Western imperialism.'[33] Said was primarily concerned with the discourse of Western scholars about Islam and the cultures of the Middle East, but his work stimulated a much broader discussion about the ways in which Western scholarship has depicted 'the other,' including the 'religious others' of Asia. In religious and cultural studies, Orientalism has come to refer to that branch of Western scholarship that uses Western categories, assumptions, and methodologies for portraying Eastern peoples and cultures, and in so doing both distorts the Eastern realities and subjugates them to Western agendas. According to Said, the depiction of Eastern peoples by Orientalists is not the strictly objective, scientific, and factual portrayal that Western scholars presumed it to be. To the contrary, it is inaccurate and serves colonialist agendas by controlling, marginalizing, and subjugating Eastern peoples and cultures to Western interests. Drawing upon Michel Foucault's provocative discussions of the relation between knowledge and power, Said claimed that the British and French depictions of the Middle East were shaped by, and also served to support, European agendas of colonialism. Although European scholars understood themselves to be merely portraying and explaining the Orient objectively, as it really is, in fact they were misrepresenting it and imposing upon Eastern cultures the categories and interests of the West. Said's claim is that the mythological constructions of such 'scholarship' were then used to marginalize and control the peoples of the East.

---

[32] Edward Said, *Orientalism* (New York: Vintage, 1978).
[33] Richard King, *Orientalism and Religion: Postcolonial Theory, India and the 'Mystic East'* (New York: Routledge, 1999), p. 83.

Our concern here is not with Said's thesis itself so much as with the broader discussion it stimulated, particularly with respect to the current understanding of Buddhism.[34] Recent scholarship has shown that much of the nineteenth- and early twentieth-century Western discourse about India, China, and Japan – and religions such as Hinduism and Buddhism – has been misleading. For example, Orientalist discourse makes a sharp distinction between 'the East' and 'the West,' with sweeping generalizations about 'the East' that ignore the many differences both within and across the many Asian societies, cultures, and religions.[35] But there is no monolithic 'East' any more than there is a uniform, homogenous 'West.' Both concepts are, to some extent, interpretive constructs which distort the diverse and messy realities denoted by the terms.

There is also in Orientalist discourse a tendency toward the reification of religions, portraying religions as clearly defined entities with sharp boundaries with identifiable 'essences.' The adoption of the term 'Hinduism' in the nineteenth century as denoting a clearly identifiable religion, rather than the astonishingly varied and loose collection of religious traditions actually practiced by 'Hindus,' is an oft-cited example of this tendency.[36] 'Hindu' was initially a term used to refer to the peoples

---

[34] Said's book has met with various responses, some positive and others not. For helpful critical discussions of his thesis, see Bruce Robbins, 'The East is a Career: Edward Said and the Logics of Professionalism,' and Richard G. Fox, 'East of Said,' both in *Edward Said: A Critical Reader*, ed. Michael Sprinker (Oxford: Blackwell, 1992), pp. 48–73, 144–56; David Kopf, 'Hermeneutics Versus History,' *Journal of Asian Studies* 39:3 (1980), pp. 495–506; Fred Dallmayr, *Beyond Orientalism: Essays on Cross-Cultural Encounter* (Albany, NY: State University of New York Press: 1996); and Philip A. Mellor, 'Orientalism, Representation and Religion: The Reality Behind the Myth,' *Religion* 34 (2004), pp. 99–112.

[35] For a classic discussion of the varieties in south and east Asian intellectual and religious traditions, see Hajime Nakamura, *Ways of Thinking of Eastern Peoples*, rev. edn., trans. Philip P. Wiener (Honolulu, HI: University of Hawaii Press, 1964).

[36] Helpful discussions of the development of the concept of 'Hinduism' as a distinct religion can be found in David Smith, *Hinduism and Modernity* (Oxford: Blackwell, 2003), parts one and two; Gauri Viswanathan, 'Colonialism

of the Indus River, so that one could speak of Christians in the area as Hindu Christians. Under British colonialism, however, the term became a way of distinguishing people who were not Christian, Muslim, Sikh, Jain, Buddhist or Parsi and giving them a unifying identity.

Moreover, there is the tendency in some Western discourse about Eastern religions to isolate one particular aspect of a religion – especially what is most different from the monotheism of Western (Christian) religion – and to use that as a central category for understanding the religion. For example, despite the enormous variety of Hindu traditions, including many theistic traditions, Western discussions frequently focus upon the non-dualism of Advaita Vedanta as defining the 'essence' of Hinduism, thereby ignoring the more theistic traditions. Or, as we shall see below, Zen is frequently understood as capturing the heart of Buddhism or 'Eastern spirituality,' although it is one of many diverse Buddhist traditions.[37]

Orientalist discourse often portrays 'the West' and 'Western religion' in favorable terms whereas 'the East' and 'Eastern religion' are depicted in negative contrasts with the West. Thus, for example, Western (Christian) religion is said to be rational, ethical, predictable, and orderly, scientific, philosophically sophisticated, and progressive; Eastern religions, by contrast, are portrayed as irrational, ethically deficient, unpredictable, primitive and superstitious, mystical and intuitive, and socially stagnant.

Both characterizations are misleading and simplistic. Thankfully, more recent scholarship is moving away from such misrepresentations and emphasizes the diverse realities in both the West

---

and the Construction of Hinduism,' and David Smith, 'Orientalism and Hinduism,' both in *The Blackwell Companion to Hinduism*, ed. Gavin Flood (Oxford: Blackwell, 2003), pp. 23–44, 45–63; and Robert Eric Frykenberg, 'Constructions of Hinduism at the Nexus of History and Religion,' *Journal of Interdisciplinary History* 23:3 (Winter 1993), pp. 523–50.

[37] For a stimulating discussion of ways in which this tendency has marginalized the study of Pure Land traditions of Buddhism, see Galen Amstutz, *Interpreting Amida: History and Orientalism in the Study of Pure Land Buddhism* (Albany, NY: State University of New York Press, 1997).

and the East. But our concern here is not simply with Western Orientalist depictions of the East and Buddhism, but also with what is sometimes called 'reverse Orientalism' or 'Occidentalism' – that is, ways in which Eastern thinkers turned the tables by utilizing the discourse of Orientalism in order to construct fresh cultural and religious identities and thereby demonstrate the superiority of the East. In Occidentalist discourse it is the West that is portrayed negatively, as crassly materialistic, crude, ethically insensitive, violent, spiritually bankrupt, and obsessed with a rationality and scientism that keeps it from cultivating spiritual truth and insight. By contrast, the East is pictured as gentle and non-violent, ethically sensitive, harmonious, wise, and guardians of an intuitive, mystical spirituality that transcends the superficial rationality of Western monotheism.[38] While such sweeping generalizations are just as misleading as those of Western Orientalists, they can be highly effective in shaping perceptions about religions such as Hinduism or Buddhism. What was introduced to the West in the early twentieth century as 'the essence of Buddhism and Eastern spirituality' was in part a construct of just such a process.

D.T. Suzuki and Zen

When most Westerners think of Buddhism what comes to mind is either Zen or Tibetan Buddhism – and for many, there is little difference between them. Zen has a longer history in America than Tibetan Buddhism, and the story of its transmission and adaptation to American culture illustrates nicely how perceptions of a religious tradition can be shaped by contemporary factors external to the tradition itself. The result can be the transformation of the tradition, as fresh perceptions replace earlier realities. David McMahan, for example, observes that the popular image of Zen in the West today is actually quite different from its historical tradition in Asia.

---

[38] See Ian Buruma and Arvid Margolit, *Occidentalism: The West in the Eyes of Its Enemies* (New York: Penguin Press, 2004).

A brief perusal of Amazon.com's books containing the word *Zen* reveals titles like *Zen in the Art of Golf* and *Zen Sex*. One also finds the word tossed around casually in more studied culture – a *New York Times* review of an art retrospective by Yoko Ono declares it 'very Zen.' Whether noun or adjective, *Zen* has, it seems, come to denote a kind of free-floating state of being, both relaxed and disciplined, engaged yet detached. While such a way of understanding the term may have something vaguely to do with the actual practice of this tradition, the use of the term *Zen* to designate a state of mind completely dissociated from the long and complex historical tradition of Chan and Zen in Asia is a unique development of the modern West and the missionary-minded Japanese.[39]

McMahan argues that what most Americans understand as Zen is actually a 're-envisioning' of various Buddhist themes as these have been filtered through the European Enlightenment and modern culture.

Europeans encountering Buddhism in the late nineteenth century read many ideas in ancient Buddhist scriptures and philosophical texts that appeared to resonate with the modern, scientific attitude. They saw in textual Buddhism an experimental attitude, a de-emphasis on faith and belief, and a sophisticated philosophy – exquisitely rational, yet soaring beyond ordinary reason. Buddhism as practiced in Asian countries, however, seemed permeated by things quite counter to the modern, rationalistic attitude – practices and beliefs that appeared superstitious, magical, and ritualistic. A number of early Western admirers and modernizing Asians tried to extract the empirically minded philosophical and practical ingredients of Buddhism from what they considered its idolatrous and superstitious elements. This 'demythologized' Buddhism – more accurately, 'remythologized' in terms of the dominant European and American attitudes and beliefs – is what most Westerners still know of Buddhism.[40]

Japanese Buddhists at the dawn of the twentieth century sought to present Buddhism to the West in such a way that it was

---

[39] David L. McMahan, 'Repackaging Zen for the West,' in *Westward Dharma*, p. 218.
[40] Ibid., p. 219.

relevant and attractive to modern, educated Western audiences. Significantly, this effort at 'contextualization' was initiated by the Japanese themselves. 'Zen was introduced to Western scholarship not through the efforts of orientalists, but rather through the activities of an elite circle of internationally minded Japanese intellectuals and globe-trotting Zen priests, whose missionary zeal was often second only to their vexed fascination with Western culture.'[41]

The Japanese effort to carry the dharma westward must be understood within the context of the social and cultural tensions of late nineteenth-century Japan, as it embarked upon an ambitious program of modernization. After some 250 years of feudal rule by the Tokugawa Bakufu, including two centuries of isolation from the outside world, Japan was forced in the 1860s to come to grips with the modern West. After Commodore Perry forced an end to the exclusion policy in 1853, the Tokugawa government fell and, with the Meiji Restoration of 1868, the emperor was restored to at least nominal rule. Japan then embraced modernization, setting itself the ambitious goal of attaining parity with the Western powers. The attempt to combine modernization with traditional ways provoked social and political upheaval. The lure of liberalizing democracy and modernity was captured in the popular slogan 'Bunmei kaika!' [Civilization and Enlightenment!]. But powerful reactionary currents pulling Japan back to traditional spiritual values were present as well, epitomized in the slogan 'Toyo no dotoku, Seiyo no gakugei!' [Eastern ethics, Western science!]. Tensions between the pull of modernity and the longing for tradition were transcended by an emerging nationalism which set out to gain respect for Japan from Western powers. The astonishing Japanese victory over the Russians in the Russo-Japanese War of 1904–5 gave an enormous boost to Japanese pride. A militant nationalism, fed by a carefully crafted manipulation of Shinto ideology and the emperor cult by militarists, thrust Japan down the precarious path of invading Manchuria and China in the 1930s

---

[41] Robert H. Sharf, 'The Zen of Japanese Nationalism,' in *Curators of the Buddha: The Study of Buddhism Under Colonialism*, ed. Donald S. Lopez, Jr. (Chicago, IL: University of Chicago Press, 1995), p. 108.

and on to the Second World War. The particular understanding of Zen that was introduced to the USA at the beginning of the twentieth century, and which has since then shaped American perceptions of Zen and Buddhism in general, was cultivated during these tumultuous and often tragic decades.

No one was more effective at shaping and propagating Zen to the West than Daisetzu Taitaro Suzuki (1870–1966). Suzuki was born in Kanazawa, Japan, and became interested in Zen while still in high school.[42] In the late 1880s Suzuki met Kitaro Nishida (1870–1945), later the founder of the Kyoto School of philosophy, and the two became lifelong friends. While a student at Tokyo Imperial University, Suzuki commuted to Kamakura to study Zen, first under Imagita Kosen and then under Shaku Soen. Throughout his long life, however, Suzuki remained a Buddhist layman.

Suzuki's mentor, Shaku Soen, participated in the 1893 World's Parliament of Religions, where he met Dr Paul Carus (1852–1919), head of the Open Court Publishing Company and editor of the journal *The Monist*. Carus, born to a Protestant minister in Germany, had rejected orthodox Christianity as incompatible with modern science and was a passionate advocate of 'a religion of science.'[43] Not only would such a religion be compatible with the latest insights of science but Carus held that it would also build upon the central insights of all the world's great religions. Buddhism

---

[42] Suzuki provides two autobiographical accounts in his 'Early Memories' and 'An Autobiographical Account,' both in *A Zen Life: D.T. Suzuki Remembered*, ed. Masao Abe (New York: Weatherhill, 1986), pp. 3–26. This is a collection of largely sympathetic and appreciative essays on Suzuki by Western and non-Western scholars. More critical assessments of Suzuki's portrayal of Zen are found in Robert H. Sharf, 'The Zen of Japanese Nationalism,' in *Curators of the Buddha*, pp. 107–60, and 'Whose Zen? Zen Nationalism Revisited,' in *Rude Awakenings: Zen, the Kyoto School and the Question of Nationalism*, eds. James W. Heisig and John C. Maraldo (Honolulu, HI: University of Hawaii Press, 1994), pp. 40–51; David L. McMahan, 'Repackaging Zen for the West,' in *Westward Dharma*, pp. 218–29; and Bernard Faure, *Chan Insights and Oversights: An Epistemological Critique of the Chan Tradition* (Princeton, NJ: Princeton University Press, 1993), chapter 2.
[43] See Martin J. Verhoeven, 'Americanizing the Buddha: Paul Carus and the Transformation of Asian Thought,' in *The Faces of Buddhism in America*, pp. 207–27.

seemed to be particularly conducive to such a project. Carus found a kindred spirit in Shaku Soen, who was eager to promote Buddhism in the West as a modern, universal religion. Writing to Carus in 1895, Soen envisioned America as the birthplace of a new Buddhism: 'Buddha who lived three thousand years ago being named Gautama, now lies bodily dead in India; but Buddhism in the twentieth century being named Truth, is just to be born in Chicago in the New World.'[44]

In 1894 Carus published *The Gospel of Buddha*, a highly sympathetic and influential portrayal of Buddhism as a rational faith, fully compatible with science. Carus reinterpreted key Buddhist notions such as no-self, nirvana, and emptiness, giving them a more theistic and ethical flavor. 'An especially articulate American apologist for Asian ideas, Carus proved instrumental in convincing many that the East might well have an answer to much that ailed the West spiritually, philosophically, and psychologically.'[45]

In 1897, at Paul Carus' invitation and Soen's urging, Suzuki moved to La Salle, Illinois to work with Carus as a translator at Open Court Publishing. Returning to Japan in 1909, Suzuki taught at several universities, eventually taking a position in 1921 as professor of Buddhist philosophy at Otani University in Kyoto. There he launched the journal *Eastern Buddhist*. But it was only after reaching the age of fifty that Suzuki's career as an interpreter of Zen to the West really got under way. He published over a hundred books and articles on Buddhism, some of the more significant English titles including *Outlines of Mahayana Buddhism* (1907); *Essays in Zen Buddhism: First Series* (1927); *Studies in the Lankavatara Sutra* (1930); *Essays in Zen Buddhism: Second Series* (1933); *Essays in Zen Buddhism: Third Series* (1934); *An Introduction to Zen Buddhism* (1934); *Zen Buddhism* (1956); *Mysticism: Christian and Buddhist* (1957); and *Zen and Japanese Culture* (1959). In 1936 Suzuki lectured at major universities in England. Returning to Japan, Suzuki lived in Kamakura during the war years. In 1949, at the age of 79, Suzuki traveled to the United States for an extended

---

[44] As quoted in Verhoeven, 'Americanizing the Buddha,' p. 216.
[45] Ibid., p. 208.

stay, lecturing at the East–West Philosophers Conference in Hawaii, teaching at the Claremont Colleges in California, and then lecturing at Columbia University from 1951–7. Suzuki returned to Japan in 1958, where he died in 1966 at the age of 95. Through his many writings, lectures, and extensive contacts with Western intellectuals Suzuki became the most influential spokesman for Zen in the West.

Suzuki's influence upon American understandings of Buddhism in the twentieth century has been enormous.[46] While he was clearly a remarkable man and did much to popularize Buddhism in the West, he was also controversial. Suzuki is often understood by Westerners to be a dispassionate, meticulous scholar whose depiction of Zen is simply an objective restatement of classical Buddhism for Western audiences. In fact, however, Suzuki was frequently criticized by other Japanese Buddhists for his portrayal of Zen. 'Japanese Zen Buddhists were often astounded at the transformations Zen was undergoing in the West, and they differentiated between the traditional form of Japanese Zen and that which they called "Suzuki Zen".'[47] Recent scholarship has highlighted the various influences upon Suzuki and his formulation of Zen, as well as the distinct stages of his thought throughout a long and prolific career. Between 1903 and 1924, for example, when his early writings on Zen were taking shape, Suzuki had strong interests in both Swedenborgianism and the Theosophical Society.[48] Suzuki translated four of the mystic Emanuel Swedenborg's (1688–1772) works into Japanese

---

[46] See Larry A. Fader, 'D.T. Suzuki's Contribution to the West,' in *A Zen Life: D.T. Suzuki Remembered*, pp. 95–108.

[47] Heinrich Dumoulin, *Zen Enlightenment*, p. 7. For a fascinating discussion of a critique of aspects of Japanese Buddhism, including Suzuki's understanding of Zen, by Japanese Buddhist scholars, see Paul L. Swanson, 'Why They Say Zen Is Not Buddhism: Recent Japanese Critiques of Buddha-Nature,' in *Pruning the Bodhi Tree: The Storm Over Critical Buddhism*, eds. Jamie Hubbard and Paul L. Swanson (Honolulu, HI: University of Hawaii Press, 1997), pp. 3–29.

[48] See Thomas Tweed, 'American Occultism and Japanese Buddhism: Albert J. Edmunds, D.T. Suzuki, and Translocative History,' *Japanese Journal of Religious Studies* 32:2 (2005), pp. 249–81.

and published a book length study of Swedenborg in 1913. In the 1920s Suzuki and his wife Beatrice opened a Theosophical Lodge in Kyoto. Rather than simply a distillation of 'pure Buddhism' for the West, Suzuki's depiction of Zen reflected multiple influences – including the rising nationalism of Japan, Suzuki's encounters with Christianity as well as more esoteric Western traditions such as Swedenborgianism and Theosophy, and his reaction to modernity and the materialism of the West. Various agendas were at work, as Suzuki was concerned not merely with transmission of the dharma to the West but also with establishing the superiority of Eastern (that is, Japanese) spirituality over Western (Christian) religious and intellectual patterns. Our purpose here is not to denigrate Suzuki but rather to illustrate how, when a religious tradition moves from one cultural context to another, perceptions about it can be shaped by factors external to the tradition itself. Three issues in particular will be noted.

First, critics have pointed out that Suzuki tends to exaggerate the paradoxical and irrational elements in Chinese and Japanese Zen, and to treat these as defining traits of Buddhism in general.[49] For example, in discussing some characteristics of the satori (enlightenment) experience, Suzuki lists 'irrationality' first. 'By this I mean that *satori* is not a conclusion to be reached by reasoning, and defies all intellectual determination. Those who have experienced it are always at a loss to explain it coherently or logically.... The *satori* experience is always characterized by irrationality, inexplicability, and incommunicability.'[50] Moreover, the experience of satori is said to be self-authenticating for the one experiencing it. Suzuki uses the term 'authoritativeness' for this characteristic of satori. 'By this I mean that the knowledge realized by *satori* is final, that no amount of logical argument can refute it. Being direct and personal it is sufficient unto itself.'[51] Suzuki

---

[49] Heinrich Dumoulin, *Zen Enlightenment*, p. 6.
[50] Daisetz T. Suzuki, *The Essentials of Zen Buddhism: Selected from the Writings of Daisetz T. Suzuki*, ed. Bernard Phillips (Westport, CT: Greenwood Press, 1962), p. 163.
[51] Ibid., p. 164.

emphasized what he took to be the 'pure,' immediate experience
of enlightenment, an experience which was said to transcend
concepts, doctrines, and rational reflection.

In elevating the 'Zen experience' Suzuki was echoing a theme
prominent in the Kyoto School of Japanese philosophy, dominated
by his friend Kitaro Nishida. The Kyoto School was a creative
intellectual movement that tried to develop a synthesis between
traditional Western philosophical concerns and Zen Buddhism.[52]
Nishida's philosophical writings put forward the notion of
'pure' or 'direct' experience [junsui keiken] which transcends
conceptualization and rational reflection, and is prior to all
oppositions such as that of subject and object. Suzuki, who was
loosely associated with the Kyoto School, understood Nishida's
philosophy as an attempt to make Buddhism, Zen in particular,
intelligible to the West.[53] With Suzuki, the pure, unmediated,
'non-dual' experience of satori becomes central to Zen. But
Suzuki has been criticized by Japanese Buddhist scholars for
elevating the notion of pure experience at the expense of critical,
rational reflection in a way that is not faithful to earlier Buddhist

---

[52] Nishida's most significant work is *An Inquiry Into the Good*, trans. Masao
Abe and Christopher Ives (New Haven, CT: Yale University Press, 1987
[1927]). On Nishida, see Michiko Yusa, *Zen and Philosophy: An Intellectual
Biography of Nishida Kitaro* (Honolulu, HI: University of Hawaii Press, 2002),
and Robert E. Carter, *The Nothingness Beyond God: An Introduction to the
Philosophy of Nishida Kitaro* (New York: Paragon House, 1989). On the Kyoto
School and its significance, see *The Buddha Eye: An Anthology of the Kyoto
School*, ed. Frederick Franck (New York: Crossroad, 1982), and Thomas
Kasulis, 'The Kyoto School and the West,' *Eastern Buddhist* 15 (1982), pp.
125–44.

[53] Robert Sharf, 'The Zen of Japanese Nationalism,' p. 127. Bernard Faure
observes that although both Nishida and Suzuki used Zen to respond to the
West, their approach was different. 'Taking their cues from Zen, the two men
offered opposite responses to the challenge of Western philosophy. Whereas
Suzuki underscored the antisystematic nature of Zen and relentlessly
expressed his contempt for Western philosophy, Nishida attempted to
systematize Zen insights in a way compatible with Western philosophy. Thus,
Nishida philosophy has sometimes been read as a "Zen philosophy" based on
the notion of "pure experience" [*junsui keiken*]' (Bernard Faure, *Chan Insights
and Oversights*, pp. 75–6).

tradition.[54] Moreover, as we saw earlier, Buddhists from the Theravada and Tibetan traditions – in contrast to Suzuki – have emphasized the importance of rational analysis in Buddhism.

Second, Suzuki's writings are said to distort the historical roots of Zen and to vacillate inconsistently between what is supposedly universal, and transcends the particularities of culture and religion, and what is culture- and religion-specific. Heinrich Dumoulin, for example, observes that in his writings Suzuki tended to 'uproot' Zen from its 'native Buddhist soil.'[55] The 'dehistoricizing' of Zen is said to be evident in the priority Suzuki gives to the Rinzai School of Zen (of which he was a member) while ignoring Soto Zen Buddhism and Dogen; his minimizing of the Chinese Ch'an tradition; and his failure even to mention Son, the Korean version of Ch'an, although he knew about it from traveling to Korea during the Japanese occupation of Korea.[56] Suzuki did not hesitate to disparage the Theravada tradition as inadequately comprehending the essential teaching of Gautama. The earlier Buddhists were incapable of grasping the exalted teaching of the Buddha's Enlightenment, and thus early Buddhist literature focuses more on the Four Noble Truths than Enlightenment itself.

> This being the case, the idea of Enlightenment was not brought forward so fully and conspicuously in Hinayana [Theravada] literature as at once to command our attention.... The earlier writers conceived the Fourfold Noble Truth or the Twelvefold Chain of Causation, or the Eightfold Path of Righteousness to be the central teaching of Buddhism, which also included on the psychological side the theory of the non-ego (*anatman*). But when we reflect, both philosophically and from the Zen point of view, on the life of the Buddha, and on the ultimate principle of Buddhahood, we cannot help thinking of his Enlightenment as the most significant and most essential and most fruitful part of Buddhism. Therefore, what the Buddha really wished to impart to his disciples must have

---

[54] See Paul L. Swanson, 'Why They say Zen Is Not Buddhism,' p. 19; and Jamie Hubbard, 'Topophobia,' in *Pruning the Bodhi Tree*, pp. 81–112.
[55] Heinrich Dumoulin, *Zen Enlightenment*, p. 6.
[56] Bernard Faure, *Chan Insights and Oversights*, p. 57.

been the Doctrine of Enlightenment in spite of the Hinayanaistic interpretation or understanding of what is known as primitive Buddhism.[57]

Moreover, we find in Suzuki a tension between two themes that are difficult to reconcile. On the one hand, Zen is said to have a universal status, transcending cultural and religious particularities, since it is 'the spirit of all religion and philosophy.'[58] David McMahan states, 'Zen, as Suzuki presented it, is the pure experience of unmediated encounter with reality, and the spontaneous living in harmony with that reality.' For Suzuki, Zen is not just a particular Buddhist tradition but rather 'an ahistorical essence of spirituality.'[59] At the same time, Zen comprises the heart of true Buddhism. Shin'ichi Hisamatsu, Buddhist philosopher of the Kyoto School and friend of Suzuki, claimed, 'Zen is not one particular school within Buddhism; it is, rather, the root-source of Buddhism.'[60] (Buddhists of the Theravada and Tibetan traditions, as well as many other Mahayanists, would of course strongly disagree.) Furthermore, Suzuki, following Paul Carus, saw in Zen the potential for a unifying common ground for all the world religions. In an editorial comment in the second issue of *Eastern Buddhist*, Suzuki stated, 'Our standpoint is that the Mahayana ought to be considered one whole, individual thing and no sects, especially no sectarian prejudices, to be recognized in it, except as so many phases or aspects of one fundamental truth. In this respect Buddhism and Christianity and all other religious beliefs are not more than variations of one single original Faith, deeply embedded in the human soul.'[61] As McMahan notes, 'The essence of Zen, for Suzuki, was mysticism,

---

[57] D.T. Suzuki, *Essays in Zen: First Series* (New York: Weidenfeld, 1961 [1949]), pp. 164–6. For a contrasting Theravada perspective on Zen, see David Kalupahana, *Buddhist Philosophy: A Historical Analysis* (Honolulu, HI: University of Hawaii Press, 1976), pp. 163–77.
[58] As quoted in Faure, *Chan Insights and Oversights*, p. 57.
[59] David L. McMahan, 'Repackaging Zen for the West,' p. 221.
[60] Hisamatsu Shin'ichi, 'Zen: Its Meaning for Modern Civilization,' *The Eastern Buddhist*, vol. 1:1 (September 1965), p. 22.
[61] As cited in Robert Sharf, 'The Zen of Japanese Nationalism,' pp. 120–21.

which he believed was common to other religious traditions as well.'[62]

And yet the universal emphasis was counter-balanced by a highly particularistic theme in which Zen was identified with the essence of a uniquely Japanese spirituality. In a typical passage, Suzuki states, '[I]n Zen are found systematized or rather crystallized, all the philosophy, religion, and life itself of the Far-Eastern people, especially the Japanese.'[63] Robert Sharf observes that for Suzuki, '[W]hile Zen experience is the universal ground of religious truth, it is nonetheless an expression of a uniquely *Japanese* spirituality.... Zen is touted as the very heart of Asian spirituality, the essence of Japanese culture, and the key to the unique qualities of the Japanese race.'[64] Suzuki's depiction of Zen draws upon late nineteenth- and early twentieth-century Japanese discourse [Nihonjinron] about the alleged uniqueness of the Japanese race, so that the Indian, Tibetan, and Chinese historical antecedents of Japanese Buddhism are minimized in favor of the 'Japanese spirituality,' said to express the essence of Buddhism. Commenting on Suzuki's influential *Zen and Japanese Culture*, Sharf states:

> Virtually all of the major Japanese artistic traditions are reinter-preted as expressions of the 'Zen experience,' rendering Zen the metaphysical ground of Japanese culture itself. Given this exalted spiritual heritage, the Japanese are said to be culturally, if not racially, predisposed toward Zen insight; they have a deeper appreciation of the unity of man and nature, the oneness of life and death and so on.... The claim that Zen is the foundation of Japanese culture has the felicitous result of rendering the Japanese spiritual experience both unique and universal at the same time.[65]

---

[62] David L. McMahan, 'Repackaging Zen for the West,' p. 221.

[63] Daisetz T. Suzuki, *The Essentials of Zen Buddhism: Selected from the Writings of Daisetz T. Suzuki*, p. 8.

[64] Robert Sharf, 'The Zen of Japanese Nationalism,' pp. 128, 111. Emphasis original.

[65] Robert H. Sharf, 'Whose Zen?,' p. 46. Sharf notes a certain irony in this discourse: '[I]t was no coincidence that the notion of Zen as the foundation for Japanese moral, aesthetic, and spiritual superiority emerged full force in the 1930s, just as the Japanese were preparing for imperial expansion in East and South-East Asia' (ibid.).

Needless to say, not only other Asian Buddhists, but also Hindus, Jains, and Daoists would dispute the identification of 'Eastern spirituality' with Japanese Zen.

Finally, Suzuki's characterization of Zen draws upon the discourses of Orientalism and Occidentalism that shaped the encounters of early modern Japanese intellectuals with modernity and the West. The universality of Zen as the ground of all genuine religious truth, regardless of culture or religion, was thus juxtaposed against the esoteric particularities of 'Eastern thought,' exemplified in Japanese spirituality – thereby rendering Zen inaccessible to the 'Western mind.'

> Having lived through the military humiliation of Japan at the hands of the 'culturally inferior' Occidental powers, Suzuki would devote a considerable portion of his prodigious energies tantalizing a legion of disenchanted Western intellectuals with the dream of an Oriental enlightenment. Yet all the while Suzuki held that the cultural and spiritual weaknesses of the Occident virtually precluded the possibility of Westerners ever coming to truly comprehend Zen. One is led to suspect that Suzuki's lifelong effort to bring Buddhist enlightenment to the Occident had become inextricably bound to a studied contempt for the West, a West whose cultural arrogance and imperialist inclinations Suzuki had come to know all too well.[66]

Furthermore, Suzuki's rhetoric essentializes both 'the West' and 'the East,' with the one depicted as the antithesis of the other. He skillfully promoted certain generalizations about 'the West' and 'the East' which, while simplistic and misleading, have become widely accepted. For example, in one passage Suzuki states,

> The Western mind is: analytical, discriminative, differential, inductive, individualistic, intellectual, objective, scientific, generalizing, conceptual, schematic, impersonal, legalistic, organizing, power-wielding, self-assertive, disposed to impose its will upon others, etc. Against these Western traits, those of the East can be characterized as follows: synthetic, totalizing, integrative, nondiscriminative,

---

[66] Robert Sharf, 'The Zen of Japanese Nationalism,' p. 131.

deductive, nonsystematic, dogmatic, intuitive (rather, affective), nondiscursive, subjective, spiritually individualistic and socially group-minded, etc.[67]

Such sweeping generalizations have little purchase upon actual realities in either the East or the West. But the attraction of Buddhism in the West is due in part to the skillful and effective use of such discourse to depict a profound and esoteric 'Eastern spirituality' as the antidote to 'Western rationalism' and materialism. Robert Sharf's comments are especially pertinent:

> While Suzuki's Zen claimed a privileged perspective that transcended cultural difference, it was at the same time contrived as the antithesis of everything Suzuki found deplorable about the West.... We read repeatedly that the 'West' is materialistic, the 'East' spiritual, that the West is aggressive and imperialistic, while the East extols nonviolence and harmony, that the West values rationality, the East intuitive wisdom, that the West is dualistic, the East monistic, and that while the West is individualistic, setting man apart from nature, the East is communalistic, viewing man as one with nature. In short, his image of the East in general, and Japan in particular, is little more than a romantic inversion of Japanese negative stereotypes of the West.[68]

It is not surprising, then, that Suzuki's Zen was especially attractive to those who were growing disillusioned with Western culture and society.

Masao Abe

Undoubtedly the most influential spokesman for Zen in the West since the time of Suzuki is the Japanese scholar Masao Abe (1915–2006). Although initially practicing Pure Land Buddhism, Abe converted to Zen and studied under Shin'ichi Hisamatsu,

---

[67] As cited in Bernard Faure, *Chan Insights and Oversights*, pp. 64–5, n. 18.
[68] Robert H. Sharf, 'Whose Zen?,' pp. 47–8.

a philosopher associated with the Kyoto School. After teaching for several years at Nara University of Education, in 1955 Abe went to New York for two years, where he assisted D.T. Suzuki at Columbia University, and studied Christian theology under Paul Tillich and Reinhold Niebuhr at Union Theological Seminary. For the next several decades Abe lived and taught in Japan, but pursued the comparative study of Eastern and Western philosophy. During this time, Abe became actively involved in Buddhist–Christian dialogue in the United States and Europe. Retiring from Nara University in 1980, Abe spent the next thirteen years in the US, teaching at various American universities and introducing Zen and the Kyoto School to American audiences. In 1993 Abe returned to Japan, where he continued to lecture and publish works on Buddhism until his death.[69]

Abe follows Nishida, the Kyoto School, and Suzuki in emphasizing a pure experience that is pre-rational and pre-judgmental, the realization of a 'positionless position,' which is also identified with the Buddhist notion of sunyata or emptiness.[70] Our concern here is not with Abe's characterization of this experience itself but rather with implications of his claims for ethics and moral judgments. For Abe makes explicit what is at least implicit in much Buddhist thought concerning the status of moral values and principles. Buddhist claims about the ultimacy of emptiness, which allegedly transcends all distinctions and dualities, relativizes the opposition between good and evil, right and wrong. Zen, in particular, has come under strong criticism, from some Buddhists as well as others, for its advocacy of a standpoint beyond moral judgments. Recent scholars argue that not only

---

[69] For an overview of Abe's life and scholarly contributions, along with appreciative essays by western scholars, see *Masao Abe: A Zen Life of Dialogue*, ed. Donald W. Mitchell (Boston, MA: Charles E. Tuttle, 1993). Among Abe's many writings are Masao Abe, *Zen and Western Thought*, ed. William R. LaFleur (Honolulu, HI: University of Hawaii Press, 1985); *Buddhism and Interfaith Dialogue*, ed. Steven Heine (Honolulu, HI: University of Hawaii Press, 1995); and *Zen and Comparative Studies*, ed. Steven Heine (Honolulu, HI: University of Hawaii Press, 1997).

[70] Masao Abe, *Buddhism and Interfaith Dialogue*, p. 23.

does Zen advocate an amoral stance but that Japanese Zen in particular, in its emphasis upon 'transcending life and death,' was used to support the warrior code of the samurai in the premodern era. Critics charge that Zen sects and prominent intellectuals also supported the extreme nationalism and militarism of Japan in the 1930s and 1940s, as they 'helped rationalize, glorify, or even promote Japanese imperialism.'[71] Although their attitudes toward Japanese nationalism and war were ambivalent, Nishida and Suzuki have been strongly criticized for statements that seem supportive of nationalistic and imperialistic aims.[72]

Before looking more specifically at Abe's position, however, we can highlight the general problem confronting Zen by considering statements by two Japanese scholars. Seiko Hirata states that

[T]he freedom espoused by Zen – and by Buddhism as a whole – is fundamentally *non*ethical (as opposed to *un*ethical) in nature. This was the very position taken by Sung dynasty Confucian scholars in their attacks on Zen. As they saw it, Zen's position that the adept's world of satori can be reached only through a transcendence of dualistic notions of good and evil is one that leaves no grounds for distinguishing the socially beneficial from the socially harmful. Not only is it bereft of social significance, it is also incapable of providing any sort of foundation for social development. Their Zen opponents countered by saying that fixation on the dualistic dimension of good and evil merely promotes delusion and cuts off all possibility of attaining the true peace of satori.[73]

---

[71] Christopher Ives, 'Ethical Pitfalls in Imperial Zen and Nishida Philosophy,' in *Rude Awakenings: Zen, the Kyoto School, and the Question of Nationalism*, p. 16.

[72] See especially Hirata Seiko, 'Zen Buddhist Attitudes To War,' in *Rude Awakenings*, pp. 3–15; Christopher Ives, 'Ethical Pitfalls in Imperial Zen and Nishida Philosophy,' in *Rude Awakenings*, pp. 16–39; Kirita Kiyohide, 'D.T. Suzuki on Society and the State,' in *Rude Awakenings*, pp. 52–75; and John C. Maraldo, 'Questioning Nationalism Now and Then: A Critical Approach to Zen and the Kyoto School,' in *Rude Awakenings*, pp. 333–62.

[73] Hirata Seiko, 'Zen Buddhist Attitudes to War,' p. 12. See also Jan Van Bragt, 'Reflections on Zen and Ethics,' *Studies in Interreligious Diaolgue*, vol. 12 (2002), pp. 133–47.

Kiyohide Kirita makes the connection between Zen and the Japanese war effort.

The emphasis on the here-and-now in Zen thought breaks the ties between before and after. It breaks with all value judgments and distinctions between good and evil. Recognizing this here-and-now and stressing it as 'non-thought' is also part of Zen thought. The distinction is important, as it is the fact that during the war [World War II] this idea in effect encouraged soldiers to push on and do battle without a thought, totally unconcerned with the historical and social circumstances. The emphasis on the here-and-now is related to the Zen idea that 'wherever you stand is the right place' and the ideal of 'becoming a master of one's circumstances.' By discouraging one from pausing to think rationally, such teaching blinds one to the realities of history and society. Any situation whatsoever, any setting can become 'true,' so that one can even murder enthusiastically. Such Zen ideas of the here-and-now are particularly efficacious in time of war, as not a few Zen Buddhists recognized during the Second World War, lending the arm of Zen to the war effort.[74]

Masao Abe was well aware of the tensions between Zen and moral judgements. Abe followed the third century Nagarjuna in positing a distinction between two levels of truth and reality – a provisional level in which we normally live and in which distinctions and duality apply, and ultimate truth and reality (sunyata or emptiness) which transcends all distinctions. Conceptual and logical categories, and dualities of any kind, do not apply on the level of ultimate reality. Moral distinctions and principles are also transcended on the ultimate level. Abe acknowledged the difficulties this raises for strong ethical agendas addressing moral problems in this world, and although he challenged Buddhists to develop grounds for ethical activism today it is difficult to see how this can be done within a Zen framework.

To say that moral values and principles apply only on the provisional level does not mean that Buddhism has no interest

---

[74] Kirita Kiyode, 'D.T. Suzuki on Society and the State,' pp. 71–2.

in ethics. To the contrary, moral values and principles have been integral to Buddhism from its inception.[75] The Buddha's Fourth Noble Truth, leading to the cessation of suffering through following the Noble Eightfold Path, explicitly calls for cultivating moral virtues in right conduct, right speech, and right livelihood. Buddhist laity are expected to adhere to the Five Precepts – not to take life, not to steal, not to speak falsely, not to engage in sexual misconduct, and not to take intoxicating liquor. Monastic discipline presupposes that cultivation of moral virtues and elimination of vices prepares one for higher levels of spiritual attainment. And central to the Mahayana tradition is karuna, or altruistic compassion for all sentient beings, exemplified in the bodhisattva ideal. The question, however, is whether a Zen ontology, which eliminates an ultimate distinction between good and evil, can make sense of such ethical precepts and values.

The issue of the status of moral values and principles was addressed by Abe in the context of discussion about the problem of evil.[76] The problem of evil is different in Buddhism than Christianity, for Abe insists that in Zen there is no God. Ultimate reality is sunyata or emptiness. 'In Buddhism *sunyata*, or emptiness as ultimate reality, is entirely unobjectifiable and nonsubstantial in that *sunyata* is neither immanent nor transcendent, being beyond even the one God.'[77] Abe claims that,

Buddhism has no need of a notion of one God because the fundamental principle of Buddhism is 'dependent origination.' This notion indicates that everything in and out of the universe is

---

[75] See Shundo Tachibana, *The Ethics of Buddhism* (Oxford: Clarendon Press, 1926); David Kalupahana, *Ethics in Early Buddhism* (Honolulu, HI: University of Hawaii Press, 1995); Peter Harvey, *An Introduction to Buddhist Ethics* (Cambridge: Cambridge University Press, 2000); and Damien Keown, *The Nature of Buddhist Ethics* (Basingstoke, Hampshire: Palgrave, 2001).

[76] See Masao Abe, 'The Problem of Evil in Christianity and Buddhism,' in *Buddhist–Christian Dialogue: Mutual Renewal and Transformation*, eds. Paul Ingram and Frederick J. Streng (Honolulu, HI: University of Hawaii Press, 1986), pp. 139–54; 'Ethics and Social Responsibility in Buddhism,' in *Eastern Buddhist* 30:2 (1997), pp. 161–72; *Buddhism and Interfaith Dialogue*, chapter 17; and *Zen and Comparative Studies*, chapters 3 and 15.

[77] Masao Abe, 'Ethics and Social Responsibility in Buddhism,' p. 164.

interdependent and co-arising and co-ceasing: nothing whatever is independent and self-existing.... The universe is not the creation of one God, but fundamentally is a network of causal relationships among innumerable things which are co-arising and co-ceasing.[78]

The concepts of good and evil, like everything else, are completely interdependent; they always co-arise and co-cease so that one cannot exist without the other. There is, then, no supreme good which is self-subsistent apart from evil, and no absolute evil which is an object of eternal punishment apart from good. Both the supreme good and absolute evil are illusions. According to Zen, although the distinction between good and evil has its use on the level of provisional reality, ultimately as one awakens to the true nature of things through enlightenment even this duality is transcended.

Ethically speaking, Buddhists clearly realize that good should conquer evil. However, through the experience of their inner struggle, Buddhists cannot say that good is strong enough to over-come evil. Good and evil are completely antagonistic principles, resisting each other with equal force, yet inseparably connected and displaying an existential antinomy as a whole. However imperative it may be from the ethical point of view, it is, according to Buddhism, illusory to believe it is possible to overcome evil with good and thereby to attain the highest good. Since good and evil are mutually negating principles with equal power, an ethical effort to overcome evil with good never succeeds and results in a serious dilemma.... In Buddhism ... what is essential for salvation is not to overcome evil with good and to participate in the supreme Good, but to be emancipated from the existential antinomy of good and evil and to awaken to Emptiness prior to the opposition between good and evil. In the existential awakening to Emptiness, one can be master of, rather than enslaved by, good and evil. In this sense, the realization of true Emptiness is the basis for human freedom, creative activity, and the ethical life.[79]

[78] Masao Abe, 'The Problem of Evil in Christianity and Buddhism,' p. 145.
[79] Masao Abe, 'The Meaning of Life in Buddhism,' in *The Meaning of Life in the World Religions*, eds. Joseph Runzo and Nancy M. Martin (Oxford: Oneworld, 2000), p. 160.

In a fascinating discussion with several Christian and Jewish theologians, Abe was pressed on the implications of his rejection of an ultimate distinction between good and evil for the Holocaust.[80] In response, Abe distinguished three dimensions of reality according to which the question of evil must be addressed.[81] The first is the non-human, natural dimension in which evil and suffering can be experienced through the sometimes tragic processes of nature. Earthquakes, floods, disease, even killing within the food chain constitute suffering on this level. The second dimension is that of the 'transnatural human dimension represented by individual morality, and collective social and historical ethics.' Here there is a distinction between good and evil, with honesty, kindness, integrity, and courage being regarded as good whereas stealing, lying, and killing are regarded as evil. While on this level the distinction between good and evil is real enough and we must do our best to promote good and eradicate evil, nevertheless, 'Ultimately the distinction between good and evil in the ethical dimension is relative, not absolute.'[82]

The ontologically highest dimension is what Abe calls 'the fundamental religious dimension,' or the level of ultimate reality, sunyata or emptiness. Ultimately, all dualities and distinctions, including that between good and evil, are transcended. The point is made explicit with reference to what has become the definitive symbol of evil – the Holocaust. On the level of human social interaction Abe speaks of the Holocaust as 'a brutal, atrocious, historical evil,' although even here he emphasizes that since all events are interrelated and co-dependent there is a sense in which the 'root karma' which caused the Holocaust is 'common to all human beings,' with good and evil interrelated in this network of causal factors.[83] Nevertheless, 'While in a human, moral dimension

---

[80] See the essays in The Emptying God: A Buddhist–Jewish–Christian Conversation, eds. John B. Cobb, Jr. and Christopher Ives (Maryknoll, NY: Orbis Books Books, 1990).

[81] Masao Abe, 'Kenotic God and Dynamic Sunyata,' in The Emptying God, pp. 46–50.

[82] Ibid., p. 47.

[83] Ibid., p. 52.

the Holocaust should be condemned as an unpardonable, absolute evil, *from the ultimate religious point of view even it should not be taken as an absolute but a relative evil.'*[84] From the perspective of ultimate reality, emptiness, we cannot condemn the Holocaust as evil since moral categories do not apply on that level.

But this strikes many as unacceptable. Zen clashes with a widely shared aspect of human experience which recognizes an irreducible distinction between good and evil, right and wrong. Any worldview which cannot condemn the Holocaust as evil is at odds with some of our deepest moral insights. In his response to Abe, the Jewish theologian Eugene Borowitz objects that

> [T]he caring Jewish community will overwhelmingly reject the suggestion that, for all the trauma connected with the Holocaust, we ought to understand that it *ultimately* has no significance; or, to put it more directly, that *ultimately* there is no utterly fundamental distinction between the Nazi death camp operators and their victims. For most Jews, a response to the encompassing evils of our day – world hunger, political tyranny, religious intolerance and warfare, the threat of nuclear destruction – cannot properly be made with a consciousness that they are truly second-level concerns, that bringing people to a higher level of understanding is the most significant way to face them. And I cannot imagine them agreeing that the ultimate response to the Nazis would have been for Jews to raise their consciousness from a radically moral to a higher, postmoral level.[85]

Four decades earlier, the Protestant theologian Paul Tillich visited Japan and engaged in dialogue with Buddhist scholars. He too noticed the moral ambivalence of Buddhism with respect to Hitler and Nazism:

> I asked someone, in this regard, about Hitler (who was the divine mouthpiece for believing Nazis), whether one doesn't have to fight against Hitler. And this that [*sic*] question caused him great distress

---

[84] Ibid., p. 53. Emphasis added.
[85] Eugene B. Borowitz, 'Dynamic Sunyata and the God Whose Glory Fills the Universe,' in *The Emptying God*, p. 83.

because he felt, on the one hand, it was inhuman to say not to fight against Hitler, while on the other hand he had no theoretical foundation on which to fight Hitler as a demonic distortion of holiness. This conflict occurs if one says that everything is a means of salvation, so to speak. This inner conflict I see in Buddhism.[86]

While in practice Buddhists often show exemplary moral character and Buddhist sacred texts call for cultivation of moral character, many have sensed a deep tension between such moral imperatives and an ontology in which moral distinctions are overcome. It remains to be seen whether Buddhism's encounter with the West, with its (diminishing) Christian heritage, will alter the traditional ontology in a way that strengthens the Buddhist basis for moral action.

---

[86] 'Tillich Encounters Japan,' ed. by Robert W. Wood, *Japanese Religions*, vol. 2 (May 1961), p. 62.

4

Aspects of Buddhist Doctrine

We have seen how Buddhism emerged in north India around the sixth century BC, then spread throughout Asia, and eventually was transmitted to the West in the nineteenth and twentieth centuries. In tracing the development of Buddhism we have given special attention to Buddhist teachings or doctrines. In this chapter we will consider further the nature of doctrine or teaching in Buddhism, and we will conclude by examining again several major Buddhist teachings introduced in earlier chapters.

Like all great religions, Buddhism not only calls for living a certain kind of life but it also makes assertions about reality, the way things are. Indeed, the Buddhist way of life is rooted in a particular understanding of what is real and what beliefs are true. Ancient Indian religious traditions often follow a pattern analogous to a medical analysis of an illness. Initially there is a diagnosis of the nature of the illness, followed by an account of the causal conditions under which the illness developed, and finally consideration whether the illness can be cured. If it can be cured, then there is the prescription showing how the cure is to be attained. This structure, of course, is clearly reflected in the Four Noble Truths of early Buddhism.[1] The medical analogy is a helpful way of looking at the major religions, for each claims that there is a basic problem affecting humankind and the cosmos at large and each offers a distinctive way of overcoming this predicament. Moreover, each religion presumes that its own diagnosis of the problem is correct and its cure efficacious.

---

[1] See Chapter 1.

If we compare Christianity and Buddhism, for example, we see that quite different diagnoses and cures are offered by the two religions. In Christianity, the 'illness' is sin; the causal conditions involve our misuse of the gift of freedom in an effort to become free from God; the disease is curable; and the cure requires God's gracious, redemptive action in Jesus Christ – his life, death for our sins, and resurrection – and our repentance and trust in God. In Buddhism, by contrast, the 'disease' is the unsatisfactory nature of existing transitorily and dependently; the cause is that we mistakenly suppose ourselves to be persons who endure through time; the disease is curable; and the cure requires the occurrence of an esoteric, profound experience in which calm lack of attachment is accompanied by deep acceptance of a Buddhist account of how things really are. Clearly, the diagnoses and cures in the two religions are different.

The medical analogy also nicely illustrates the utter seriousness with which devout believers in Christianity and Buddhism have taken the teachings of the respective religions. If one is ill – one needs a coronary bypass, for example, or has cancer of the lymph nodes, or has a dangerously low level of red blood cells – it is essential that one receive the correct medical diagnosis and be given appropriate treatment. Placing one's arm in a splint will not open up the arteries. A knee brace will not control the spread of cancer. Taking an aspirin will not remove anemia. These are serious matters, since mistakes in diagnosis or treatment can be fatal. Both Buddhism and Christianity assume that humankind is afflicted by a spiritual disease and in desperate need of a cure. But they disagree about the nature of the disease and, not surprisingly, they differ on what will provide the cure.

Religious Exclusivism

The seriousness with which believing Christians and Buddhists historically have treated these matters, combined with the conviction that their own perspective is true, results in the problem of conflicting truth claims, and the tendency toward an exclusivism which insists that the diagnosis and cure offered in one's own religion is distinctively accurate and efficacious. That Christianity is exclusivistic in this sense is widely acknowledged and often deplored. In the Gospel of John, for example, Jesus states, 'I am the Way, and the Truth, and the Life; no one comes to the Father but by me' (Jn. 14:6). The Gospel goes on to claim that 'he who believes in the Son has eternal life; he who does not obey the Son shall not see life, but the wrath of God abides on him' (Jn. 3:36). The apostle Peter asserted, 'There is salvation in no one else [but Jesus Christ], for there is no other name under heaven given among men by which we must be saved' (Acts 4:12). Such themes in Christianity have been the subject of extensive debate in recent years, and are often taken as evidence that Christianity is exclusive in ways that other religions – such as Buddhism – are not.[2]

But it is important to recognize that other major religions, including the Indian religions, also have exclusivistic tendencies in that each regards its own perspective as uniquely true and superior to other alternatives.[3] Buddhism does not offer itself as merely one among many possible choices in the smorgasbord of religious options. It claims to tell the truth about how things are, and to tell the truth as to how best to deal with things being that way. Other accounts that are incompatible with Buddhist teachings are said to be mistaken, resulting in ignorance and further suffering; only Buddhism leads to release from suffering and the ignorance from which suffering arises.

---

[2] The literature on Christian approaches to other religions is vast. Helpful introductions to the subject include Paul Knitter, *Introducing Theologies of Religion* (Maryknoll, NY: Orbis Books, 2002); Veli-Matti Kärkkäinen, *An Introduction to the Theology of Religions* (Downers Grove, IL: InterVarsity Press, 2003); Paul Griffiths, *Problems of Religious Diversity* (Oxford: Blackwell, 2001); and Harold Netland, *Encountering Religious Pluralism* (Downers Grove, IL: InterVarsity Press, 2001).

[3] A religion can be exclusivist in maintaining its own distinctive truth while also acknowledging that other religious or philosophical perspectives contain important truths. This has been characteristic of both Christianity and Buddhism. On Buddhist attitudes and perspectives on other religions, see K.N. Jayatilleke, *The Buddhist Attitude to Other Religions* (Kandy, Sri Lanka: Buddhist Publication Society, 1975); and Kristin Beise Kiblinger, *Buddhist Inclusivism: Attitudes Towards Religious Others* (Burlington, VT: Ashgate Publishing Company, 2005).

Among the Indian religious traditions there were vigorous debates over rival religious claims.[4] Shankara (d. 820), who shaped Advaita Vedanta Hinduism, forthrightly states that, 'if the soul ... is not considered to possess fundamental identity with Brahman – an identity to be realized by knowledge – there is not any chance of its obtaining final release.'[5] In other words, only if one accepts Shankara's perspective, as expressed in Advaita Vedanta, can one be liberated. Shankara dismissed the Buddha by saying that 'Buddha, by propounding the three mutually contradictory systems, teaching respectively the reality of the external world, the reality of ideas only, and general nothingness, has himself made it clear either that he was a man given to make incoherent assertions, or else that hatred of all beings induced him to propound absurd doctrines by accepting which [people] would become thoroughly confused.' He then declares that 'Buddha's doctrine has to be entirely disregarded by all those who have a regard for their own happiness.'[6] Similarly, a text from the Jaina Sutras, the authoritative texts of Jainism, bluntly informs us that, 'Those who do not know all things by Kevala (knowledge), but who being ignorant teach a Law (of their own), are lost themselves, and work the ruin of others in this dreadful, boundless Circle of Births. Those who know all things by the full Kevala knowledge, and who practicing meditation teach the whole Law, are themselves saved and save others.'[7] In other words, those who accept Jain doctrine can be enlightened and liberated from rebirths; those who do not cannot be enlightened. A Buddhist text is equally exclusive in rejecting non-Buddhist teachings: 'If one does not proceed in this manner [to "proceed in

---

[4] See Richard King, *Indian Philosophy: An Introduction to Hindu and Buddhist Thought* (Washington, DC: Georgetown University Press, 1999).

[5] Sankara, 'The Vedanta-Sutras, with commentary by Sankaracarya,' IV.3.14, translated by George Thibaut, Part II, in *Sacred Books of the East*, ed. F. Max Müller, vol. 38 (Delhi: Motilal Barnarsidass, 1968 [1904]), pp. 399–400.

[6] Sankara, 'The Vedanta-Sutras,' with commentary by Sankaracarya, II.2.32, translated by George Thibaut, Part I, in *Sacred Books of the East*, ed. F. Max Müller, vol. 34 (Delhi: Motilal Barnarsidass, 1968 [1904]), pp. 400–428.

[7] 'Jaina Sutras,' translated by Hermann Jacobi, in *Sacred Books of the East*, edited by F. Max Müller, vol. 45 (Curzon: Richmond, Surrey, 2001), p. 418.

this manner" is to "develop the understanding which results from the study of (Buddhist) teachings"], inasmuch as meditation on some erroneous idea cannot even clear away doubt, recognition of reality will not arise and consequently meditation will be profitless like that of Tirthikas (i.e. non-Buddhists, especially Jains).'[8] Those – such as Jains – who do not accept Buddhist doctrine will remain unenlightened.

This should not merely be dismissed as an ancient perspective that modern Buddhists have outgrown. The Dalai Lama, for example, in responding to the question whether only the Buddha can provide 'the ultimate source of refuge' stated, 'Here, you see, it is necessary to examine what is meant by liberation or salvation. Liberation in which "a mind that understands the sphere of reality annihilates all defilements in the sphere of reality" is a state that only Buddhists can accomplish. This kind of *moksha* or *nirvana* is only explained in the Buddhist scriptures, and is achieved only through Buddhist practice.'[9]

The theme in these passages is clear enough: Beliefs matter, and proper acceptance of the relevant teachings is essential for attaining the soteriological goal. The stakes are high. To put it in a particular idiom: there is a heaven to gain and a hell to shun; there is only one way to gain heaven and shun hell, but there are plenty of ways to shun heaven and gain hell. This perspective, among the most 'politically incorrect' and allegedly intolerant beliefs and attitudes in the view of many today, is in fact utterly understandable if one actually examines what the religions claim. If one believes that these are the stakes at issue, then taking seriously the idea that there is a path to take and many paths to shun makes perfect sense. If a particular diagnosis of the spiritual disease is accurate, then we desperately need the efficacious cure.

Now a secularist, who rejects not only Christianity and Buddhism but other religions as well, will not think that there

---

[8] Geshe Sopa and Elving Jones, *A Light to the Svatantrika-Madhyamika*, p. 62; privately circulated.

[9] His Holiness The XIVth Dalai Lama, '"Religious Harmony" and The Bodhgaya Interviews,' in *Christianity Through Non-Christian Eyes*, ed. Paul J. Griffiths (Maryknoll, NY: Orbis Books Books, 1990), p. 169.

is any deep spiritual disease in need of cure, and thus will
find the utter seriousness with which believing Christians and
Buddhists take these matters to be at best error, if not simply
superstitious ignorance. But simply to assume that the secular
view is correct, and therefore to conclude that sincere Christians
and Buddhists are intolerant for taking their respective views
with such utter seriousness, is a particular perspective which
itself needs justification. Moreover, there is no reason to accept
the suggestion that deep commitment to a particular view about
the spiritual disease, whether Christian or Buddhist, is necessarily
intolerant. Why suppose that skepticism or secularism is required
for tolerance on these matters? Tolerance and intolerance are not
functions of degrees of commitment to religious views about
the spiritual disease and cure, nor are they matters of accepting
or rejecting certain beliefs. Rather, they concern the appropriate
treatment of people whose beliefs or actions one does not fully
accept. Believing that there is a deep spiritual disease of which we
need desperately to be cured neither justifies nor permits using
violence or any disrespectful means to induce others to accept
one's views, nor does it sanction mistreatment of those with whom
one disagrees.

To repeat, Buddhism and Christianity offer strikingly different
diagnoses of the problem afflicting humankind and thus different
cures. A basic Buddhist theme is that our most fundamental
disease is a kind of ignorance. The cure for this is the right kind of
understanding or knowledge. Buddhism promises enlightenment
as the cure. For the Buddhist tradition, the question 'What must
I do to become enlightened?' is thus analogous to the Christian
tradition's question, 'What must I do to be saved?' (Acts
16:30–31). The Christian tradition answers, 'Believe in the Lord
Jesus Christ and you will be saved.' By contrast, the Buddhist
tradition answers, 'Come to see how things really are, especially
concerning what actually lies behind talk about persons, and
you will become enlightened.' According to Buddhism, this
ignorance is rooted in false views about oneself as a person,
and the relevant knowledge concerns the truth about what we
mistakenly take to be our selves. The goal is to 'see things as they
are,' particularly concerning the reality behind our ordinary talk

of persons. Having the correct understanding here is not simply a matter of being able to provide the correct answers on a true–false exam. It involves a transforming understanding of reality, having one's view of the world radically altered, and has far-reaching implications for how one thinks, feels, and acts.

Buddhist Doctrine and Truth

It is popular today in the West to minimize the significance of doctrine or truth claims in religions.[10] What really matters in religion, it is said, is personal experience and doctrines are important only as they help to bring about desired experiential states. Buddhism is often held up as an example of a religion in which doctrines are merely pragmatic tools to prod one toward enlightenment. Thus, it is said, we should not focus upon specific metaphysical claims but rather upon the experience of enlightenment towards which they point.

The minimizing of doctrine is evident in the discipline of Religious Studies as practiced in many Western universities. Religious Studies tends to emphasize things that can be observed by those studying the religious tradition – the rites, ceremonies, architecture, formal and informal organizations, and so on. Doctrines are not items that can be seen or heard. Their centrality to a religious tradition is thus often underestimated. There is also, to some extent, a curious anti-intellectualism in much of the academic study of religion. Moreover, matters of doctrine – although (to use a Buddhist way of putting things) they 'perfume' rites, rituals, ceremonies, etc. – tend to be in the charge of the

---

[10] Although a Buddhist, Stephen Batchelor, for example, claims that the Four Noble Truths of Buddhism 'are not propositions to believe; they are challenges to act.' Similarly, 'The Dharma is not something to believe in but something to do.' Batchelor maintains that one need not believe the classical Buddhist teaching on rebirth (Stephen Batchelor, *Buddhism Without Beliefs: A Contemporary Guide to Awakening* [New York: Riverhead Books, 1997], pp. 7, 10, 17, 19, 37–8). See also Stephen Batchelor, 'Life As a Question, Not a Fact,' in *Why Buddhism? Westerners in Search of Wisdom*, ed. Vickie Mackenzie (London: Element, 2002), pp. 142–62.

community leaders, the religious elite. The strong tendency to favor what is accessible – even to those who least understand their tradition – operates to further support a minimizing of the importance of doctrine.

These factors are joined by some traits of Buddhism itself which can be seen to reduce the significance of doctrine. For example, nirvana is said to be ineffable – to be 'beyond concepts and descriptions.' This is, of course, doctrinally counterbalanced by the fact that achieving nirvana is held to be of immense value, and this high assessment of nirvana is partly based upon negative features that it is said to lack but also on positive features that it is said to possess. But insofar as the idea of ineffability is stressed, nothing doctrinal concerning nirvana is on the table.

Mahayana Buddhism also puts forward the idea of 'skillful means' (upaya), which claims that the Buddha taught different things to different people in accord with what they were able to understand.[11] The suggestion is not that the Buddha was deceptive, but that people vary in their capacity to grasp the truth: one person might be able only to understand a distant approximation of a given doctrine; another might manage a closer approximation; and only a few will grasp the full doctrine itself, stated literally and straightforwardly. This suggestion leads to thinking of Buddhism as teaching various levels of doctrine. The idea, roughly, is that the true doctrine is D, while doctrines A, B, and C are closer and closer approximations to D. Only a very few will be able to comprehend D, while A can be grasped by many more, B by somewhat fewer, and C by fewer still. Obviously this raises a problem for interpreting Buddhist teachings. One has to figure out which version of teaching is the one that says how things *really* are. This issue arises frequently within the Buddhist tradition itself. The importance of where the deepest, not-in-need-of-correction teaching lies is a matter of what doctrine one must believe in order to become enlightened.

---

[11] Skillful means is a central theme in the *Saddharma pundarika*, or *Lotus of the True Law*, arguably the most influential Mahayana text (Paul Williams, *Mahayana Buddhism: The Doctrinal Foundations* (New York: Routledge, 1989), pp. 143–5; Richard King, *Indian Philosophy*, pp. 95–6).

Finally, given the vast number of texts taken as authoritative by Buddhist traditions, a literal interpretation of all scriptures yields multiple inconsistencies. The common Western assumption that Indian, Chinese, and Japanese religious and philosophical traditions happily embrace acknowledged contradictions, in religion or elsewhere, is unwarranted. This misleading assumption has been supported by a tendency to look to certain expressions of Zen as manifesting the 'essence' of Buddhism or even 'Eastern thought' in general. But, with possibly an exception or two, Buddhist traditions and sub-traditions, like other religious traditions, will want a reading of their authoritative texts that is logically consistent. But to arrive at such a reading, it is necessary to treat some passages as literal and others as non-literal, and to regard some passages as expressing the true doctrine and other passages as merely expressing the closest approximation to the true doctrine that the original audience could grasp.

The distinction between the literal statement of true doctrine and non-literal statements, and between exact statements and approximations, assumes that there are true doctrines that can be stated, and thus does not provide evidence against there being such doctrine. The entire application of skillful means explanations of textual differences has the same presupposition, plus the supposition of significant differences in people's abilities to grasp doctrines. Moreover, the acceptance of the idea of rebirth removes much of the urgency of 'getting things right' within this lifetime. After all, one might always be in a better position in the next life to apprehend and act upon the true doctrine. Finally, the importance attached to consistency also argues for the idea that there are at least some important doctrines that can be stated.

Now it is certainly true that early Buddhism was not interested in abstract metaphysical speculation or doctrine merely for its own sake. Buddhist teachings are soteriological – they are intended to guide people toward enlightenment and liberation. This is illustrated in a famous simile attributed to the Buddha, in which Buddhist teachings are compared to a raft used to cross a river. In the Majjhima Nikaya the Buddha tells of a man who is on a journey and comes to a vast stretch of water. He needs to get to the other side, but there is no bridge or boat available. So the man gathers grass, wood, branches, and leaves and makes a raft. Boarding the raft, he pushes himself to the other side of the river. But suppose, asks the Buddha, that after successfully crossing the river the man were to do the following: 'Having crossed over and got to the other side, he thinks: "This raft was of great help to me. With its aid I have crossed safely over to this side, exerting myself with my hands and feet. It would be good if I carry this raft on my head or on my back wherever I go."' We would think the man foolish if he were to carry the raft around with him once he was on the other side. Having served its purpose, the raft should be left at the shore. The Buddha concludes, 'In the same manner, O *bhikkus* [monks], I have taught a doctrine similar to a raft – it is for crossing over [to Nirvana] and not for carrying.'[12] Walpola Rahula summarizes the point of the story: 'From this parable it is quite clear that the Buddha's teaching is meant to carry man to safety, peace, happiness, tranquility, the attainment of *Nirvana*. The whole doctrine taught by the Buddha leads to this end.'[13]

Moreover, the Buddha systematically discouraged speculative questions which, in his mind, were not conducive to attaining enlightenment. On one occasion a disciple named Malunkyaputta became dissatisfied with the Buddha's unwillingness to answer a series of metaphysical questions. Among the questions he wanted answered were whether the world is eternal or not eternal, the world is finite or infinite, the soul and body are identical or distinct, and whether one exists after death or not. So Malunkyaputta approached the Buddha, demanding answers. But the Buddha responded by noting that he never promised answers to these questions and that demanding that they be answered before putting into practice the Buddha's teaching would mean one never attains enlightenment.

Malunkyaputta, any one who would say, 'I will not lead the religious life under The Blessed One until The Blessed One shall elucidate to me either that the world is eternal, or that the world is not eternal,

---

[12] As cited in Walpola Rahula, *What the Buddha Taught*, rev. edn. (New York: Grove Press, 1974), pp. 11–12.

[13] Ibid, p. 12.

... or, that the saint either exists nor does not exist after death;' – that person would die, Malunkyaputta, before the Tathagata had ever elucidated this to him. It is as if, Malunkyaputta, a man had been wounded by an arrow thickly smeared with poison, and his friends and companions, his relatives and kinsfolk, were to procure for him a physician or surgeon; and the sick man were to say, 'I will not have this arrow taken out until I have learnt whether the man who wounded me belonged to the warrior caste, or to the Brahman caste, or to the agricultural caste, or to the menial caste.' Or again he were to say, 'I will not have this arrow taken out until I have learnt the name of the man who wounded me, and to what clan he belonged.'

The Buddha insisted that overcoming the causes of suffering – attaining enlightenment and nirvana – does not depend upon settling such questions. Rather than speculate about such matters, the Buddha kept the focus upon suffering and the elimination of suffering.

And what, Malunkyaputta, have I elucidated? Misery [*dukkha*], Malunkyaputta, have I elucidated; the origin of misery have I elucidated; the cessation of misery have I elucidated; and the path leading to the cessation of misery have I elucidated. And why, Malunkyaputta, have I elucidated this? Because, Malunkyaputta, this does profit, has to do with the fundamentals of religion, and tends to aversion, absence of passion, cessation, quiescence, knowledge, supreme wisdom, and Nirvana; therefore have I elucidated it.[14]

It does not follow that no metaphysical questions are of ultimate religious importance, or that no metaphysical beliefs are required for reaching enlightenment. The understanding of Buddhist teaching as primarily pragmatic and conducive to attaining enlightenment, and the Buddha's reluctance to engage in metaphysical questions, should not be taken as meaning that correct understanding or belief is not important in Buddhism. For many in the West, Buddhism is primarily a matter of engaging

---

[14] *Majjhima Nikaya* 63, in *A Sourcebook in Asian Philosophy*, eds. John M. Koller and Patricia Koller (New York: Macmillan, 1991), pp. 243–6.

in meditation practices that lead to certain mystical experiences, a set of therapeutic exercises resulting in calming experiences. Questions about doctrine or correct belief are minimized, if entertained at all. But in classical Buddhism rejecting certain incorrect beliefs and embracing certain correct beliefs is regarded as essential to overcoming the causes for suffering and rebirth. As Robert Gimello reminds us, meditation and even mystical experiences were never ends in themselves; they were a

> necessary prelude to an analytic discernment of the 'truths' of dependent origination (*pratityasamutpada*) and impermanence (*anitya*) as they apply to the 'self.' It is this sort of analysis which is the true culmination of the [meditative] exercise … There is wide agreement in the systematic treatments of meditation that pride of place belongs to doctrinal analysis as practiced in the supramundane path. In fact, this is a point often made to distinguish Buddhism from other meditative traditions. It is acknowledged that even the highest absorptive attainments are available in the practice of the heterodox paths (e.g. those taught by some of the Buddha's own pre-enlightenment teachers), but the qualification is always made that without insight into the 'truths' formulated by the Buddha these infidel yogis are still confined to *samsara* [the cycle of rebirth].[15]

Gimello states that, contrary to popular perception 'there is an intellectual or analytic component of meditation' that 'consists in the meditatively intensified reflection upon basic categories of Buddhist doctrine and the application of them to the data of meditative experience.' An essential part of such analysis is the refutation of false views. 'The final key to liberation for the Buddhist lies with this analytic destruction of false views.'[16]

Nor should the pragmatic emphasis in Buddhist views on doctrine be taken as indicating that Buddhism embraces a strictly pragmatic theory of truth. The Buddhist scholar Jayatilleke states, '[W]e have to stress the fact that the Buddha confined himself to

---

[15] Robert Gimello, 'Mysticism and Meditation,' in *Mysticism and Philosophical Analysis*, ed. Steven T. Katz (New York: Oxford University Press, 1978), pp. 181, 187.

[16] Ibid., p. 188.

asserting statements, which were true and *useful*, though pleasant or unpleasant, so that the Dhamma is pragmatic although it does not subscribe to a pragmatic theory of truth....'[17] After noting the Buddha's parables of the arrow and the raft, Jayatilleke concludes, 'Even the true statements in the Dhamma are not clung to. They are to be used for understanding the world and overcoming it.... The value of the Dhamma lies in its utility for gaining salvation. It ceases to have value to each individual *though it does not cease to be true*, when one's aims have been realized.'[18]

Rebirth and Karma

As we saw in the first chapter, the Buddhist tradition tells a simple story which includes a doctrine of rebirth. Without any beginning, each of us has lived one embodied lifetime after another for countless ages. We have lived and died millions of times. Unless we become enlightened, we will continue to do so forever. Moreover, this is not a happy state of affairs. Rebirth brings with it a suffering, or a pervasive dissatisfaction. The first Noble Truth, from the Buddha's First Sermon, expresses this well:

> Now this, O monks, is the noble truth of pain: birth is painful, old age is painful, sickness is painful, death is painful, sorrow, lamentation, dejection, and despair are painful. Contact with unpleasant things is painful, not getting what one wishes is painful. In short, the five *khandas* [the elements that together compose a person, or what talk of a person refers to] of grasping are painful.[19]

This is not an attractive picture. Life within the cycle of rebirth is viewed as inherently undesirable.

In Buddhism life in this world is seen to be profoundly unsatisfactory. This theme is typically put in terms of life inevitably involving suffering, but this way of stating things can be

---

[17] K.N. Jayatilleke, *The Message of the Buddha*, p. 46. Emphasis original.
[18] Ibid. Emphasis added.
[19] *Samyutta-nikaya* v. 420, cited in *A Sourcebook in Indian Philosophy*, p. 274.

misleading. The term 'painful' was used in the text quoted above to translate the Pali term 'dukkha.' The term 'dukkha' includes the notions of pain and suffering, but is broader than these words in speaking of a pervasive unsatisfactoriness or discontent. Imagine, for example, two parents at the wedding dinner of their only child. The child is deeply in love with her groom, as he is with her. They are perfectly matched. She is beautiful and he is handsome. Both are intelligent and have good jobs. The entire family is in good health, the food and drink are excellent, the weather perfect, no troubles threaten the family's unity, and everyone is joyous. These people are not suffering in the ordinary sense. But each may contract a dreadful disease. The jobs may be lost and poverty ensue. The family members may come to hate one another. The food and drink will be consumed, and overindulgence has its price. In any case, all will die and their bodies will decay. Even the greatest joy is fleeting. Anxiety about one's place in the world, the purpose of living, the fear of altogether ceasing to exist, the uncertainty of the future, the inevitability of aging unless one dies young, the awareness of the ravages of war and disease, the ever present possibility of something terrible occurring to you and those you love – these compose a small part of the evils that threaten us all. The bottom line is that no good that you receive in this life completely fulfills your needs and hopes, and every good one experiences in this life will be utterly lost. No good that you can lose is satisfactory, and every good this life offers will be lost. This is true of the present lifetime, and of every other lifetime, in the absence of your becoming enlightened. Simply dying will not free you from this unsatisfactoriness, and suicide is not permissible. The Buddhist teaching is that you need an effective way of escaping the unsatisfactoriness of not just this life but all lives.

A doctrine of karma is also an integral part of the Buddhist account.[20] The doctrine of karma claims that one's actions in this and all previous lives have consequences. If they are right

---

[20] See Bruce R. Reichenbach, *The Law of Karma: A Philosophical Study* (Honolulu, HI: University of Hawaii Press, 1990).

actions, then the consequences will be relatively desirable; if they are wrong actions, then the consequences will be undesirable. Each right or wrong action has its own set of consequences and there is no escaping them – one performs the action and receives the consequences. If some of the consequences, desirable or undesirable, come in the same lifetime in which the action that leads to them is performed, others do not. So when one's body dies, one still has consequences coming. Thus one must be reborn so as to receive these consequences. But then in this new lifetime one also performs actions and thereby initiates yet further consequences. The consequences again are not exhausted within one's current lifetime. So again one must die and be reborn in still different circumstances. So it goes, forever, unless something radical happens to break the cycle. Buddhist doctrine offers such a radical 'something' through the experience of enlightenment. Although various sub-traditions within Buddhism differ on their understandings of enlightenment and the conditions for its attainment, the escape from the otherwise unending cycle of birth–death–rebirth–redeath–forever is not typically conceived as coming by way of an unembodied or disembodied continued existence of a soul, self, mind, or person.

If one approaches the story of beginningless birth and death, repeated over and over again, from a common-sense viewpoint, or from an orthodox Christian (or Jewish or Islamic) perspective, one will likely understand it in terms of the travels of a soul from one life to another. But none of these traditions accepts these ideas. If one retains the idea of a soul, and transfers it to the rebirth–karma perspective, the resulting view is that there is a conscious being that is distinct from the body and exists without a beginning. It lives in one body after another. But no condition the enduring soul is ever in is actually satisfactory. To a degree that varies greatly in intensity, each enduring soul suffers a sort of cosmic claustrophobia from which it seeks relief. Relief will come when the cycle of rebirths ceases. At that point, one's enduring soul will be in something like heaven or hell, or perhaps purgatory. One will not re-enter the cycle of rebirths. While variations of this scenario are found in Hindu and Jain traditions, it is important to emphasize that this is *not* the classical Buddhist perspective.

The Buddhist perspective, even at its surface, is quite different. There are various heavens or places of pleasant (although still unsatisfactory) afterlife, and various ghastly hells. But none of these is permanent. Furthermore, according to Buddhist accounts, one can be reborn as a worm, a ghost, or a god or goddess. There are many other possibilities, and 'you' have not always been a human being. In fact, in the fabulous number of past existences through which 'you' have gone, 'you' have had the lives of an incredible variety of beings.

The most important way in which the 'transmigrating soul' understanding of the birth–death–rebirth–redeath cycle is deeply non-Buddhist is that the Buddhist tradition rejects the idea that there is a soul, or enduring mind, self, or person.[21] For Buddhism, no soul travels from life to life, or even exists within a single lifetime. To believe in an enduring soul is to cling to ignorance and prevent enlightenment. This raises the question of what, for the Buddhist, replaces the concept of the soul. If there is a cycle of rebirth, *something* or other must be reborn. The most straightforward Buddhist answer is that what you are is simply a collection of momentary states. Over time, you are simply a series of these collections, each collection causing the next. If the reincarnation-karma story is taken literally, this series is what the typical Buddhist tradition asserts does the transmigrating from lifetime to lifetime.

But perhaps the talk of a cycle of rebirth is not to be taken literally. What if it is seen as merely a first, rough approximation of something very different – as a way of getting people started on a journey of religious learning that leads to enlightenment? Talk of rebirth would then be a kind of 'skillful means,' intended to prod people along the spiritual journey to the point where they are in a position to attain enlightenment.

In sum, one literal way of reading the doctrines of rebirth and karma says that an enduring soul migrates from lifetime to lifetime receiving the consequences of his earlier actions. This is the way

---

[21] See Steven Collins, *Selfless Persons: Imagery and Thought in Theravada Buddhism* (Cambridge: Cambridge University Press, 1982).

that monotheistic Hinduism, and Jainism, understand the story. The central way in which this reading is eminently non-Buddhist, however, lies in its idea that there is an enduring soul. The question for the Buddhist tradition – Personalism aside – is *not* how exactly to conceive of this enduring entity, but rather how to reductively analyze or replace the mistaken idea of such a soul. This is true for both those versions of the Buddhist tradition that take the story of rebirth and karma literally and those that do not.

Impermanence, No-self, and Dependent Co-origination

The Buddhist tradition contains various accounts of how the escape from rebirth provided by enlightenment can be attained. Although they differ in some respects, the accounts agree that becoming enlightened has as its centerpiece 'seeing things as they are.' The ordinary 'common sense' view of how things are is rejected by almost all of the Buddhist traditions. One core mistake of common sense is said to be the belief that people are, or have, enduring minds or souls. You believe that you were born a certain time ago and have existed continuously, as numerically one enduring thing, from then until now. You of course have changed. Change requires something that changes. That you have changed, however much, in the years from your birth until now, is true only if you have endured from your birth until now.

Another basic error of common sense belief is said to be the idea that things have natures or essences, what the tradition often calls 'own being.' There are features that a cow, for example, must have in order to be a cow. The features that are necessary and sufficient for Bessie, the cow out in the field, to be a cow constitute Bessie's nature. So common sense holds.

But the Buddhist tradition typically denies that anything denies that any composite has a nature. Furthermore, nothing, with or without essence can exist independently. Any such thing exists in mutual dependence on other things that also are essenceless. To believe otherwise is to fail to see things as they are, to be ignorant, and to be unenlightened. Indeed, it is to be incapable of enlightenment until these beliefs are replaced by proper Buddhist belief.

Now it is by no means obvious that nothing endures, that there are no enduring souls or minds, or that nothing has a nature. The Buddhist tradition grants, what seems obvious in any case, that belief in enduring things, including ourselves, and that things belong to kinds, barring enlightenment, is present in us all. But much Buddhist effort has been spent on trying to show that these very natural beliefs are in fact false. There have developed within Buddhism strategies for dealing with the fact that we have these beliefs – of trying to account for our having them in a way that does not include reference to anything in virtue of which these beliefs would be true after all. Here, then, are some central concepts that are relevant to the Buddhist strategies for dealing with the idea that there is any such thing as an enduring soul, mind, self, or person.

First, there is the concept of a construct. A construct, as the term suggests, is something constructed. Constructs are concepts that do not fit anything that actually exists; what actually exists is very different from what the constructs represent as existing. One common Buddhist strategy is to treat the concept of a soul, mind, self, or person as only a construct. This is a typical Buddhist move, used not only to deconstruct the notion of a soul but also to analyze away physical objects.

Second, there is the concept of reductive analysis. In this case, the individual parts of a complex thing are listed, and then it is asserted that the complex thing just is the parts – that the whole is nothing more than the parts together. This is illustrated in a famous exchange between the Buddhist Nagasena and King Milinda, in the Milindapanha. Nagasena asks the King whether he arrived on foot, to which the King responds by saying he came in a chariot. Nagasena proceeds to try to show the King that there is no chariot as such, beyond the various constituent parts associated with the word 'chariot.'

> 'Your majesty, if you came in a chariot, declare to me the chariot.
>   Pray, your majesty, is the pole the chariot?'
> 'Nay, verily, *bhante* [lord].'

'Is the axle the chariot?'
'Nay, verily, *bhante.*'
'Are the wheels the chariot?'
'Nay, verily, *bhante.*'
'Is the chariot-body the chariot?'
'Nay, verily, *bhante.*'

Nagasena proceeds to ask about each part of the chariot, each time eliciting from the King the answer that that particular part does not constitute the chariot. Finally, Nagasena asks,

'Is it, then, your majesty, something else besides pole, axle, wheels, chariot-body, banner-staff, yoke, reins, and goad which is the chariot?'
'Nay, verily, *bhante.*'

Nagasena draws the desired conclusion: there is no chariot beyond the parts enumerated. He then applies this analysis to the conventional idea of an enduring person or soul.

Your majesty, although I question you very closely, I fail to discover any chariot. Verily now, your majesty, the word chariot is a mere empty sound.... In exactly the same way, your majesty, in respect of me, Nagasena [the name] is but a way of counting, term, appellation, convenient designation, mere name for the hair of my head, hair of my body ... brain of the head, form, sensation, perception, the predisposition, and consciousness. But in the absolute sense there is no ego here to be found.[22]

A whole or complex – a person or a chariot – is nothing more than the parts that constitute it. Just as there is no chariot beyond the constituent physical parts associated with what we call a 'chariot,' so too there is no soul or mind or person beyond the constituent parts associated with the idea of a person. The process of reductive analysis begins with making a list of what are regarded as all the parts of the thing being analyzed, and then proceeds to say that the item in question has no further parts and is simply identical to the parts that are listed.

---

[22] Milindapana, II.i.1; in *A Sourcebook in Indian Philosophy*, pp. 281–2.

Third, there is the concept of an item lacking its 'own being,' or its not having an essence. Some make the claim that anything that cannot be analyzed into other things has its 'own-being' or essence. The non-complex – the simple item that has no parts – has an essence, insofar as there are such things. Whether anything at all has an essence is a matter of some dispute among Buddhist sub-traditions,[23] but that nothing complex has an essence is a matter of agreement. Having an essence and existing in a manner not dependent upon the existence of other things are sometimes linked. Whether anything at all has its own essence is not a point on which all Buddhist traditions agree. But that lacking an essence and being dependent are inherently linked is a shared view.

Fourth, a claim very basic to the Buddhist tradition is that everything, or almost everything, depends for its existence and properties on the existence and properties of something else. This is the doctrine of 'dependent co-arising' or 'dependent origination' (pratitya-samutpada). Other than nirvana, everything is changing and impermanent; all appearances are interdependent and condition or affect one another in a continual process of coming into being and ceasing to be. The Buddha described dependent origination as follows: 'If this is that comes to be; from the arising of this that arises; if this is not that does not come to be; from the stopping of this that is stopped.'[24] All things arise and pass out of existence due to certain interrelated conditions, linked through causal relationships. When the necessary and sufficient conditions are present, a particular thing comes to be. When the conditions change, the thing changes. When the necessary conditions are

---

[23] Some of the Abhidharma schools, for example, maintained that dharmas, or the fundamental elements comprising the basic constituents of mental and physical objects, have essences, whereas conventional things such as tables or persons do not. See Donald W. Mitchell, *Buddhism: Introducing the Buddhist Experience*, 2nd edn. (New York: Oxford University Press, 2008), pp. 134–8. The Madhyamaka school, by contrast, regarded all the dharmas as 'empty' and devoid of 'own being' or essences.

[24] Samyutta-nikaya II, 64–65; in *Buddhist Texts Through the Ages*, trans. and ed. by Edward Conze, I.B. Horner, David Snellgrove, and Arthur Waley (Oxford: Oneworld, 1995), p. 66.

removed, the thing ceases to be. The 'thing,' in accord with the doctrine of the previous paragraph, is either a non-composite momentary state or event, or a causally linked complex collection of such states or events.

Two lines of dependence are included here. Suppose item X (whatever X might be) comes to exist at a given time T1. In that case, X came into existence at a time T1 only because something (or things) existing prior to time T1 caused X to do so. Furthermore, while it exists at T1, X depends for its existence and properties on at least some of its colleagues that also exist at T1. So dependence is both successive (on some things) and simultaneous (on other things). The further claim is then added that whatever is dependent is momentary, so that nothing dependent can endure.

The Buddha used the doctrine of dependent origination to explain the origin and elimination of suffering (dukkha). This was done through the twelve-linked chain of cause and effect (the wheel of life), which connects the effects of past lives to the present, and links past and present to the future. Experiences in the present, including the appearance of enduring selves, are produced by the twelve-linked chain of causation. The first and most basic cause of these experiences is ignorance, from which then emerge the other causal conditions.

> On ignorance depends karma; on karma depends consciousness; on consciousness depend name and form; on name and form depend the six organs of sense; on the six organs of sense depends contact; on contact depends sensation; on sensation depends desire; on desire depends attachment; on attachment depends existence; on existence depends birth; on birth depends old age and death, sorrow, lamentation, misery, grief and despair. Thus does this entire aggregation of misery arise.[25]

Ordinary experiences in this world are rooted in ignorance, especially that ignorance associated with the idea of an enduring self. The wheel of life resulting in rebirth can be broken if the

---

[25] *Samyutta-nikaya* XXII, 90; in John M. Koller and Patricia Koller, eds., *A Sourcebook in Asian Philosophy*, pp. 233–4.

causal chain is interrupted. The cessation of the cycle of rebirth is 'awakening' or nirvana.

The claims that result from applying these general strategies are quite radical in their consequences for the common sense view of the world. On that view, there are lots of enduring things – oneself, one's friends, and family included. Typically, at least many of these things are thought of as having essences. On a widely accepted view, biology and chemistry study these. But for the Buddhist tradition, all of that is only conventional and constructed, and will not survive critical analysis. For example, the concept of a mind or a body can be analyzed without remainder into the concepts of parts that are not themselves concepts of minds or bodies. The idea is that if a concept of some X can be analyzed away into concepts of things that are not Xs, then the 'X itself' – the thing of which the concept of X is a concept – is composed of non-Xs, and is nothing more than a collection. A collection of ten coins is simply coin one, coin two ... coin ten. The collection is not something more than its composite parts. The same thing is true of a chariot, a tree, a cow, or a human being – each of these is a mere collection. This is, of course, a controversial claim, and one typically denied by Jains and Hindus. There is some disagreement among Buddhist traditions themselves over how to understand whether the parts that have no parts themselves survive analysis and have essences. For some varieties of Buddhism, such as the Abhidharma schools, at least the simple parts of which physical objects and souls, minds, selves, or persons are composed, exist and survive analysis; they even have their essences. But for other varieties of Buddhism, even these simple parts lack an essence, are merely conventional, and do not survive analysis.

There are other themes that lie deep in the Buddhist tradition. They include the doctrine that there are some absolutely simple things out of which the world is made. Among these simple things, everything is impermanent; nothing lasts very long. How long is 'not very long'? If we refer to the smallest temporal unit as a moment, one Buddhist answer is that while a strong man snaps his fingers, some 65 impermanent simple items come and go, 65 moments pass. No single item of whatever sort retains existence for as long as two moments. Every simple thing is impermanent. Further, it is typically held that no simple thing exists independently; each simple item is caused to come into existence by something else, is affected by other items during its short appearance, and then goes out of existence. Those who accept co-origination and simple entities having essences cannot consistently hold that having an essence precludes dependent existence. Anything that is complex – that is made up of simples – is made up of simples each of which of course exists momentarily.

The claims that we have been discussing are metaphysical claims – claims concerning the most basic things that exist and how they are related. They seem to have no religious interest or importance. If one wants to understand Buddhist religion, however, one must realize that these claims are of enormous significance. The Buddhist criterion for what has religious importance is not necessarily what seems to have importance to contemporary Westerners, let alone what university Religious Studies departments find most interesting. The Buddhist criterion for what is religiously significant is what is taught by the texts that are acknowledged as authoritative and what is conducive to attaining enlightenment. For typical Buddhist traditions, having true beliefs regarding certain matters in metaphysics is a necessary condition of one's deep spiritual disease being cured.

Now the Buddhist assumption that anything that exists dependently must be impermanent, existing only for a while and then going out of existence, is not a necessary truth. For example, if an omnipotent God wished to create something – say, an angel – that always existed dependent only on God, and on nothing else, God could do this. Noting this is true does not assume that God does exist, or that God does not exist. The point here is simply that it is not logically impossible that God exist, and if God does exist this is something that God, as omnipotent, could do. So there is no logically necessary connection between dependence and impermanence. For a secular materialist, elementary particles endure for vast periods of time, and there seems to be nothing self-contradictory about this view. Indeed, just the claim that there are material particles that exist for vast periods of time can be accepted by Jews, Christians, Muslims, Hindus, and Jains as well as by secularists. There seems to be good reason to accept it. But most Buddhist traditions reject any such duration.

Appearances and Reality

The assumption that anything that exists dependently necessarily lacks a nature or essence is also not a necessary truth. A palm tree exists dependently on its physical parts, but still has a nature or essence. A human body is composed of cells which in turn are composed of particles, but nonetheless has an essence or belongs to a kind. At this point, a defender of Buddhist doctrine is likely to introduce another basic Buddhist teaching. Although often called the 'doctrine of two truths,' this is a misleading way of putting things.[26] The tradition makes a distinction between 'conventional truth' and 'ultimate truth.' A proposition is true if and only if things are the way it says they are. Such a proposition is an ultimate truth. A proposition is conventionally 'true' if and only if it says how things *seem to someone* but is not true about the way things actually are. Thus, in plain English, conventional 'truths' are false. The locution 'ultimate truth' is redundant and 'conventional truth' is an oxymoron. The relevant distinction here is between *the way things appear to be* and *the way things are*. This requires, of course, that there also be a truth about how things appear. That things appear in a certain way, whether they are that way or not, entails that propositions that accurately describe the way things appear – propositions of the form 'It appears to the unenlightened person that A' – are true if what replaces 'A' – is a correct account of how things appear to the unenlightened. In other words, there is a fact of the matter as to how things appear as well as a fact of the matter as to how things are. According to the tradition, knowing the truth about how things appear to the unenlightened is not part of becoming enlightened. It is, we might say, mundane truth – but it is true nonetheless, and it is easy to neglect this fact.

The relevance of these considerations to the matters of dependent co-arising, and the claim that if an item is dependent

---

[26] See Paul Williams, *Mahayana Buddhism*, pp. 69–72.

then it has no nature or essence, is as follows. While there appear to us to be trees and human bodies, there really are no such things. There are different ways of making this idea more specific. One might, for example, hold that what lies behind talk of physical objects is merely the sensory content of certain conscious states. One would then be an idealist, maintaining that there are only minds and their mental states (or that minds reduce to mental states). Or one could hold that there are fundamental particles, and the things that we call trees and human bodies are nothing more than collections of these particles. Alternatively, one could hold that there are not even any elementary elements, either mental or physical. But the relevant point here is that if there are not any trees or human bodies then there are not any essences or natures of trees or human bodies. So the basis of the dependent co-origination and the dependent-then-no-essence claims entails the idea that ordinary, everyday experience is radically misleading, in that it includes belief in the existence of enduring physical and mental things, when there really are not any. This is obviously very different from claiming that *necessarily*, what is dependent is transient and lacks a nature.

Typical Buddhist doctrines nonetheless require that *there is something or other of which the doctrines are true*. Within the Buddhist traditions there is more than one account of what that is. But whatever is said to exist in virtue of which the basic Buddhist doctrine of co-origination is true, it must be multiple and not just one thing, and the multiple items in question must be causally related in such a way that what happens next depends for its existence on other items that exist now. The point is simple: if no causality, then no dependent co-origination; and if no dependence then no inference from it to lack of natures or essences.

There is a genuine risk that a tradition that makes a sharp distinction between appearance and reality, that says how things appear is radically different from how they are, and adds that we make up how things appear to us, falls into a certain conceptual pit. The basic point is simple and straightforward: if these are constructions, then there are constructors that are not themselves constructions. However far removed from the everyday view the final Buddhist account of things may be, there still must be *some* account or other of *something* that the revised story does fit – of which it is true. It can't be 'constructions all the way down.'

For the Buddhists, there are constraints on what sort of 'something' that can be. Minimally, there cannot be enduring persons, lest enlightenment be impossible. It is this belief – that if there are enduring selves then enlightenment and escape from the cycle of rebirth is impossible – that makes the no-self doctrine so essential in most of the Buddhist tradition. (Properties of enduring persons are not parts, and change presupposes something enduring that undergoes change. One thing going out of existence and being replaced by something else is replacement of that thing, not change in it.)

More generally, nothing non-composite can endure, where to endure is to last for as long as two moments in any other way than in virtue of having one part that exists at one time and another part that exists at a succeeding time. If non-persons can endure, then perhaps persons can endure, which would be unthinkable in Buddhist traditions. Nor can even the items that compose composite items endure. Components fare no better.

There are various strategies for giving an account of things that excludes any one item actually enduring rather than being made of successive momentary items. Before considering them, however, it is worth remembering that historically there have been some Buddhist traditions which considered it necessary that there be enduring agents which are reincarnated and on which karma operates. The Pudgalavadins (or Personalists), for example, were a third-century AD school that apparently had a great many adherents at one time. This sub-tradition held that the pudgala, a self or soul over and above the five aggregates (skandhas), exists and is reborn through the life cycles.[27] But these perspectives are regarded as heretical by most Buddhists because of their denial of the central Buddhist doctrine of impermanence. Those variations of Buddhism that deny the impermanence doctrine by supposing that there are things of which it is false, of course, take there to be sufficient reasons within Buddhist thought for restricting the

---

[27] See Richard H. Robinson and Willard L. Johnson, *The Buddhist Religion: A Historical Introduction*, 4th edn. (Belmont, CA: Wadsworth, 1997), pp. 58–60.

doctrine to only some of what exists. They have thought that something must exist of which the impermanence doctrine is false, lest other Buddhist doctrines turn out not to be true. It is worth emphasizing again that concern with what a doctrine entails and whether different doctrines are logically consistent is of significant concern within most Buddhist traditions, as it is throughout Indian and 'Eastern thought' generally.

There is, from a Buddhist perspective, great danger in believing that one is a permanent, or at least an enduring, being. According to Buddhism, such belief is false and must be abandoned in order for enlightenment to be attained. If we take ourselves to be selves or souls, permanent or enduring, then whatever must exist in order for us to possess that belief must exist. It is thus crucial for the Buddhist tradition that *there being an enduring conscious mind* is not a necessary condition of *there being the belief that there is an enduring conscious mind*. Suppose that what must exist in order for us to possess that belief is that we must be enduring conscious beings. Then any view that admits that we have this belief, but denies that it is true, must be false. In that case, one who wishes to accept the standard 'no self' view must hold that the very conditions that standard Buddhist diagnoses describe as creating the disease that Buddhism addresses must exist in order for one to have diagnosed the disease. But the condition is a disease only if the view that there are enduring minds is false. Then a condition of having the diagnosed disease is that it not be a disease after all. So, for most Buddhist traditions, the supposition must be false – it must not be the case that there being beliefs requires enduring believers.

Dependent Co-origination and Determinism

The doctrine of dependent co-origination is relevant to many other themes in Buddhist teachings. One feature of this doctrine is that, applied consistently as it is in typical Buddhist perspectives, it entails determinism. The basic idea is that each item that comes into existence is caused by preceding causes. The world is thus seamless causally. But causality in this context is somewhat more complex than in typical deterministic systems. The usual deterministic view – often held in connection with some variety of physicalism – maintains that each event that occurs at a given time cannot fail to occur at that time, given what has gone before. To put it more precisely, suppose that there are three things: (1) a description of the entire condition of the world at a given time, with no detail left out; (2) a statement of all the laws of nature, that is, all of the laws that the sciences seek to discover; (3) a statement of all of the laws of logic – or, if one prefers, all of the principles of correct inference. Given (1) – (3) one could, if sufficiently well informed and intelligent, infer every detail of the description of the world at the next moment, and the next, and so on, for as long as there is a world. In standard versions of determinism, no moral element causally enters into this view. The complete description of every event lacks any reference to being good or bad.

On the typical Buddhist view, however, the determinism that is true of the world does contain a moral element. Good actions yield positive consequences. Bad actions yield negative consequences. So it is not only the weight, location, velocity, direction, and so on, of causes that determine what effects arise. The moral quality of actions, which typically is held to be decided on the basis of the intention with which the action was performed, is also relevant. Causality here includes karmic causality. (Karmic considerations play no role in the standard versions of determinism.) In Buddhism, the karmic connections – positive consequences for good actions, negative consequences for bad actions – are not based upon the hidden hand of a powerful moral agent who sees to it that the proper consequences for actions occur. That the proper consequences – the ones that fit the action – occur is simply a brute fact of nature. The introduction of a karmic element into a deterministic view does not make the view less deterministic; it simply makes the determinism more complicated, not less rigid.

A contention that follows from determinism is that whenever an event occurs, there is in fact an explanation of the event (whether we ever discover what the correct explanation is or not). On the dependent co-arising view of things, that explanation will simply refer to prior events, not to a cosmic agent. No person, human or divine, is ever a cause, save as the word 'person' is merely a way of referring to a series of momentary states. This perspective thus denies that there is any creator – any being to which everything else owes its existence but which does not owe its existence to anything else.

Buddhist traditions typically assume that there is such a thing as human freedom – that what it is that talk of 'persons' refers to is free to seek enlightenment. Ultimately, for the most typical view, what must be free is conscious states. They (perhaps along with non-conscious states) are all that Buddhist Reductionism – discussed in some detail in our next chapter – allows that there is. It appears that 'freedom' then refers to the possibility of sequences of conscious states being different from the way that they actually are. It refers to its being somehow possible that a given sequence go in some way other than it does go. Given the way the sequence itself was at an earlier time, and other sequences were at an earlier time, and are at the present time, however, this – given dependent co-origination – seems to be ruled out.

On a Buddhist account of things on which a rebirth-karma view is taken literally, the bundles of states or events that comprise all that you are is as it is in part due to the states or events that occurred earlier and caused the current 'you sequence' to exist. It is also affected by simultaneous states or events. For this view, the chain of sequences is without beginning; there is no temporally first member of a chain. There is also no agent – no mind, self, soul, or person – which transcends or is something over and above the constituents of the series and possesses freedom of the will, or anything else. So what could freedom of choice possibly mean in this context? What could have it?

It seems that what can lie behind a doctrine of freedom of choice, or its replacement, that is compatible with dependent co-arising will be characterized by two claims. In describing this we neglect the fact that a given state likely will have more than one causal antecedent, and is causally affected by simultaneous states. One claim is that there are conscious states whose content is of the form 'let X occur,' where X is some event or state that can be caused by some state that has a 'let X occur' content. At least it can have this effect in the context of the collections that are simultaneous to the one containing the 'let X occur' content, plus the other members of that state's collection. Second, it must be the case that the 'let X occur' state, as a result of which X does occur, is caused by a conscious state that had a 'let a thought of the form "let X occur" occur.' This will be the replacement for a subject who chooses to do something. (For cases in which an agent does something intentionally and does not think about whether to do it or not, the replacement need not include reference to the 'let a thought of the form "let X occur".')

To review: what replaces an agent's choice, on this theory, is a state that has as its content a will that a state that has 'let X occur' as its content. This, on the theory, replaces an agent's choice to do X. The state with a 'let X occur' as its content replaces the agent's doing X. That state causes a state with an 'X' content. Each state will be preceded by a series in which conscious states, whose content was caused by prior states, whose content in turn is caused by yet other states, in an endless chain that goes back forever. The result is that there is a beginningless causal chain of states, each of which is caused by a previous state by which it is caused and which itself is a cause of another state. In this fashion there could be conscious states that caused other states, some of which caused states will have content that correspond to its own in the way that 'let a thought of the form "let X occur" occur' corresponds to 'let X occur,' which corresponds to X's occurring. This, however, will not be freedom of the will since there is, on this view, no will or person to have a will, whether determined or free. Yet it might be claimed that this is what lies behind talk of freedom, and should be a replacement for it.

The replacement requires a second order state – the 'let there be a thought whose content is "let X occur".' If this state can be other than caused by prior or simultaneous states, it can cause a first order state and not itself be determined. The tradition does not typically concern itself with second order states or countenance states (nirvana aside) not caught in the net of dependent co-origination, which is held to be seamless, and not subject to intervention from 'outside.' Then each mental state that was a cause was caused by another mental state. Short of accepting a compatibilist account of freedom, for which our being free and determinism being true are logically compatible (and hence means something different by 'freedom' than has been assumed here), it is hard to see what account might be given that is compatible with dependent co-origination. Even so, on this account, freedom is more a matter of freedom *from* than freedom *to* – if a sequence is so fortunate as to have its future unsatisfactory states limited to whatever time is left to it in this lifetime, there will have occurred in it an enlightened state that allows detachment to dominate and brings the sequence to an end of rebirths. That is what the tradition most cares about. 'Freedom' in any sense matters only if it makes this possible.

Nonetheless, the Buddhist tradition does suggest that there is a degree of freedom not available in a strictly deterministic world. Paul Griffiths, having noted that, on the typical Buddhist view, one is influenced by one's parents, one's mental capacities, and much more besides, states that, 'within these parameters, it is still possible to act well or badly, to make the best possible use of what has been determined for one or make things worse by bowing to one's limitations. So Buddhist theory is certainly not strict determinism.'[28] Putting the point in a way that is compatible with the metaphysics most typically held in the tradition, the sequence that lies behind talk of 'you' can contain states that are themselves not fully caused by prior states. The conscious states will be states with 'intending-to-bring-about-some-later-state' content and at least may make a difference in how the sequence within which it occurs, and even other sequences, continue. This seems to require a 'looseness' in the causal connections between prior and posterior states that is hard, if not impossible, to make consistent with affirmation of the doctrine of dependent co-origination and the absence of any agent whose conscious states are involved.

The tradition is sometimes interpreted as committed to compatibilism (a popular theory in contemporary philosophy). Compatibilism is the view that the only freedom we can have, or

---

28 Paul Griffiths, 'Notes Towards A Critique of Buddhist Karmic Theory,' *Religious Studies* 18 (1982), p. 187.

that we need, is compatible with the truth of determinism. This does not seem to be at all the dominant perspective in the tradition, though it may well be a route that, were the tradition to take it, would at least render dependent co-origination compatible with a sort of freedom, or perhaps the closest a determinist can come. To whatever degree there is not a single detailed determinate theory, or a set of detailed determinate theories, of freedom, this may be in part due to its being freedom from suffering or unsatisfactoriness that matters most. Freedom *from* rather freedom *to* is what counts, and the latter is significant only insofar as it may be necessary for the former. There is also the noted reluctance on the part of the Buddha to engage in metaphysics more than simply stating what the disease and cure require. Also such matters are discussed in the everyday terms that the tradition needs to communicate with all but a tiny number of initiates, but which it also must strongly reject because of the tradition's commitment to the doctrine of no-self. This shifts attention away from any problem there might be in fitting freedom into a world that contains only what actual Buddhist thought says exists.

Conscious States

Buddhists traditions offer different accounts of what there really is. They agree, however, that knowing what there really is, 'seeing things as they really are,' constitutes the essence of becoming enlightened. But given the accounts of what really exists, the story that Buddhism tells about compassion, peace, and relief of suffering or unsatisfactoriness must be revised. It cannot mean what it seems to mean. For the story seems to be about actually existing enduring persons. But according to classical Buddhism, there are no enduring persons. What the story about compassion, peace, and relief from suffering actually amounts to, then, cannot be taken literally as it stands. So what does it mean?

The central factor in determining what the story actually means is what is held to really exist. If there are no enduring persons, then what is there? As noted earlier, the most frequent Buddhist answer is that there are momentary states. These states dependently co-arise and they exist momentarily in mutual dependence upon other states. They vanish as soon as they appear. They come in causal sequences. Some or all of these states are conscious states, but states that are not the states of any conscious being that has them. Some of these states may be mere sensations – states like sensing pain, states that have unpleasant feeling content. Now sensations are not complex. One would ordinarily say that they are simply ways of feeling, though since this suggests someone whose ways of feeling they are, this cannot be the Buddhist account. Sensations, nonetheless, have simple content – nausea, dizziness, euphoria, warmth, and the like are sensations. So are itches and headaches. Generalized feelings – generalized euphoria, anxiety, depression, panic, and the like – are also sensations. In these cases, one does not feel happy about something, anxious that some particular thing may happen or not happen, depressed by something, panicky at something. Sensations simply have feeling contents. The feeling content of a sensation can be highly unpleasant or highly pleasant.

In contrast, at least some conscious states are more complex. Contrast generalized feelings with their more prosaic cousins. One who is just plain (not merely generalized) euphoric is delighted by something, or at some prospect, or in light of some expectation. Ordinary (non-generalized) euphoria is euphoria *about* something, real or imagined. Ordinary fear is fear *of* something – say, of being hit by a car, or being in high places, or of finding oneself in unfamiliar surroundings. Ordinary depression is a matter of feeling down about something, real or imagined. Ordinary panic is panic at something – say, at one's room being on fire, at the prospect of having to give a speech, or having to find a new job.

There is not an entirely familiar way to make a distinction that is relevant here, but there is a non-complicated way of doing so. We begin by defining 'object relative to Kim,' where Kim is a person. Something X is an object relative to Kim if and only if X exists distinct from and independent of Kim and Kim's experiences, provided it exists at all. So a cat, the weather, and Kim's sister are objects relative to Kim. Kim's headache or her fear of snails are not objects relative to Kim. Then we distinguish between conscious states that are just sensations and conscious states that are not just sensations. Kim is having a sensation if and only if Kim is in a conscious state that has some feeling-content and that feeling-content is not, and does not seem to Kim to be, even partly a matter of its seeming to her that she is experiencing something that is an object relative to herself. Kim is having a conscious experience that is not a sensation if and only if Kim is in a conscious state which, at least partly, is a matter of it at least seeming to her that she is experiencing something that, if it exists, is an object relative to herself.

Conscious states that are not sensations are 'outer-directed' – that is, they are, or seem to be, of something external to the person whose experiences they are. They have an internal complexity lacking in mere sensations. We will call them simply complex states. Of course, complex states can, and often do, have some feeling content. But they do not have *only* feeling content. So Kim's feeling dizzy or having a panic attack (feeling generalized panic) are not complex experiences – they are sensations – but her consciously drinking a cup of coffee or her seeing a tree are complex states.

It is important to Buddhism that there are complex states as well as sensations. For whether a given action is right or wrong is importantly influenced, if not determined, by the intention with which it is performed. Intending is a complex state. States of knowledge are complex. So are believing, hoping, wishing, inferring, and wondering. Knowing that seven plus two equals nine and believing that there are no enduring persons are complex states. At least insofar as it involves knowledge, enlightenment is a complex state. Complex states too, short of enlightenment, are unsatisfactory from a Buddhist perspective.

What is involved then in release from suffering is that a sequence of conscious states comes to no longer contain any conscious states that are unsatisfactory. This is what a person being released from suffering amounts to – a series of conscious states no longer containing any states of suffering. In principle, this can occur in either of two ways. One way is that the series continues but is free from states of suffering. The other way is that the series simply cease altogether.

There is, especially in Mahayana Buddhism, the idea that the Buddha[29] (or Buddhas or bodhisattvas) provides help to those in need of enlightenment. Part of this help is said to come from the merit that the Buddha has earned in the process of becoming enlightened. This perspective, of course, is most prominent in the Pure Land tradition of Mahayana Buddhism. The Pure Land tradition is often said to have teachings reminiscent of the Christian notion of divine grace – it is the grace of Amida Buddha that makes rebirth in the Pure Land possible. But there are lingering questions about the language used here: is it all to be understood literally? Or is, perhaps, some of it to be understood non-literally? Or is none of it to be understood literally? If it is not to be understood literally, what does this language mean?

An issue relevant to this theme comes by way of accounts in which the Buddha is said to act in order to aid others in becoming enlightened. The Buddha is viewed as having enormous soteriological powers – as being able to act in such a way that any given seeker after enlightenment is aided in the search. This involves possession of omnipotence and omniscience. Thus, in this respect, the Buddha is regarded as having powers that resemble those attributed to God in Christianity.

Now it is deeply held in Buddhist traditions that all cognitive states in which there is any sense of self are illusory and lead to attachment. Thus no Buddha can be in such a state, for to be in such a state would require that the Buddha be unenlightened. So the Buddha can be in no cognitive state in which there is any sense of self.

The difficulties alluded to in these sorts of considerations, however, arise much more widely. In some philosophical traditions, mental states have been divided into three types: thoughts, choices, and emotions – reflecting the cognitive, volitional, and affective dimensions. But this threefold distinction is not particularly apt. Choices, after all, include thoughts. Roughly speaking, a choice is a choice to make the way that things come to be correspond to some thought. Emotions are ways of feeling

---

[29] We are not concerned here whether 'the Buddha' is more appropriate than 'a Buddha.'

about things – being pleased at the odor of a chocolate cake, repulsed by the sight of a decaying flower, and so on. So volitions and affective states are also cognitive states; choices and emotions include thoughts. But this need not detain us here. Part of the relevant point here is that, according to Buddhism, thoughts (in principle) can be mistaken, so that a being that can have thoughts (in principle) can be mistaken.[30] So the Buddha has no thoughts. This, by itself, entails that the Buddha makes no choices and has no emotions. In any case, according to Indian Buddhism, the Buddha makes no choices and has no emotions. If all conscious states are thoughts, choices, or emotions, then the Buddha has, or is in, or is composed of, no mental state whatever. A further minor point is worth brief mention. In addition to the sorts of mental states already noted there are sensations – such things as headaches, tickles, dizziness, aches, and the like. The Buddha, of course, lacks these as well.

There are other ways of classifying mental states, but there is no need to pursue the issue further. According to implications of teachings in the Buddhist tradition, the Buddha has no mental states. But then the story of the Buddha acting on behalf of the unenlightened, in any sense of intentionally rendering any help to anyone, of the Buddha being compassionate, and the like are not accurate. Given the nature ascribed to the Buddha, it is not even possible that the Buddha have a mental life at all. If the Buddhist tradition is to choose between the view that any being that has thoughts can be mistaken and the view that the enlightened Buddha can help sequences reach enlightenment, it is the latter view that is likely to triumph and the former likely to fall by the wayside.

---

[30] This seems to be an assumption of the tradition. See Paul Griffiths, 'Why Buddhas Can't Remember Their Previous Lives,' *Philosophy East and West* 39:4 (October 1989), pp. 449–51. But it does seem that it is possible that a being have thoughts without it being possible that it have mistaken thoughts. An essentially omniscient being that has beliefs necessarily has only true beliefs. To be essentially omniscient is to fit this description. A being B is essentially omniscient if it is logically impossible that it exist and not be omniscient, and if it has beliefs, it has every true belief, and no other beliefs. This notion seems perfectly consistent.

Enlightenment and Nirvana

The question as to what becoming enlightened amounts to is of central interest in Buddhism. There is agreement among Buddhist traditions that being enlightened is incompatible with still having attachment to anything. The term 'nirvana' means, at least in part, snuffing out, as in the extinguishing of a candle flame. An enlightened state is one without desires, all attachment having been extinguished.

A further question is what else, if anything, is extinguished in the realization of enlightenment. As we have seen, the majority of Buddhist traditions agree that there is not, in any ordinary sense of the word, any self – any enduring mind or soul or person. So there is no enduring person to become extinguished. In a famous passage in the Majjhima-nikaya, the Buddha responds to questions about the survival of the self by rejecting four proposed alternatives.[31] The alternatives are as follows: the self survives in nirvana; it does not survive in nirvana; it both survives and does not survive; and it neither survives nor does not survive. This rather cryptic response is generally understood as teaching that since there is no soul, it cannot be either true or false that it survives, and if it is neither true nor false that a self survives, it is not both true and false that it survives, and not both true and false that it does not survive. But this provides no help in answering the question of what the Buddhist position is regarding what happens to that which, on a Buddhist account, exists and to which the ordinary use of 'person' misleadingly refers.

A possible answer is that 'attaining nirvana' involves annihilation of what the Buddhist traditions typically take ordinary talk of 'persons' to be misleadingly referring to (the sequence of bundles of mental states ends), and that is all.[32] But Buddhism generally has been highly critical of this way of describing nirvana. The idea that annihilation expresses a central Buddhist concept

---

[31] See Majjhima-nikaya, I, 483–8, in *A Sourcebook in Indian Philosophy*, pp. 289–91.
[32] See Thomas E. Wood, *Mind Only: A Philosophical and Doctrinal Analysis of the Vijnanavada* (Delhi, India: Motilal Banarsidass, 1994).

is highly unpopular and has historically been flatly rejected by Buddhists. One reason for this is that this suggests that Buddhism is a variety of nihilism – a tradition from which Buddhism has been careful to dissociate itself.[33]

One thing that makes the subject of nirvana difficult to discuss is the claim that it is ineffable, that is, that it is literally true of nirvana that no concepts apply to it. If this claim is taken as it stands, that should end all discussion of nirvana. However, it should also preclude any beginning of discussion of nirvana. If it is literally ineffable, then it is not better described in one way than in another. It is as accurate to describe it as hell in which torture is carried out by gods and goddesses who are masters of their wicked trade as it is to describe it in terms that might make it desirable to a sane person. But Buddhist traditions, of course, do describe it in positive terms, assuming attainment of nirvana to be the long-term goal of becoming Buddhist in the first place. As is the case in many religious traditions, the claim that some item X of great religious importance is ineffable is never allowed to prevent X from being described in honorific ways. But if X is literally ineffable, then it lacks any properties that would justify the honorific descriptions, since for any such property that we know of, we have a concept of that property. So a being having that property would be correctly described by saying that it has that property, and so such an item would not be ineffable. To say that it has lots of properties that justify honorific language but that we do not know what any of them are, is doubly self-defeating. First, if we have no idea of what these properties might be, what justification do we have for supposing that the item has any properties that would justify the honorific language? Second, if it is true of the item that it has properties that justify honorific descriptions, then the item is not ineffable after all. It is true of it, for example, that it exists, that it has properties, and that those properties (whatever they are) justify honorific descriptions of the item.

---

[33] See Walpola Rahula, *What the Buddha Taught*, pp. 62–6; and David Kalupahana, *Buddhist Philosophy: A Historical Analysis* (Honolulu, HI: University of Hawaii Press, 1976) pp. 29 and 41.

Furthermore, a literally and strictly ineffable item would be something of which it was true that it does not exist, does not fail to exist, does not both fail to exist and not fail to exist, and does not both not fail to exist and fail to exist. The suspicion is not unfounded that, if this is true, then the explanation of its truth is that there is no nirvana to which one can refer. This is obviously not a tack that most Buddhist traditions will take – the Mahayana Ineffabilist tradition being in effect an exception.[34]

Another approach is to hold that when what talk of persons actually refers to reaches enlightenment in the present lifetime, it must choose between not being reborn and being reborn. Furthermore, suppose that the choice will be to be reborn – to 'come back' and aid others in achieving enlightenment. The question then arises as to when the other choice – the choice not to be reborn – will be made. The answer is, when the referent of what all that we ordinarily speak of as 'persons' has become enlightened. But when will that time come? Here there are two answers. One is, never. Given this answer, no one actually ever ceases to be reborn. On this view, nothing ever actually 'enters' nirvana, so the nature of nirvana is not as important as it seemed. The answer to the question, 'What makes this unceasing cycle of rebirths anything other than hell?' is that the states included in being enlightened, in sharp contrast to those involved in not being enlightened, are satisfactory – they do not involve suffering. The other answer concerning when the state of universal enlightenment comes is: not for a very long time. This answer at least puts off the urgency of figuring out what the nature of nirvana is.

Still another approach is that there is no such thing as nirvana as a state to be sought, since there is nothing to which talk of persons – or of anything else – actually refers. Strictly speaking, there is no one to have the religious problem that the Buddhist tradition diagnoses and to which the tradition offers a cure. What nirvana amounts to is the realization that all this is true. There is, then, no possible answer to the question, 'Who or what is it that

---

[34] This will be discussed further in Chapter 5.

learns this truth?' that is consistent with the truth of what is said to be learned in enlightenment experience. A still further answer is that nirvana is samsara looked at with detachment – it just is the dreaded cycle of birth and rebirth, no longer dreaded but looked at with complete detachment.

In this chapter we have endeavored to provide a general map of some relevant Buddhist doctrines concerning the ignorance which is said to be our disease and the general content of the enlightenment which is said to be our cure. In the next chapter we will consider the major varieties of some Buddhist sub-traditions and the differing specific notions that they offer as accounts of 'how things really are' – of what one must believe or 'come to see as true' in order to be enlightened. What knowledge, exactly, is it possession of which, along with its affective feeling content, constitutes becoming enlightened?

5

Some Buddhist Schools and Issues

The Buddhist tradition is rich and complex. We cannot summarize here the bewildering variety of Buddhist schools of thought, but we can explore briefly some representative Buddhist schools or sub-traditions, and the central aspects of those views. The criterion for what within the teachings of these schools gets our attention is simply its relevance to the proposed Buddhist diagnosis of our fundamental religious disease and its proposed cure. We will look at the Pudgalavada or Personalist tradition, then the Madhyamaka tradition, and finally consider some versions of what we might call Buddhist Reductionism. These perspectives cover a wide range of what the Buddhist tradition says concerning what, exactly, our deep religious problem is, and how it is to be solved. The problem, as discussed earlier, is rooted in ignorance about the way things really are – in particular, ignorance about the impermanence of all things and thus the unreality of an enduring soul or person. Clinging to and craving for that which is enduring and permanent results in the causal chain producing continual rebirth. The cure is said to be enlightenment, involving a radical reorientation so that one sees things as they actually are, but just what this means varies significantly with different Buddhist schools. Some aspects of these differences are examined in this chapter.

Since it stands alone, and provides a convenient contrast to other Buddhist schools of thought, we begin with Personalism. To understand the intense opposition it receives from other varieties of Buddhism, it will help to remember the context within which Indian Buddhism arose.

As we saw in Chapter 1, Buddhism emerged from within an Indian intellectual and religious context that shared certain assumptions about karma and the rebirth of the atman, or soul. But while the Buddha accepted the ideas of karma and rebirth, he rejected prevailing views about the atman. The Hindu view about the atman that the Buddhist tradition typically rejects is put in these terms:

> It is like this. As a caterpillar, when it comes to a tip of a blade of grass, reaches out to a new foothold and draws itself onto it, so the self [atman], after it has knocked down this body and rendered it unconscious, reaches out to a new foothold and draws itself onto it.
>
> It is like this. As a weaver, after she has removed the coloured yarn, weaves a different design that is newer and more attractive, so the self, after it has knocked down this body and rendered it unconscious, makes for himself a different figure that is newer and more attractive.[1]

Elsewhere, the analogy of a rider and a chariot is used to illustrate the relation of the soul to the body.

> Know the self as a rider in a chariot, and the body, as simply the chariot. Know the intellect as the charioteer, and the mind, as simply the reins. The senses, they say, are the horses, and sense-objects are the paths around them. He who is linked to the body, senses, and mind, the wise proclaim as the one who enjoys.[2]

The point is more simply put in the popular Hindu text, the Bhagavadgita: 'Just as a person casts off worn-out garments and puts on others that are new, even so does the embodied soul cast off worn-out bodies and take others that are new.'[3] Jainism agrees with Hinduism on the reality of souls which transmigrate from one

---

[1] Brhadaranyaka Upanishad 4.4.3–4, in *Upanishads*, trans. and ed. by Patrick Olivelle (New York: Oxford University Press, 1996), p. 64.
[2] Katha Upanishad 3.3–4, in *Upanishads*, pp. 238–9.
[3] *The Bhagavadgita*, II.22, trans. by S. Radhakrishnan (New York: Harper Colophon, 1973), p. 108.

life to another.[4] On these views, an enduring person travels from one life to another, retaining personal identity from a past without beginning into a future without end within the transmigratory cycle, unless liberation is attained.

As noted in Chapter 4, the Buddhist tradition, like the Hindu, illustrates its view of the self by referring to a chariot. But the Buddhist use of the chariot example makes a quite different point: just as there is no 'chariot' which underlies the constituent parts of what we conventionally call a chariot, so too there is no soul distinct from the constituent elements of consciousness. The chariot is said to be nothing over and above its parts – when you list the parts, there is nothing further to list. Similarly with consciousness. And this has been the dominant view within Buddhism, although there was an early significant exception.

Personalism

Personalism is a school of Buddhist philosophy which emerged in the third century AD and asserted that a self or soul (pudgala) exists which cannot be reduced to the five aggregates (skandhas). The Pudgalavadins, as they were called, maintained that the Buddha spoke of a person in three contexts in such a way that it could not be understood simply as a conventional way of referring to the five aggregates.[5] The three contexts the Pudgalavadins cited were the cohesion and integrity of experiences in the present life, rebirth in the next life, and attainment of nirvana. In these contexts, it was argued, something beyond just the five aggregates was necessary to make sense of our experience and Buddhist teaching. Personalism posited the existence of enduring pudgalas, or persons, in this life which continue on in the cycle of rebirths until final liberation in nirvana. Personalism was for some centuries quite popular in India but it did not take root beyond

---

[4] See Geoffrey Parrinder, *The Indestructible Soul: The Nature of Man and Life After Death in Indian Thought* (London: George Allen & Unwin, 1973).
[5] See Richard H. Robinson and Willard L. Johnson, *The Buddhist Religion: An Historical Introduction*, 4th edn. (Belmont, CA: Wadsworth, 1997), pp. 58–60.

India's borders, and it disappeared with other Buddhist schools from India around the thirteenth century. Personalism was vigorously attacked by other Buddhist schools and condemned as heretical.

It is easy enough to see how Personalist views could develop. Suppose that you are a sincere Buddhist with an interest in becoming enlightened in your present lifetime. The question of how you are to interpret the Buddhist texts then becomes crucial. You become enlightened only if you come to see things as they are. But how are they? The question concerns what the Buddha himself knows in virtue of his having become enlightened. When error is removed, constructions recognized as such, attachment to the things of this world overcome, what is it that you know? On this point, there is some disagreement among Buddhist traditions. The disagreement between Personalists and other Buddhists is captured in the Abhidharmakosha, a work attributed to the fourth century Buddhist Vasubandhu. The Personalist is portrayed as appealing to an earlier Buddhist text which seems to suggest the reality of persons: 'Moreover, another Sutra says: "One person, when he arises, when he is born in the world, is born for the weal [happiness] of the many. Who is that one person? It is the Tathagata [the Awakened One or Buddha]."'[6]

Personalists, understandably, claimed that this passage tells us that there are people. People perform actions and are responsible for them. They either attain enlightenment or not. If there aren't any people, then there can't be any religious problem to be solved or disease to be cured. Nor can there be anybody to teach how to attain the cure. The Buddha himself, the Worthy One, says that he is a person. There being rebirth, karma, suffering, or enlightenment presupposes that there are people. Moreover, it must be the same person who does the deed, receives the karmic consequences for the deed, and who successfully follows the path and enters nirvana. So say the Personalists.

Personalism differs from other Buddhist perspectives by rejecting the no-self (anatman) doctrine, holding instead that

---

[6] Abhidharmakosha, 9, in *Buddhist Scriptures*, trans. and ed. Edward Conze (New York: Penguin Books, 1959), p. 195.

there are enduring selves of some sort. But from other Buddhist perspectives, this looks altogether too similar to Hindu and Jain views. Nonetheless, Personalist Buddhists held that this doctrine of an enduring self was taught by the Buddha, is found in the Buddhist scriptures, is justified by evidence and argument, and clearly is presupposed by central Buddhist doctrine. It is true, however, that their claim to find the doctrine that there is an enduring person in what is said to have been taught by the Buddha, and in the Buddhist scriptures to which they appeal, is difficult to maintain. Yet they do appeal to certain texts which they claim support their position. A favorite Personalist verse refers to the five skandhas, or the elements that Buddhists typically claim compose persons, as burdens that have to be carried. For in the Abhidharmakosha, the Personalist argues as follows:

> Why then if the word 'person' means nothing but the five Skandhas which form the range of grasping, did the Lord teach the 'Burden Sutra,' which says: 'I will teach you the burden, its taking up, its laying down, and the bearer of the burden. The five Skandhas, which are the range of grasping, are the burden. Craving takes up the burden. The renunciation of craving lays it down. The bearer of the burden is the person: this venerable man, with such and such a name, born so and so, of such and such a clan, who sustains himself on this or that food, experiences these pleasures and pains, lives for just so long, stays here for just so long, terminates his life in just this way.' For, if 'person' were only another name for the Skandhas, if 'person' and Skandhas were actually identical, then the burden would carry itself, and that is absurd.[7]

The argument is that if the elements are a burden to be carried, then there must be a carrier distinct from the burden. Burdens do not carry themselves. Other Buddhists, however, maintain that this is a metaphor, expressing what could be stated more literally as 'The elements are unsatisfactory' or 'Life is a burden.'

It is when one considers what fundamental Buddhist doctrine presupposes or entails that the Personalists' case appears strongest.

---

[7] Ibid.

Their arguments can be put in terms of performing an action in the context of rebirth and karmic responsibility, memory, and seeking and finding enlightenment. We will look briefly at each. The force of their arguments is best understood if we keep in mind the view that Personalists are opposing – a view that can properly be called Buddhist Reductionism.

Action, Karma and Rebirth

Consider the ordinary person as traditional Buddhism conceives her. She comprises collection after collection of momentary states whose contents are unsatisfactory. But no one momentary bit of her lasts long enough to suffer unsatisfactoriness, for each collection lasts barely long enough to exist at all. On the typical Buddhist view, it is not as if a single enduring person has to push the heavy stone up the hill. Each collection that exists during the pushing period lasts barely long enough to be there at all. The misery of a migraine headache that lasts for ten minutes is spread out over some 39,000 or so collections of 'unowned' conscious states, each having painful content. But no one thing endures, or is, anything vaguely like all of the pain.

The idea that rebirth and karma occur is commonsensically expressed in terms of, say, Ananda living a life in which he often acts wrongly and thus in his next life being born in sad circumstances in which he suffers. According to typical Buddhism, however, what really occurs is that a short-lived collection of unowned states is succeeded by another short-lived collection of unowned states, which in turn is succeeded by yet another, with each being part of the cause of the next, for long enough to fill out a series that makes up a lifetime of whatever length it may be. An action that is performed thus requires the successive presence of many collections of unowned states that have whatever content is relevant. No one collection lasts nearly long enough to take up the period required for what we standardly describe by saying, 'Good morning, how are you doing?' Nor does a single collection come close to lasting long enough to reap the relevant karmic consequences. In addition, there is a long period of collections that come temporally and causally between what the tradition must view as the action-composing states and the consequence-comprising states. There is no numerical identity between these temporally adjacent collections, let alone temporally separated collections. But, say the Personalists, unless there is numerical identity between the doer of the deed and the receiver of proper karmic result, we do not have rebirth and karma. Yet the Buddhist tradition says that rebirths and karmic results do occur. Exactly parallel comments apply to responsibility for one's actions within a single lifetime.

Rebirth and Karma Fine-Tuned

As has been noted, the idea of karma is that actions performed in earlier lifetimes yield proper consequences in later lifetimes. The relevant point is that karma requires that there be causal connections. Put in everyday terms, actions performed in an earlier life have consequences in a later life. This can be expressed in Buddhist Reductionist terms as follows: A sequence of collections that occur at a time T1 may have causal impact on a sequence of collections that occur at T1000, provided the causality is carried through each of the collections in the series in between T1 and T1000. Strictly, the format will be something like:

> BR1. If in a series (of the sort that lies behind talk of persons) collections of events or states occur in sequential causal relations over time in such a manner as to constitute, for example, what is referred to by the unenlightened as stealing a purse, then the effects of the occurrence of those collections in the series occur at a later time in such a manner as to constitute what is referred to by the unenlightened as someone receiving the karmic results of her theft. A series is understood here as nothing more than simply one collection causing another causing another, and a collection is nothing more than elements – events or states – in causal relations to each other.

The connection between the former collections and the latter collections is a matter of the latter being an inevitable causal result of the former. Buddhism typically does not explicitly embrace a deterministic view of the world, but how exactly freedom is to be understood by a Buddhist Reductionist is not obvious. The idea can be put in ordinary terms by saying that while a person's moral or immoral actions inevitably bring about determinate consequences, the actions themselves are not ones that the person could not fail to perform, given her past history and her circumstances. In terms of what Buddhist Reductionism actually believes exists, this can be expressed as follows.

> BR2. A sequence contains a temporally successive grouping A of collections that causes a later temporally successive grouping B of collections, but A might not have caused B.

As noted in the previous chapter, it is not at all clear how this is to be related in a logically consistent fashion to the doctrine of universal dependent co-origination.

Talking about such scenarios in terms of agents who are in or have conscious states is one thing. Speaking of such scenarios in terms of unowned conscious states is quite another. It is hard to see how BR2 can be read as saying anything more than that the causal connections between A and B make up an unbroken sequence and that there are possible worlds in which this is not so – that is, ways the world might have been in which the sequence did not occur and perhaps some other sequence might have occurred instead. But where in any of this is freedom to be found?

Memory

The standard account of event memory goes something like this: a person remembers an event only if the event occurred, the person observed the event, the person's beliefs about the event are (near enough) accurate, and the event that comprises the memory is caused by the remembered event. This requires that numerically the same person who originally observed the event does the remembering. If nothing endures from one nanosecond to the next, then in the common sense of the term, memory never occurs.

The most typical Buddhist account of memory, by contrast, involves something along these lines: a collection (C2) of unowned states occurs later in a causal sequence of collections in which a collection (C1) of unowned states occurs earlier, C2 contains a state that represents a state that was included in C1, and (to make things fully explicit) C1 causes another collection which causes another which causes yet another until C2 is reached. The Personalist critique of this account is that, whatever this might be, it isn't memory. They maintained that our experience of memory is more in line with the standard account above.

Seeking and Finding Enlightenment

What are the implications of the traditional no-self doctrine for what we typically speak of as someone seeking and finding enlightenment? Suppose that twenty-year-old Ananda begins to seek enlightenment, and that sixty-year-old Ananda achieves enlightenment. How should we understand this? A typical Buddhist account would amount to the following: There is a sequence of momentary unowned collections containing states whose content is intending to become enlightened that continues until there occurs a collection of unowned states none of which has any content of attachment or desire, none that have belief in an enduring self or person, but which does contain a belief that there is no self. Moreover, no temporally later collection in this sequence than the one just described contains any state that has any content of desire or attachment or belief in an enduring self or person, and yet it continues to contain belief that there is no self.

How long does each element or state (collection of aggregates) last? Although this should not be pressed as a precise measurement, the fleeting nature of such states is indicated by the Buddhist saying that more than sixty-five come and go in the time it takes a strong man to snap his fingers. Suppose that, in conventional language, Nagasena begins at age twenty to seek enlightenment and over a rigorous course of discipline, study of texts, and meditation, he reaches enlightenment at age sixty. Suppose it takes a strong man one second to snap his fingers. Within that period, sixty-five (collections of) non-overlapping elements come and go. The forty-year period during which he was seeking enlightenment involves some 81,993,600,000 collections arising and disappearing, each collection being nothing more or other than its elements or aggregates, with no enduring person underlying these collections. It is surely understandable that the Personalists questioned whether this amounts to numerically the same being that sought liberation later finding it. Similarly, there will be reason for doubt that the performance of an action by a series of collections over one time period earns a karmic consequence that comes to another series of collections that arise only significantly later, with the only connection between the earlier collections and the later ones being that there is a large number of collections causally connecting the earlier sequence and the later sequence. This applies to cases in which one sequence occurs in what is ordinarily referred to as one lifetime and the later sequence occurs in what is ordinarily referred to as another, later lifetime, as well as those occurring in what is ordinarily referred to as a single life. For one thing, the matter of deciding to seek enlightenment requires, not one collection, but a sequence of them. The same thing holds for performing an action. Deciding and acting are products of sequential and numerically distinct items. The Personalist's point is that the standard Buddhist account does not provide even a possibility that the doer(s) of a deed be identical with the one(s) receiving its karmic consequences, or that the seeker(s) of enlightenment is numerically identical to what later achieves it.

It is sometimes suggested that these collections come and go so fast that no one can observe their fleeting procession, and so it is just as if it were all one undivided experience. But it should be obvious that this is not a typical Buddhist view. For there exists nothing whatever that might observe any fleeting procession. The procession itself is a sequence of collections, and nothing more. Each collection is 'itself' only the aggregates that compose 'it.' It is out and out cheating to describe what occurs in terms of an enduring thing observing fleeting unowned conscious states when one also proclaims that there is no observer at all. The closest that typical Buddhism can allow is that a collection at time T2 contains a representation of at least part of the collection at T1 that caused it, and that new tokens of momentary unowned states contain similar representational content for some extended period. But this cannot amount to anything observing or being aware of the whole sequence which goes by so quickly that the observer does not notice the gaps that occur when one collection of states passes away and another makes its tenuous appearance – for that would require an enduring observer.

The Personalist view maintains that only something that has at some point been in a conscious state can be a person. Nonetheless, there is no particular mental state that one must be in at any given time in order to be the person that she is, and there cannot be an unowned conscious state. The first claim notes that persons are necessarily sometimes conscious. The second claim notes that someone being the same person over time does not require that there be some one state in which a person must always be in order to continuously be the single thing that she is. The contrary assumption is often made – it is thought that a given person Kim must have exactly the same properties at every moment at which Kim exists, and perhaps also be unflinchingly aware of having exactly the same properties at each moment. But this is a case of stating requirements for a view being true that one knows in advance are not met, without showing that they must be met in order for that view to be true. Those who believe that there are enduring persons typically do not suppose that such a person cannot lose properties and gain others. Nor do they typically hold that a person is uninterruptedly aware of herself. Some have held that there are subconscious or unconscious mental states had even during sound sleep, or that in sound sleep the candle of one's consciousness burns low as opposed to one's waking states. But conscious life involves change, and change occurs only if something remains the same – retains numerical identity – over time. No one holding this view is going to require uninterrupted awareness of some single state on the part of a continuing self, nor need one holding this view require uninterrupted awareness of any sort.

The Personalist is famous for saying that the self or enduring person is neither distinct from, nor identical to, its elements. This is sometimes treated by other Buddhists as simple inconsistency, as can be expected from anyone who denies the no-self doctrine. There is, however, a straightforward way to read this remark. The elements in question are conscious states. A person is not identical to her conscious states (she could, after all, have had quite different ones and still have been herself). Joice, who spent her day in the library researching methods of tea production in Sri Lanka might instead have gone to a water park with her friends. She is the same person either way. But an alleged person who is never in any conscious states is not a person at all. So a person is not simply identical to her conscious states (she could have had others) nor distinct from them (she can be a person at all only given that she sometimes has some conscious states or other). The situation expressed by Joice's current conscious states – which include an enjoyment of Oolong tea and reflection of Paul's argument in the Letter to the Romans, chapter two – does not refer to conscious states that might have graced our world even though Joice did not. She need not have been in those states, but she is a person only if she sometimes is in some conscious states or other. The connection is intimate but not one of identity. This view seems perfectly intelligible.

It is not difficult to see why this view, expressed by the Personalists, was for centuries popular within Indian Buddhism. If belief in an enduring self is needed to make selfishness even a possibility, it seems no less true that belief in an enduring self is needed to make compassion even a possibility. Furthermore, the belief that enlightenment is not only possible but can actually be reached, and that it can be numerically the same person who achieves it as sought it in the first place, provides a forceful reason to seek enlightenment. In addition, if there are other enduring persons then there is strong motivation to regard them as appropriate objects of compassion. It is not difficult to see how belief in enduring persons might support compassion, and one might even wonder whether the much repeated insistence on compassion to be found within Mahayana reflects a need to support a motivation that was somewhat undercut by the no-self view.

Other Buddhist groups, however, categorically and firmly rejected the idea that there are persons. Accepting this idea was regarded as a Hindu or Jain error that prevents one from becoming enlightened. Believing that there actually are persons condemns 'one' to continued suffering, prolonged unsatisfactory existence, and ties one firmly to the cycle of birth-death-rebirth-redeath. In the passage cited earlier, it was said, the Buddha is simply speaking in conventional terms to people not capable of understanding anything more profound. He was saying in conventional terms what can only be put in doctrinally acceptable form by recognizing that persons are mere constructs – that there really aren't any persons or enduring beings who have conscious states and are aware of themselves as distinct from all else.

The disagreement here between the Personalists and other Buddhist schools is deep and basic. It concerns the core of the Buddhist message. Both sides cannot be right. Both sides claim to be correct concerning what the Buddha ultimately taught and right as to the knowledge that becoming enlightened requires one to have. The point here is not that this disagreement somehow refutes Buddhism. The sheer presence of disagreement in matters of textual interpretation, even when how enlightenment can be reached is the topic under dispute, does not show that neither side can be correct. Nor does it eliminate the possibility of other readings of the text – there are other Buddhist readings.

Interpretations of Madhyamaka: Nihilism

Madhyamaka, or the school of the 'middle way,' is a Buddhist philosophical school founded by Nagarjuna in the first or second century AD. It has been enormously influential within Mahayana Buddhism.[8] There are two competing and controversial interpretations of Madhyamaka thinking. On one account, it is

---

[8] See p. 43 in Chapter 2 on Nargajuna and the Madhyamaka tradition.

nihilistic – it denies that anything really exists. Neither the cycle of rebirth and karma nor nirvana exists. The cycle of rebirth, if it existed, would contain all that changes. Nirvana would include what does not change. But neither the cycle nor nirvana exists. It is tempting to simply reply: who then says this? Nonetheless, it is interesting to see why anyone would hold this position, and what its religious implications, if any, might be.

One way of seeing the development of the idea is to begin with the early Buddhist no-self doctrine. This concerns only the non-existence of a self – of a mind or person in a non-technical, ordinary sense of these terms. At that point, the items that compose what is said to exist are what is behind ordinary talk about persons; the constituent elements are the real referent behind our ordinary talk of 'persons.' But if one takes this line regarding persons, it raises the question of whether it might not be also correct concerning physical objects. If one decides that it is, then the irreducible elements of which objects are composed are also real. Add to this mix the idea that the elements, whether mental or physical, exist only momentarily, so that an element makes its appearance in the world only to exit existence immediately. Thus at any time there exists only items that last for just a tiny period of time. Suppose one also thinks that the elements themselves lack any essence, and worse – so far as there really being elements goes – are nothing more than constructions we make. They are nothing over and above items posited by us due to a disposition to do so. This last move of course implicitly reintroduces a mind that does the constructing, but suppose for the moment that there might be a way of successfully dealing with this.

According to this version of Buddhism, then (i) nothing has an essence or nature; (ii) anything that lacks a nature is only a construction; and thus (iii) everything is a construction. As other varieties of Buddhism pointed out, however, this cannot be right. For constructions require a constructor. The world cannot be constructions 'all the way down.' As an account of what there really is, this view is obviously mistaken. A necessary condition of there being any constructions is that something that is not a construction construct them. After all, anything that is a construction does not actually exist; it is only *thought* to exist. But nothing that is only thought to exist can do anything. So nothing that is only thought to exist can construct anything. Without belaboring the point any further, the incoherence of this view was recognized within the Buddhist tradition by other versions of Buddhism which flatly rejected it – it is not even logically possible that the view be true.

There is also another religious problem with this version of a possible form of Buddhism. Mahayana Buddhists put great emphasis on compassion for people, and on the role of bodhisattvas – enlightened ones – in alleviating suffering. These ideas are central to what makes Buddhism seem so attractive to many. They are at the heart of what Buddhism presents itself to the world to be about. But if everything is a construction, the fact is that there aren't any persons. Nor is there anything – person or not – that could either feel compassion or suffer or be freed from suffering. The following text, already cited in chapter one, is typically taken at least very closely to literally:

> Misery only doth exist, none miserable,
> No doer is there; naught save the deed is found.
> Nirvana is, but not the man who seeks it.
> The Path exists, but not the traveler on it.[9]

The text is to be taken only very closely to literally because, for a consistent constructivism, misery vanishes as well. Nevertheless, it is clear that not only is there no traveler on the path, there is nothing that replaces the traveler – nothing else that the traveler really is. There is only what the traveler seems to be. But there is also nothing to which anything at all could even seem to be. Consider the following text from the Diamond Sutra, which depicts a bodhisattva thinking as follows:

> 'As many beings as there are in the universe of beings, comprehended under the term "beings"… all these I must lead to Nirvana, into that Realm of Nirvana which leaves nothing behind. And yet, although

---

[9] Cited in *A Sourcebook in Indian Philosophy*, eds. Sarvepalli Radhakrishnan and Charles A. Moore (Princeton, NJ: Princeton University Press, 1957), p. 289.

innumerable beings have thus been led to Nirvana, in fact no being at all has been led to Nirvana.' And why? If in a Bodhisattva the notion of a 'being' should take place, he could not be called a 'Bodhi-being.' And why? He is not to be called a Bodhi-being, in whom the notion of a self or of a being should take place, or the notion of a living soul or a person.[10]

Strictly speaking, there are no beings to be guided to nirvana, nor is there a being to guide them. So the incoherence of the view is again clear, but now the religious consequence of this view is also apparent: there is no reason to worry about suffering beings, for there aren't any. There is no basis for trumpeting how compassion plays a central role in Buddhism; there isn't any compassion. There isn't anybody, or any thing, that might suffer or be compassionate. Bodhisattvas are constructions; so is everything else. There isn't any religious problem to be solved, since there isn't anyone or anything that might have a religious problem. This version of Buddhism makes itself religiously irrelevant as well as incoherent. It proposes to solve a problem that – on its own terms – is impossible. One can embrace this sort of view only by simply ignoring its consequences, denying them, or being unaware of them. Since the consequences are obvious, it is hard to ignore or deny them if one understands the view.

There are deep problems, of course, with this view. Philosophically, taken literally, were it true, no one could hold it. Religiously, were it true, there could be no religious disease and no cure. There would be nothing of which Buddhism might be true. The story about how anyone might come to hold this sort of view is not relevant to our purposes here. Whether it is a correct interpretation of a genuinely Buddhist view is disputed. It is not held, by much contemporary thought about Buddhism, to be a proper account of Madhyamaka. In any case, it is not a typical Buddhist view.

---

[10] As cited in John M. Koller and Patricia Koller, *A Sourcebook in Asian Philosophy* (New York: Macmillan, 1991), p. 258.

Interpretations of Madhyamaka: Absolutism

The other controversial interpretation of Madhyamaka is Absolutist. On this view, which has a Hindu version, what exists is a qualityless unchanging reality. There seem to exist all sorts of things, from cabbages to kings. Even the Buddhist Reductionist holds that there are elements, items without parts. For the Absolutist, all distinctions are mistaken. Nothing is related to anything else. One obvious philosophical problem is that if things seem to be distinct, then there are those to whom things so appear. At least there is something that appears to something, and so there are distinctions and things that are related to one another. Religiously, once again there is nothing to have the disease Buddhism diagnoses or to receive its proposed cure. Even if one says that the problem is that we think that there is a problem, the same problems that plague the nihilist view arise here as well.

Interpretations of Madhyamaka: Ineffabilism

It seems more likely that the Madhyamaka view is a version of something found in various religious traditions. The core idea here is that language is radically inadequate to express how things really are, whereas 'getting things right' is a condition of becoming enlightened, and constitutive at least of becoming enlightened 'in this lifetime.' This emphasis on 'getting it right' – seeing things as they really are, knowing the truth about the world – is obvious in the Four Noble Truths. These concern the fact of suffering, its origin, its cessation, and the means to its cessation. The Four Noble Truths, then, function as a kind of creedal statement, making truth claims concerning the origin and cessation of suffering.

Creedal statements such as the Four Noble Truths – statements of doctrine essential to the tradition that they define, the acceptance of which is required for formal admission into the tradition – do not play the sort of role in Buddhism that they do in Christianity. But it does not follow from this that there are no Buddhist doctrines, or that these doctrines are never taken to define a type of Buddhism by those who practice it, or that there are not doctrinal positions that are held within the Buddhist tradition that others in the tradition regard as utterly incompatible with Buddhist doctrine and therefore view as actually non-Buddhist. To speak of a creed is to talk about a formal doctrinal statement that plays a particular sort of role in the development of an institution.

Creedal statements such as the Four Noble Truths make truth claims. It is helpful here to distinguish truth claims, which are embedded in such creedal statements, from the states of affairs to which the claims refer. That these are different is plainly true. A 'truth claim' is simply some proposition that is true or false, and said by someone to be true. Probably no one has ever confused the proposition 'I have a splitting headache' with the splitting headache itself, the existence of which makes the proposition true. If any one of the Four Noble Truths is true, the proposition that expresses it is one thing, and the state of affairs that makes the proposition true is another. The point, however, is that these two matters are necessarily paired. If the state of affairs, the 'actual thing' or 'reality' that would make a Noble Truth true, does not exist, the Noble Truth is in fact false; and conversely. If a Noble Truth is true, then the state of affairs that makes it true does exist; and conversely. We cannot have one without the other.

Further, if one did not think that the Four Noble Truths were true, why would one try to act as the Buddhist commends us to act? To believe that a Noble Truth is true and to believe that what makes it true exists are not separate, detachable beliefs. They are the same belief, differently described, or at the very least, they are mutually necessarily connected. One cannot obtain without the other. So the two senses of 'truth' amount to this: necessarily a proposition is true if and only if what it says exists is real – that is, does exist.

So we do have a series of 'truth claims' on the part of the tradition, and the Four Noble Truths are among them. They concern, as noted above, the fact, origin, cure, and means to cure, of suffering – of unsatisfactoriness, of inescapable discontent. Not surprisingly, what is said about these matters are claims about how things are. Furthermore, the fourth of the Noble Truths describes an eightfold path to the cessation of suffering, the first part of which is right view and the last two parts of which are right mindfulness and right meditation. These reflect the importance of understanding how 'things really are.'

One proper place to begin in a presentation of an ineffabilist reading of Madhayamaka Buddhism is with an account of reincarnation and karma. Buddhist Ineffabilism, then, claims that there is a reality that is ineffable – indescribable, completely inexpressible. The term 'indescribable' is not to be thought of as meaning what it does when you say that chocolate ice cream is indescribably delicious. When you say that, the idea is that it is extremely delicious, and if it is delicious it is not inexpressible because it has qualities that can be described – it is chocolate, ice cream, and very delicious. The term 'inexpressible' here is not to be thought of as meaning what it does when you say that using a dentist's drill without nerve-numbing medication or its equivalent would produce inexpressible pain. When you say that, the idea is that pain would be produced that would hurt a lot, and such pain is not ineffable because it can be described – it is pain, and a lot of it. For an ineffabilist view, 'inexpressible' and 'indescribable' are to be taken literally. No description we can give will fit reality – not merely will any description not be exact or complete, but it won't fit reality at all, not even a little.

On this reading, the Madhyamaka tradition takes a 'middle way' in the sense that, for anything we might say about reality, what we say is neither true nor false. Reality does not even either exist or not exist. If you do not know this, then you are not enlightened. If you do not come to know it, you will not become enlightened.

The fundamental problem here is this. If what must be known in order for you to become enlightened is actually true, then it is not true of you that you need enlightenment. You are, after all, part of reality. If reality is ineffable, this includes you – you are ineffable. But then a description of you that says that you are not enlightened – as well as a description of you that says that you are enlightened – will not be true. If we read the Madhyamaka as seeking a supposed middle way in the manner mentioned earlier, then you are neither enlightened nor not enlightened. It is not at all clear that it is even possible to be neither.

The idea is not that enlightenment has degrees, and even if it did you would either be fully enlightened or not. But if it is not either true or false that you are not enlightened, then it is not true that you are enlightened. Further, a description that is neither true nor false is meaningless, and so not a description after all. In any case, 'not being enlightened' is not a problem that you have. So, on this interpretation, there is not anything to be cured. For that matter, such minimal and unexciting descriptions as 'you are you' are neither true nor false of you. Thus it is not true that there is any 'you,' enduring or not enduring, to need or receive enlightenment. Thus the Madhyamaka seems to be religiously self-defeating. Its being true will make its path to enlightenment itself not-existent – since it is describable, it cannot be part of reality – and there is nothing to take the path. The point here is not merely that there is no self, mind, or person to take the path. The point is that there is nothing of any sort whatever that might take the path – reality is such that it is neither true nor false that it is or contains a possible path-seeker or path-follower.

This view has consequences that can be explained as follows. Statements such as the following are, on the view on which the defense of an ineffable reality is based, neither true nor false.

1a. Collies are planets.
1b. Collies are not planets.
2a. Rose bushes are angels.
2b. Rose bushes are not angels.
3a. Rocks are clouds.
3b. Rocks are not clouds.

Then the defender of the idea of an ineffable reality takes this idea and generalizes by holding that:

D. Every sentence of the form *Item X has property Q* fails to be either true or false.

But D entails:

E. Every statement which, if it is either true or false, ascribes a property to anything that exists or to reality as a whole, fails to be either true or false.

Claims D and E face insuperable problems. For whatever exists and whatever property you pick, that thing either has that property or not. Either the moon has donkey ears, or it does not. Either New York City contains only cream cheese, or it does not. The same holds for anything else, and any property, whatever. But then there is a simple proof that nothing is ineffable. Consider the property of being made of lead. Either reality as a whole is made of lead, or not. Reality as a whole is made of lead only if everything in it is entirely made of lead. But not everything in reality is made entirely of lead. So reality as a whole lacks the property of being made of lead. But then the proposition *Reality is entirely made of lead* is false, and hence reality is not ineffable.

There is a slightly more complex argument. Either reality is entirely made of lead, or it is not made of lead to any degree at all, or some of it is made of lead and some of it is not made of lead. All lead, no lead, part lead – this exhausts the alternatives. One of these things is true of reality. But anything of which one of these three things is true is not ineffable. So reality is not ineffable.

A still further argument: sixteen is not a prime number, and it could not be one. Given E, it ought not to be either true or false that it is a prime number. But to claim that sixteen is a prime number is to claim something that is false. *Sixteen is not prime* is an elementary arithmetic truth. The same problem about saying that sixteen is a prime number, as we have seen, arises quite generally. (Note that whether there are essences – 'own beings' – or not, these arguments against E hold; they need no assumptions about anything having an essence.)

Ineffabilism's problems can be illustrated in another way. Either something exists, or it does not. Further, in order to actually have a property, you have to exist. To ascribe properties to non-existent items is either to make false claims or to make a claim about what properties this sort of item would have if it did exist. Those who claim that there is an ineffable, indescribable item ascribe to it the properties of (a) existing independent of our thoughts and descriptions of it, and (b) being such that none of our concepts fit it, and hence we cannot give any true descriptions of it. But if (a) is true of reality then (b) is false of reality, and if (b) is true of reality then (a) is false of reality. The ineffabilist wants both to say that reality is ineffable and have what they say be true. What this amounts to is excepting certain concepts from the embargo on their use in describing reality – the embargo itself is therefore arbitrary. Neither the metaphysical content of the ineffability view, nor the attempt to state the view in non-contradictory terms, look even slightly promising. So far as the nihilist interpretation goes, if it is true then there is nothing for it to be true of, no one to know its truth, and no method of discovering its truth. Were there a method for discovering it to be true, there would be nothing that could even try to use the method. Ineffabilism is no more compatible with the core Buddhist diagnosis and cure than are Nihilism and Absolutism.

Buddhist Reductionism

Not surprisingly, then, as we have seen, there are other versions of Buddhism. One of these takes the less radical line that while there are indeed constructs, not everything is a construct. Something or other must exist to do the constructing. This raises, of course, the question: what does do the constructing? What is it that does not merely appear to exist, or is mistakenly believed to exist, but actually does exist?

On one less radical Buddhist view, the answer is that momentary states (skhandas) exist. These are the elements that make up a mind or person. For some sub-varieties of this view, there are both mental and physical elementary states. There are conscious and non-conscious elementary states – states not composed of other states. The Yogacara (Mind-only)[11] variety of Mahayana Buddhism

---

[11] Yogacara, also known as Vijnanavada, is a school of Buddhism founded by the two fourth-/fifth- century AD brothers Asanga and Vasubandhu. Yogacara teaches that consciousness itself is the fundamental reality, hence it is known as 'Mind-only' (see Donald W. Mitchell, *Buddhism: Introducing the Buddhist*

and the Abhidharma Theravada[12] schools are versions of Buddhist Reductionism. The Mind-only view holds that there are only conscious states (unowned mental states) and the Abhidharma schools hold that there are also non-conscious states (unowned physical states). This difference, of course, has its own importance, but it does not affect our concerns here. Since it will make no difference for anything that needs to be said here, and it will be a bit simpler, we shall be concerned only with mental states.

The account we are offered, then, goes as follows. Each of these states is strongly momentary, lasting for only about as long as they must last in order to exist at all. Further, each state is co-dependent on other states. Some of the states on which a given state depends existed just before it did; some of the states on which a given state depends co-exist with it. Every state that exists at a given time is co-dependent on other states that exist then, and no state fails to be dependent on others. Everything that really exists as opposed to merely seeming to exist – as opposed to being a construct – has an essence. So each of the elementary states has an essence. A mind or person – what some other religious traditions would call a self or a soul – is made up of some of these elements. While, on this view, the mind or person – or self or soul – is merely a construct, its constituent elementary parts are not.

So consider Kim at a given moment in her life. She is made up of many momentary states. At the next moment in her life, she is made up of many other, new momentary states. Of course none of the states that compose Kim at the earlier time are included among those that compose her at the later time. The central connecting

---

Experience, 2nd edn. [New York: Oxford University Press, 2008], pp. 149–53; and Richard H. Robinson and Willard L. Johnson, The Buddhist Religion: An Historical Introduction, pp. 91–6).

[12] The Abhidharma schools emerged out of attempts to understand the metaphysical implications of the Abhidarma texts, one of the three major divisions of Buddhist texts. Abhidharma schools taught that existence could be analyzed into fundamental elements, called dharmas, which were either physical or mental in nature. See Donald W. Mitchell, Buddhism, pp. 134–8; and Mark Siderits, Buddhism as Philosophy: An Introduction (Indianapolis, IN: Hackett Publishing Company, 2007), pp. 105–37.

relationship between the 'Kim-composing collection of causally co-dependent states' at one moment and 'the Kim-composing collection of causally co-dependent states' at the next moment is itself causal. Let the first collection be Collection 1 and the second collection be Collection 2. Collection 1 causes Collection 2. (At least Collection 1's causal role in causing Collection 2 is more productive of the fact that Collection 2 exists than is any other previous collection of states.)

On this type of account, although there isn't temporally much to any state, it is crucial that there really be elementary states. Otherwise there can't be anything that is composed of them, and there can't be any co-dependence between them. Further, the collections of states that, at a given time, compose what we – according to this view – mistakenly refer to as a mind must have various capacities. There must, in ordinary parlance, be some kinds of things that they can do in virtue of being minds and certain kinds of things that can be done to them. When it comes to mere collections – say, a collection of six pens – it seems unproblematic to view the collection as simply the pens, and nothing more. If the pens are on a table, there aren't thereby seven things on the table – the six pens and the collection. Remove or add a pen and you have a different collection. But if you have non-living elements and when they are together in the right arrangement something living comes to exist, then it seems that the living thing is something new. A brief indication as to why is in order. There are at least two main considerations:

1. When you put all six of your pens on the table, you can create a collection of pens, but 'the collection' has no property that is not additive, not simply a sum of properties that you had before. The collection has six pens as members and none of the pens do. But 'the collection' weighs what pen one weighs, plus what pen two weighs, and so on. 'The collection' takes up only that space which pen one, pen two, and so on, take up. 'The collection' is six-membered given that there are pens one through six. Speaking of 'the collection' is nothing more than a convenient way of referring to the pens. But if a living thing – a thing that has the property of life – comes

from putting non-living things together, then that new thing has a property that is not merely additive. It is something new. Speaking of 'the living organism' is more than a short way of referring to the non-living things that compose it. It refers as well to the life that they together support.

2. The living thing is able to do things that non-living things cannot do and have done to it things that cannot be done to non-living things. Its acting-potential and its receptive potential are radically different from the acting-potential and receptive-potential of its components. A lot more could be said about this matter, but it raises a strong barrier to the universal truth of reductionism – that wholes are always mere collections, mere sums of their parts.

An obvious counter-view, widely held in non-Buddhist Indian thought, is to say that of course there are minds and physical objects. If something is complex, it is made up of smaller things that get together in collections of things. But the collections exist, and (save for artifacts) we do not construct them. They exist mind-independently, and they do not depend for their existence on our even so much as knowing that they are there. The human mind is marvelously creative regarding plays, poems and parties. It is not creative with regard to rocks, carrots and trees. These items are just 'out there,' without any creative activity on our part. The most we can do is to move rocks around, or experiment with new strands of carrots, plant or uproot pine trees, with these things already there before we got to them. But with this view the claim that everything complex is a construction has been abandoned, and this claim is a central element in the reductive version of Buddhism we have been considering. Without it, that version cannot be correct. We are left, then, with a basic Buddhist claim to the effect that if an item is composed of elements, then 'it' is neither more nor less than the elements.

The net effect of all of this is that reductionism about organisms faces some real problems. Similar problems confront the view that a conscious mind is nothing more than non-conscious states. What is most relevant here is that a significant problem arises for the reductionist view that a self-conscious mind is nothing more than conscious states, and a unity of consciousness – a simultaneous awareness of several states of consciousness – is nothing more than the states of consciousness that are objects of awareness. In each case, what is said to be nothing more than its components has some new feature that its components singly do not have. Neither is the new feature that comes into existence just a sum of the properties of the components. But if that is the case, then it seems that the new feature's coming into the world is a matter of *something* coming into existence that is a new sort of thing. If this is so, then the question is whether it can be justifiably maintained that the new feature does not have to be a feature of something that is itself something over and above its components. The problem, however, is that there is no room in a reductionist view of things for such a 'something.'

Meditative experience is among the considerations offered for thinking that there are only conscious states. We will consider this alleged source of evidence below. For now, the point to notice is that if there are experiences in which there is awareness of conscious states, then either there is someone who is aware of those states, or there are still other complex conscious states that are aware of their kin. Imagine, for example, that you are walking across the street and a car comes close to hitting you. You observe your great relief that the car missed you. The feeling of relief is a complex state – you are relieved that the car missed you. Your observation that you feel relief is another complex state – you are aware of having the complex conscious state of being relieved at not being struck by the car. This observation is a second-order complex conscious state, and is an awareness of a first-order conscious state. (There is a complication here that will be addressed shortly.) If there are no awarenesses of first-order conscious states – if there are no second-order conscious states – then no meditation ever occurs. Buddhist meditation that reports that the only objects of awareness are conscious states includes and requires second-order states. These are the complex states that make possible any report as to that of which 'one's' experience is composed.

But, as noted earlier, for a Buddhist Reductionist, it cannot be the case that anyone has or is in these states, either first-order or second-order. Thus reference to persons must be understood in terms of the Buddhist distinction between ordinary or conventional language and language used of what is actually the case, the way things actually are. The former is not to be understood literally, whereas the latter is. Thus, Buddhist teaching that refers to persons is to be understood nonliterally, whereas teaching that refers to impermanent elements and unsatisfactoriness is to be taken literally. The non-literal teaching uses the common sense view of the world – a view that takes there to be persons who endure, act, reflect, perceive, believe, know, and the like. It includes the notion that there are enduring conscious substances. In the cultural contexts in which Buddhism developed and to which it spread, it was typical to believe in gods and goddesses – this too was part of the common belief, the view accepted by unenlightened people. Within this view, some propositions are taken to be true and others are taken to be false. It is true that people are responsible for their actions but not true that people typically can move mountains by simply wishing that they would move. This distinction between what is true and what is false is made within the system of beliefs accepted by the unenlightened, within the view that enjoys community consensus. Strictly speaking, however, such 'truth' is not true. It is merely 'regarded as true by the unenlightened' or 'true if the common sense view of the world is true' – which, it is held, in fact it is not. Conventional truth is ultimately false. There are no enduring persons. There is no God. There aren't any enduring trees or oranges.

By contrast, it is 'ultimate truth' which is actually true. One who accepts ultimate truth sees things as they are and is no longer in need of correction. Those who are enlightened know the ultimate truth; they are not limited by conventional 'truth' but actually see things as they really are. In sum, what the Buddhist tradition teaches as ultimate truth is true. Anything incompatible with this is false, no matter who happens to accept it, how widely accepted it is, or whatever evidence there might be in its favor. Talk of conventional truth is simply an accommodation to accepted perspectives, however inaccurate they might actually be.

The religious significance of Buddhist Reductionism lies in the fact that there is, from a Buddhist perspective, great danger in believing that one is a permanent or enduring being. Anyone who is conscious and unenlightened has one or another of these mistaken beliefs. According to the Buddhist Reductionist tradition, these beliefs are false or meaningless. Buddhist tradition typically maintains that the mistaken belief in an enduring self must be abandoned in order for one to become enlightened.

If there is such a belief – if we take ourselves to be selves or souls, permanent or enduring – then whatever must exist in order for us to possess that belief must exist. Suppose that what must exist in order for us to possess that belief is that there be enduring self-conscious beings. Then any view that admits that we have this belief, but denies that it is true, must be false. In this case, one who wishes to accept the standard Buddhist 'no-self' view must hold that the conditions that standard Buddhist diagnoses describe as creating the disease that Buddhism wants to cure have this feature: one can neither offer the diagnosis nor proffer the cure unless one has the alleged disease. Thus it is crucial to Buddhist Reductionism that it be false that what must exist in order for us to possess the belief that there are enduring persons is that there be enduring self-conscious beings.

What reasons might be offered in favor of a 'no-self' view? As we have seen previously, there certainly are various passages in the Buddhist scriptures in which this view seems to be taught. What is contained in these passages, however, is not offered as true simply because it occurs in a scripture. The authority of the scriptures rests solely on their being what the Buddha taught. Their being authoritative depends upon the Buddha having been enlightened and the idea that being enlightened includes knowing the truth about the correct diagnosis and cure. Thus the fundamental reason for accepting the 'no self' perspective is the enlightenment experience itself. The core of this as a defense of the 'no-self' doctrine is the idea that, in 'having' such experience, 'one' observes nothing more than elements, and the idea that, were there something more there, 'one' would see it. It is on this basis that the appeal to the claim that none of the elements is the self or enduring person, nor are all of them together, nor is any group of them, is made. In sum, one is given a list of things that everyone agrees are not identical to enduring persons, and then it is pointed out that none of them is identical to the self. Only if there is agreement that the elements are all there is (nirvana aside) does this line of reasoning have the slightest force. There is also the further matter of the assumption that all that we are will be accessible to enlightenment experience. If one wishes simply to define 'enlightenment experience' so that this is included in the definition, then Jains and Personalists can do likewise for their respective meanings of the term, although their meanings will be significantly different from those of the Buddhist Reductionists.

As we have noted, 'seeing' that all there is to 'oneself' is a collection of causally connected states requires that this is seen by something or other – and if all that exists are states, then what does the seeing is one or more states. A state that 'sees' other states is a second order state. That there be such states obviously does not violate the contention that only states exist. Still, a couple of interesting things follow.

A Jain enlightenment experience, for example, is said to be one in which a mental subject – a conscious being that has or is in the states – is (directly, non-inferentially) aware of itself as being in those states. Hence it is experientially confirmed that there is a self after all. The Buddhist enlightenment experience, on the other hand, is said to be one in which there is an awareness that all that there is to the 'self' is states – and we have noted that the Buddhist's awareness seems to require that at least one state is aware of other states and of no non-states. Buddhists and Jains agree, we have noted, that common sense is with the Jain in this regard. Thus the Jain trusts common sense as well as (Jain) enlightenment experience on this issue, and the typical Buddhist distrusts common sense and trusts (Buddhist) enlightenment experience in this regard. Curiously, perhaps, the Jain can accept the Buddhist description of what the phenomenology – the experienced content – is as Buddhistically described, and appeal to a common sense principle to the effect that *It is not possible that there be an experience without an experiencer* (free-floating, unowned experiences cannot occur). The Jain can then infer that there is a subject that has enlightenment experience even though phenomenologically there does not seem to be. The typical

Buddhist, in contrast, must take it to be true, not only that her description of the phenomenology of enlightenment experience is correct but that what there is to a 'self' is only what appears in that phenomenology. This is in addition to the fact that what Buddhistically prevents second-order states from being subjects or substances is only their momentary nature – their instantaneous existence. This cannot be phenomenologically confirmed – if it is true then there is nothing to observe that there is replacement of one state by another and nothing to observe that there is not. Either would require an enduring observer. There could be an appeal to memory as reliable, but memory seems to confirm the view that one has endured for some time. Moreover, memory cannot literally observe the past and compare it with the present, and there is no reason to think that what memory can only amount to on a reductionist view is reliable or that its content even favors the no-self view.

In this chapter we have examined some ways in which various Buddhist schools understand the fundamental religious disease and its proposed cure, especially as this relates to the core Buddhist teaching on no-self. Difficulties with these interpretations have been noted. Paul Griffiths, at the close of *On Being Mindless*, sums up the situation well when he remarks that, 'Causally connected continua [sequences] of events [or states] seem to have been found, by the Buddhist tradition in India, inadequate to perform the explanatory tasks required of them. It is more difficult than it seems to dispose of mental substances, and the debates among the Indian Buddhist schools concerning the attainment of cessation make this especially clear.'[13]

---

[13] Paul Griffiths, *On Being Mindless* (LaSalle, IL: Open Court, 1986), p. 113.

6

The Dharma or the Gospel?

In considering the relation between Christianity and Buddhism we face a curious paradox. As Buddhism becomes better known in the West, in certain quarters there is an intense interest in emphasizing commonalities between the religions, often with the result that Buddhism and Christianity are regarded as complementary religions. Much of the Buddhist – Christian dialogue of the past several decades exemplifies this search for common ground. Yet, if each religion is taken seriously on its own terms, as understood by traditional Buddhists and Christians, it is clear that the two religions offer very different perspectives on the religious ultimate, the human predicament, and ways to overcome this predicament.

There are, of course, some striking similarities between Christianity and Buddhism. Both religions look to highly attractive historical figures as founders of their respective movements. Jesus and Gautama were both critics of aspects of prevailing religious practices. Each faced opposition from the religious establishment and led a reform movement which eventually developed into a separate religion. Both Jesus and Gautama used short, pithy sayings and parables to communicate their teachings. Both called their followers to adopt radically different ways of living, marked by compassion and love for others. Both Christianity and Buddhism have been missionary religions, each regarding its message as truth that applies to all people. There is also a kind of structural similarity between Buddhism and Christianity that can be illustrated by considering the Buddhist 'Three Refuges.' Traditionally, it has been accepted that being a Buddhist involves embracing the following affirmations:

(1) I take refuge in the Buddha (the Enlightened One).
(2) I take refuge in the Dharma (the teaching).
(3) I take refuge in the Sangha (the community).

Theologian and missionary statesman Stephen Neill, who lived and ministered in India for many years, observes that a parallel declaration can also be worked out for the Christian faith, summarizing what it means to be a follower of Jesus Christ:[1]

(4) I take refuge in the Christ (the Light of the world).
(5) I take refuge in the Gospel (Christ's teaching).
(6) I take refuge in the fellowship (the body of Christ the Lord, the Church).

However, despite such similarities we must also acknowledge that there are significant differences between Buddhism and Christianity. For example, the nature and role of the Buddha in Buddhism is quite different from that of Jesus Christ in Christian faith, so that 'taking refuge in the Christ' means something very different for Christians from what 'taking refuge in the Buddha' means for Buddhists.

In this final chapter we will explore some of the fundamental differences between Christianity and Buddhism. We will focus upon the questions of God's existence and the identity of Jesus Christ, for these two issues not only take us to the heart of the Christian message but also reveal the points of greatest divergence between Christian and Buddhist understandings of the universe and the human predicament. Our purpose here is not to argue comprehensively for the truth of Christian claims as opposed to Buddhist perspectives, but rather to clarify the differences between the two sets of claims and, at points, to suggest, in a very

---

[1] Stephen Neill, *The Supremacy of Jesus* (Downers Grove, IL: InterVarsity Press, 1984), p. 52.

preliminary manner, why Christian theism is more plausible than Buddhism.

The Gospel and the Dharma

In speaking of 'the gospel' we are presupposing that there is an identifiable teaching that is essential to the Christian faith, and this, of course, is rejected by some today. There is, we are told, no single normative set of beliefs which define Christianity; there are many alternative understandings of the gospel. Now there is some truth to this. There are various authors of the parts of the New Testament, and early Christianity took root in different places. It attracted leaders with different personalities, and impacted a culture in which traditional Judaism mixed in various degrees with Hellenism, so that Jewish and Greek thought blended and contrasted. Thus there were indeed variations in the way in which the central Christian ideas were expressed.

There is nonetheless a consistent Christian gospel that the earliest Christian apostles and evangelists taught and preached. While fully recognizing the rich diversity in expression in the early church, we maintain that there is an identifiable core to Christian teaching which is embedded in the New Testament and which has been acknowledged as normative for Christians. It is only within the past century or so that there have been significant numbers of those identifying themselves as Christian who also explicitly deny what mainstream Christian communities have embraced for nineteen centuries. Mainstream Christians throughout the centuries, whether Roman Catholic, Russian Orthodox, Greek Orthodox, Calvinist, Lutheran, Anabaptist, Methodist, or Pentecostal, despite their differences on subsidiary matters, have shared certain general beliefs regarding God, sin, salvation, and Jesus Christ.

This common belief is captured concisely in the statement by the apostle Paul, that 'God was in Christ reconciling the world to himself' (2 Cor. 5:19). Paul's statement is embedded within a broader set of commitments which include belief in an all-powerful, all-knowing God who is both holy and loving, who created the world, and providentially governs it. Christian faith maintains that God has given us capacities which we can use in ways that we know are wrong. The fundamental commandment is that we are to love God with all our heart, soul, mind, and strength, and to love our neighbors as we love ourselves (Mt. 22:34–40). Love of this sort includes respecting each other, and ourselves, as persons. Sadly, we have proven that we are expert in *not* doing this, repeatedly allowing ourselves escape clauses which supposedly excuse us from doing what we ought. It is God's will that we do what we ought, and, when we do not do so, we sin. A holy and loving God cannot, and does not, simply dismiss our sins, and our bent toward sinning, as tolerable defects in us. Sin as deed and sin as habit prevents us from flourishing as beings created in God's image. It is not something simply to be overlooked with a benign neglect or dismissal; that would be incompatible with love. Sinners need to repent of their sins and ask God for forgiveness. God, as holy, cannot simply dismiss our sins, as if they did not matter. God, as merciful and loving, makes it possible that our sins be forgiven.

For this reason, the second person of the Christian Trinity became incarnate in a human body – became a human being, though not merely a human being – in the person of Jesus Christ, who lived as an example, died for our sins, and was raised from the dead on the third day. The cure for our sins – both sin as particular deeds and sin as habit – is what the early Christian preaching called 'repentance toward God and faith in our Lord Jesus Christ' (cf. Acts 2:38–39). This means genuine and deep sorrow for our sin and acceptance of what God has done for us in the death and resurrection of Jesus. It means living under an Authority that we had hitherto not acknowledged. It means continuing to repent and ask forgiveness for the sins we continue to commit. It means sharing in the resurrection to everlasting life that comes when Christ initiates His kingdom. The *gospel* is thus the good news of what God has done in the person and work of Jesus Christ on our behalf, and the proclamation of the gospel involves a call for sinful human beings to repent and embrace Jesus Christ as Lord and Savior, thereby entering into a new life empowered by God the Holy Spirit. This is one way of expressing basic Christian teachings which, with some nuancing, is common to classical Christian traditions.

As we have seen in previous chapters, at the heart of the Buddha's teaching is a diagnosis of the causes of suffering and rebirth and a way in which such causes can be overcome. Following this way results in the elimination of suffering and the realization of liberation, or nirvana. Both the diagnosis and proposed cure for suffering are based upon what is taken to be a correct understanding of reality. Central to this correct understanding is elimination of false views, especially regarding persons, and adoption of a true perspective on impermanence and the interrelatedness of all things. Now if we think in the broadest cosmic terms, the typical Buddhist account of things goes as follows. There have always been simple material items and simple immaterial items, or perhaps only the latter. These items have always come in simultaneous collections whose members are causally linked in ways sufficient to distinguish metaphysically one collection from another, though the collections themselves are causally linked to other collections. These collections have always been successively related so as to compose sequences whose collections are causally linked in ways sufficient to metaphysically distinguish one sequence from another, though the sequences are causally linked to other sequences. Typically, the sequences are nothing over and above the collections, and the collections are nothing over and above the simple items. There was no beginning to the process in which simultaneous momentary, fleeting states or events merge into collections and in which successive collections form sequences.

Some, or all, of these sequences contain conscious states. Conscious states are not states of consciousness – states of some conscious being. They are 'unowned' states, states that have conscious content without that content being the content of any self's or person's states. Such states are among the, or are the only, irreducible items in the world – items of which other things are made. The closest things there are to enduring persons are sequences of collections that contain, or are entirely composed of, conscious states. The religious disease that plagues sequences is that the collections of which they are composed contain unsatisfactory conscious states. Indeed, enlightenment aside, they contain only unsatisfactory states. This state of affairs is inherently defective. What would not be inherently defective would be a series of collections, none of which contained any unsatisfactory state, linked into a sequence. Even this state of affairs is fully satisfactory only if it ends without this sequence being continued in a cycle of rebirth. This pair of conditions – no unsatisfactory states and escape from the rebirth cycle – will arise only if a portion of the sequence is composed by conscious states that include belief that the Buddhist view of persons is true, accompanied by states of peace and bliss without accompanying states of attachment to anything. Once a series of collections of this sort occurs in a sequence, the sequence does not again contain unsatisfactory states and does not continue causing later segments that continue the rebirth cycle. Such a sequence has become enlightened.

From a Buddhist perspective, the core religious disease is the occurrence of unsatisfactory states in collections, and thus in sequences, potentially without end. For Christianity, by contrast, the core religious disease is sin – both intentional actions known to be wrong and a propensity to so act. Christianity views this world as 'fallen' – things are 'not as they are supposed to be.'[2] The Christian teaching on sin, as well as the Christian gospel itself, presupposes the reality of enduring persons. There is no sin apart from persons who sin. Sin is a type of rebellion against our own nature and against God. Sins are self-destructive, preventing our flourishing, and set a barrier between us and God, making God seem irrelevant to life.

For Buddhism, the cure for the occurrence of unsatisfactory states is enlightenment – seeing things as they are. If a series contains a conscious state whose content includes belief that everything is impermanent, that series will not contain attachment to what is impermanent. Put in everyday terms – which are defective in that they presuppose the existence of selves or persons – if we see that everything is impermanent, then we will no longer be attached to anything. Put in terms of a revised Buddhist narrative that is consistent with what Buddhism holds to actually exist, the idea is

---

[2] See the very fine treatment of the subject by Cornelius Plantinga, *Not the Way It's Supposed to Be: A Breviary of Sin* (Grand Rapids, MI: Eerdmans, 1995).

that no collection can contain both a conscious state that is a belief that the Buddhist analysis of things is correct and a conscious state that is a feeling of attachment to anything.

In Christianity, cure for sin is thought of in terms of repentance, often described as genuine sorrow for one's sin with a declared intention, so far as it is within one's power, to cease sinning. The idea is that one's repentance be made to God, along with prayer for God's grace and strength to carry through on one's intention. A holy God forgives one's sins on the basis of one's repentance and the atonement provided by the death and resurrection of Jesus Christ. Salvation from sin is provided by God's grace.

Buddhism and Christianity agree that life is lived under highly imperfect conditions. We face dangers, frustrations, disappointments, illness, and death. We feel anguish and fear concerning the fact that we will die, losing all that we have and care about. However much we imagine that we are in control – captains of our fate and masters of our soul – we are fragile and dependent. Furthermore, there is what existentialist philosophers have emphasized – a sense of *angst*, deep anxiety in the face of fragility and death. *That* things are not right is a point on which Buddhism and Christianity agree. *The ways in which things are not right* is a matter of disagreement between Buddhism and Christianity. Correspondingly, there is deep disagreement about how things can be made right. There is agreement that there is disease and cure, accompanied by disagreement as to what the disease is and what will provide the cure.

God

The difference between the Christian gospel and the Buddhist dharma is most evident when we consider the question of God's existence. The gospel presupposes the reality of God, and makes no sense if God does not exist, whereas the notion of God plays no role in the Buddhist dharma.

That the concept of God plays no role in Buddhism is clear. Paul Williams, a former practicing Buddhist and leading scholar of Buddhism who converted to Roman Catholicism, states that

'Buddhists do not believe in the existence of God. There need be no debating about this. In practicing Buddhism one never finds talk of God, there is no role for God, and it is not difficult to find in Buddhist texts attacks on the existence of an omnipotent, all-good Creator of the universe.'[3] The Buddhist rejection of theism has many religiously significant consequences: the world was not created; there will be no final judgment; there is no divine providential care of anything; and there is no sin, since there is no God to sin against. Thus there are no sins of which to repent. There is no forgiveness of sin. Jesus Christ is not God incarnate. Jesus did not die on the cross that we might be reconciled to God. There is no hope of resurrection of the body and everlasting life in God's presence. Persons are not created in the image of God. Prayer to God is religiously pointless, for there is no one to hear and respond.

It is not uncommon today to hear the claim that the Buddhist tradition is agnostic rather than atheistic concerning the existence of God. On this account, the central teachings of Buddhism simply do not address the question whether there is a God. What gods or goddesses there may be are religiously irrelevant. Even if God, in the Christian sense, did exist, this would not remove the need for enlightenment. Thus, given the view that whether God exists or not is religiously irrelevant, the Buddhist tradition is at least atheistic in practice. For even if a Buddhist allowed as an unlikely theoretical possibility that God exists, she would not take that to be relevant to her search for enlightenment. Breaking the causal chain of karma and rebirth is not something that God enables us to do; for most forms of Buddhism, we do this on our own.

---

[3] Paul Williams, *The Unexpected Way: On Converting From Buddhism to Catholicism* (Edinburgh: T&T Clark, 2002), p. 25. There are some forms of Mahayana Buddhism, especially the Pure Land traditions, that do resemble monotheism in some respects. Broadly, in this type of Buddhism, the idea seems to be that one considers what features a perfect being would have, and then one describes the Buddha as having these features. The Buddha is thereby conceived as capable of receiving worship – of being aware of being worshiped, of being worthy of worship, and as different in kind from anything or anyone else. And certainly on the level of folk Buddhism there are many who do regard the Buddha as a kind of deity and who worship him accordingly. But the dominant Buddhist traditions have clearly rejected theism.

But a careful examination of both the implications of Buddhist metaphysics and Buddhist texts themselves indicate that Buddhism is more than merely agnostic on the question of a creator God; it rules out the possibility of there being such a God. Williams observes that, 'To portray Buddhism as agnostic in this way seems to me a modern strategy. In ancient times Buddhists were quite clear that they denied the existence of a personal creator God as taught in rival theistic systems.'[4] Moreover, there is the deep-seated Buddhist teaching that, nirvana aside, *nothing* enjoys independent existence, that is, an existence not dependent on the existence and activity of something else. This, of course, rules out the Christian understanding of God, since nirvana is not conceived as personal or capable of action.

It is not surprising, then, that Buddhist thinkers throughout the ages have rejected theism as being incompatible with Buddhist metaphysics.[5] K.N. Jayatilleke, for example, a devout Buddhist, writes that 'the Buddhist is an atheist and Buddhism in both its Theravada and Mahayana forms is atheism.'[6] The Dalai Lama states that the Christian understanding of an everlasting, uncreated God who is the creator of the universe is incompatible with Buddhist ontology.

> The entire Buddhist worldview is based on a philosophical standpoint in which the central thought is the principle of inter-dependence, how all things and events come into being purely

---

[4] Ibid.

[5] On Buddhist critiques of theism, see Gunapala Dharmasiri, *A Buddhist Critique of the Christian Concept of God* (Antioch, CA: Golden Leaves Publishing Company, 1988); Arvind Sharma, *The Philosophy of Religion: A Buddhist Perspective* (Delhi: Oxford University Press, 1995), chapters 1–3; Paul Williams, 'Aquinas Meets the Buddhists: Prolegomenon to an Authentically Thomas-ist Basis for Dialogue,' in *Aquinas in Dialogue: Thomas for the Twenty-First Century*, eds. Jim Fodor and Christian Bauerschmidt (Oxford: Blackwell Publishing, 2004), pp. 87–117; K.N. Jayatilleke, *The Message of the Buddha*, ed. Ninian Smart (New York: The Free Press, 1974), chapter 8; and A. L. Herman, 'Religions as Failed Theodicies: Atheism in Hinduism and Buddhism,' in *Indian Philosophy of Religion*, ed. Roy W. Perrett (Dordrecht, The Netherlands: Kluwer Academic Publishers, 1989), pp. 35–60.

[6] K.N. Jayatilleke, *The Message of the Buddha*, p. 105.

as a result of interactions between causes and conditions. Within that philosophical worldview it is almost impossible to have any room for an atemporal, eternal, absolute truth. Nor is it possible to accommodate the concept of a divine Creation.[7]

Walpola Rahula asserts that, 'According to Buddhism, our ideas of God and Soul are false and empty.'[8] Buddhism does not deny that deities of some kind exist; it simply domesticates them, including them within the causal nexus determining all existents, and rendering them irrelevant to the task of seeking enlightenment. What is clearly rejected is the existence of an eternal creator God.[9] The Buddhist scholar José Cabezón summarizes Buddhist reasons for rejecting the notion of a creator God.

(1) Buddhists repudiate the notion of a creator god, since they maintain that the universe is beginningless. (2) They reject the idea of a being who is primordially pure from beginningless time, since all beings, even enlightened ones, must at one point in time have been fettered in the cycle of suffering and rebirth. (3) They reject the notion of an omnipotent being. (3a) Especially when such a deity is said also to be omnicompassionate, Buddhists sees these dual qualities as contradictory to the existence of suffering in the world (the problem of evil). (3b) More specifically, most Buddhists balk at the idea that any deity is capable of granting liberation to a being who suffers in samsara. Salvation from suffering is earned through the process of self-purification, not bestowed on one as a gift from above. There is no god who is the creator of the universe, who is originally pure and primordially perfected, who is omnipotent and who can will the salvation of beings.[10]

---

[7] His Holiness the Dalai Lama, *The Good Heart: A Buddhist Perspective on the Teachings of Jesus*, edited by Robert Kiely and translated by Geshe Thupten Jinpa (Boston, MA: Wisdom Publications, 1996), p. 82.
[8] Walpola Rahula, *What the Buddha Taught*, 2nd edn. (New York: Grove Press, 1974), p. 52.
[9] See Paul Williams, 'Aquinas Meets the Buddhists,' pp. 90–91.
[10] José Cabezón, 'A God, But Not a Savior,' in *Buddhists Talk About Jesus, Christians Talk About the Buddha*, eds. Rita M. Gross and Terry C. Muck (New York: Continuum, 2000), p. 26.

We might consider several Buddhist critiques of the idea of an omnipotent, all-good, creator God. There is, for example, what we might call the Puppet Argument: 'If God designs the life of the entire world – the glory and the misery, the good and the evil acts, man is but an instrument of his will and God [alone] is responsible.'[11] The idea is that if there is an omnipotent and omniscient God, then God determines everything that happens and is really the only agent that exists – the only one who acts as opposed to merely being used as a means of another's action. One Christian response to this is that creating agents whose actions are not determined is a perfectly possible exercise of divine omnipotence. So is creating a universe the fundamental physical laws of which are probabilistic rather than deterministic – in other words, an omnipotent God can, but need not, create a deterministic world if any world is created.

Furthermore it is worth noting two things about this appeal to freedom of choice relative to Buddhism. First, Buddhism accepts the doctrine of dependent co-arising which says that every event is caused by events that precede it as well as depending on events that occur at the same time as it does, and it is difficult to see how this allows for individual freedom and responsibility. Second, Buddhism denies that there are any enduring agents to have freedom. It is, it would seem, appropriate to ask what freedom means when put in terms that refer to things whose existence the tradition denies. For with the exception of the Personalist view, it isn't clear that among the things the tradition thinks actually exist, there is anything that might possess freedom.

Another argument against theism concerns the existence of evil. Thus we read:

If Brahma [God] is lord of the whole world and Creator of the multitude of beings, then why has he ordained misfortune in the world without making the whole world happy; or for what purpose has he made the world full of injustice, falsehood and conceit; or is

---

[11] The Jataka, V. 238; as cited in K.N. Jayatilleke, *The Message of the Buddha,* p. 108.

the lord of beings evil in that he ordained injustice when there could have been justice?[12]

The basic form of the argument from evil is simple:

(1) If God exists, then there is no evil.
(2) There is evil.
(3) Therefore, God does not exist.

If one offers this argument, one takes on the task of giving some reason for thinking that it is true that if God exists, then there is no evil. It is obvious that *God exists* and *There is evil* are not explicitly contradictory as are *There are cows* and *There are no cows*, where the one denies what the other asserts. *God exists* says nothing about evil, and *There is evil* says nothing about God. Thus far, we have no basis for thinking that the existence of God entails the non-existence of evil. If one makes the claim that *If God exists, there is no evil*, what basis is there for accepting the claim?

Various answers have been proposed, and the literature on the problem of evil and Christian theism is enormous.[13] One of the most popular responses is to argue that if God creates, then God will create the best possible world, and the best possible world will contain no evil. But there are problems with this line

---

[12] Jataka VI. 208; as cited in A.L. Herman, 'Religions as Failed Theodicies: Atheism in Hinduism and Buddhism,' p. 55. It is interesting that in one of the earliest accounts of an encounter between a Christian and a Buddhist, in Mongolia in 1254, the issue of evil and the Christian God was pressed by the Buddhist. See Richard Fox Young, '*Deus Unus* or *Dei Plures Sunt?* The Function of Inclusivism in the Buddhist Defense of Mongol Folk Religion Against William of Rubruck (1254)', *Journal of Ecumenical Studies* 26, no. 1 (1989): 100–35.

[13] Helpful discussions of the issues include John Stackhouse, Jr., *Can God be Trusted? Faith and the Challenge of Evil* (New York: Oxford University Press, 1998); Richard Swinburne, *Providence and the Problem of Evil* (Oxford: Clarendon Press, 1998); Daniel Howard-Snyder, ed., *The Evidential Argument from Evil* (Bloomington, IN: Indiana University Press, 1996); and Alvin Plantinga, *God, Freedom and Evil* (New York: Harper & Row, 1974).

of reasoning. Why think that the notion of a 'best possible world' even possibly refers to anything? Consider the notion of a 'highest possible number.' It sounds impressive, but for any number you pick, there is a higher number. There isn't, and cannot be, a highest number. Why think there is a best possible world? Why, if God is omnipotent, isn't it true that for any world God created, God could create a still better one? Perhaps a price of being omnipotent is that there is no best you can do. Furthermore, it is reasonable to think that the best possible world, if there were any such thing, would include moral agents, and hence persons possessing freedom. But God cannot determine how free agents choose, and their existing as moral agents is a significant good so that the wrong choices they make do not outweigh the value of there being moral agents. There is obviously much more to be said about this issue, but our point here is simply this – it isn't at all clear that the first premise is true. So it isn't at all clear that the argument shows that God does not exist.

The passage from the Buddhist text quoted above does not actually offer an argument. It simply asks three questions – why would God allow misfortune and unhappiness, injustice and other evils, and even ordain injustice? Christians typically will deny that God *ordains* injustice, but not deny that God allows it. They have offered various suggestions as to possible reasons an omnipotent good God might have for allowing various kinds of evil. Necessarily, the discussions are general in nature. They do not concern particular evils that occur to a particular person at a particular time, save as the general considerations are relevant to them. Were this a detailed discussion of the problem of evil, it would be necessary to consider these matters. For present purposes we need not do this. Instead, we ask a question of our own: Why think that, if God exists and has good reasons for allowing the evils that God allows, we would know what those reasons are? We offer a three-step argument.

(1) That we do not know what reason God would have for allowing the evils that occur is reason to think there is no God only if, if there are such reasons, we would know them.

(2) It is false that, if there are such reasons, we would know them.

(3) Therefore, that we do not know what reason God, if God exists, has for allowing the evils that God allows, is not reason to think that God does not exist.

There are other Buddhist arguments against God's existence.[14] We will consider two from the influential dialectician Nagarjuna, who, in a work entitled, *A Refutation of the View of God Being the Creator of the World*, writes:

[It is claimed by some that] there exists a God, who is the creator [of the world]. Let ... this be examined by us also. The creator is one who creates. One who performs a [known] action is called the creator [in relation to that action]. In this regard, we argue [as follows]. He can create something which we know as existent ... or which we know to be non-existent ... He cannot be the creator of something which we know as existent, because the concept of the creator cannot be applied to such an object. For example, we know that man exists. Creating him further cannot be an act of creation, because his existence is already established. But it may be argued that God creates something which is [already] known to us as non-existent ... But he does not have the power of creating these objects. Why? Because these are known to us as non-existent ... Now [it may be argued that] He makes the non-existent [i.e., God creates an object which was previously non-existent but which becomes existent as a result of this divine creation.] But this is also impossible ... Something which exists is existent ... And that which does not exist is never other than the non-existent.[15]

The argument here seems to be this: Either X exists or X does not exist. If X exists, it cannot be created, for it exists already. If X does

[14] For consideration of other arguments against a creator God, see Paul Williams, 'Aquinas Meets the Buddhists,' pp. 87–117.

[15] Nagarjuna, 'Refutation of the view of God being the creator of the world and of the view of Visnu being the sole creator of the whole world,' in *Papers of Th. Stcherbatsky*, translated by Harish C. Gupta, edited by Debiprasad Chattopadhyaya, Soviet Indology Series No. 2 (R.D. Press: Calcutta, India, 1969), pp. 10–11.

not exist, it cannot be created, for it doesn't exist. So, nothing can be created.

The obvious objection is considered in the quoted passage, namely that what will happen in creation is that God, so to speak, begins with nothing and brings into being something not made from pre-existent materials. The reply that is offered says that if something does not exist at one time it never comes to exist – to exist at all is to always exist and not to exist at a time is to not exist at every time.

Nonetheless, there is no contradiction in something existing sometimes but not always. If there were, the typical Buddhist view that what exists are momentary elements would not be even possibly true. Nor is there any contradiction in the idea of something not existing for some time and then coming to exist. All of us at least certainly seem to have done exactly this, and there is nothing inherently problematic about this. Thus the original objection to the argument stands and the reply to the objection fails.

Looked at from another angle, the argument seems to be simply this: Whatever ever exists always exists, and whatever sometime does not exist never exists. What always exists is not created and what never exists is not created. Existing and not existing are the only alternatives. So nothing is created. But Hindu monotheism typically holds that the basic things – the non-composite things – always exist because God has always been creating them – always making it the case that they exist. Thomas Aquinas, working in a very different tradition, holds that there is no proof that there must be a beginning to the existence of dependent things in order for God to be the creator. What is necessary, for Aquinas, is that what exists and might not have existed depends on God for its existence. If that is true, then God is creator in the sense that matters most religiously. Why should an omnipotent being not *always* be making beginningless things exist that might never have existed, if he so choose? Hindu monotheists and Aquinas thus deny that things that never begin to exist must be uncreated. There is nothing contradictory in this idea. Nor is there anything problematic about something existing only for a while – say, about a cake that lasts only for a short period during a party. But then it is false that if something does not exist at one time, then it does not exist at any other time.

Perhaps part anyway of what lies in the background is that something cannot come from nothing. So either there has always been something or there never would be anything. A monotheist can cheerfully agree, but will point out that God is something.

Another argument from Nagarjuna involves him typically assuming something for the sake of a 'reductio' argument, in which one begins with an opponent's premises and then draws from them conclusions the opponent cannot accept.

> Does the creator, who creates something external to Him, create it being Himself born or unborn? He cannot create something external to Himself being Himself unborn. Why? Because He is Himself something unborn, like 'the son of a barren woman,' who being unborn cannot perform any action ... [Now we shall analyze the other case.] He creates the external things after being Himself born. But wherefrom is He born? ... He cannot be born out of Himself ... Assume that God originates from something else. But this cannot be assumed, because in the absence of God there will also be the absence of anything else.[16]

The argument here seems to be that either God is born or unborn. God cannot be born, for His nature precludes that. So if God exists, God is unborn. If God is unborn, God does not exist. So if God exists, then God does not exist. This is typical of Nagarjuna's dialectical efforts to reduce his opponent's positions to absurdity. Of course, Nagarjuna does not only appeal here to things that the Indian monotheist will accept. The argument, for example, requires that anything unborn does not exist – that 'unborn' means 'never comes to exist' and that *anything that exists must come into existence*. The monotheist, of course, denies that God is born of anything. She denies that God comes into existence. But that God is not born does not entail that God does not exist. It is false that everything that exists must come into existence – must have sometime begun to exist.

---

[16] Stcherbatsky, p. 11.

The best that can be said for these arguments is that they make assumptions that no clear-headed monotheist will grant. Nor is there any good reason why she should grant them. Theism is plainly not refuted by these considerations. Nonetheless, these considerations reinforce our point: Buddhism is an atheistic religion.

It is not our purpose here to provide positive arguments for God's existence.[17] But it is worth including here the comments of Paul Williams, who for twenty years was a practicing Buddhist before converting to Christian theism. Among the factors involved in his eventual rejection of Buddhism were his growing intellectual dissatisfaction with some central Buddhist metaphysical and epistemological claims, including the inability of Buddhism to account for the contingency of the universe. Among other things, it was Buddhism's failure to address satisfactorily the question posed by the German philosopher Leibniz, 'Why is there something instead of nothing?' which prompted Williams to look again at theism. As he puts it, 'I have come to believe that there is a gap in the Buddhist explanation of things which for me can only be filled by God, the sort of God spoken of in a Christian tradition such as that of St. Thomas Aquinas.' Williams is worth quoting at length on this point:

> Why is there something rather than nothing? Why is there anything at all? And why is there a world in which, among other things, the processes (causation, etc.) detected by the Buddha are the case? Why is it that this way of things *is* the way of things? As the Buddhist scriptures (*sutras*) have it: 'Whether Buddhas occur or do not occur, the true way of things (Sanskrit: *dharmata*) remains.' Why? Why is it like that? The *dharmata* is not what we call 'necessarily existent.' That is, there is no logical *contradiction* in a world in which things are not like that. . . . Thus the *dharmata*, the

---

[17] On arguments for God's existence, see Keith Yandell, *Philosophy of Religion: A Contemporary Introduction* (London: Routledge, 1999), chapters 10–11; Stephen T. Davis, *God, Reason and Theistic Proofs* (Grand Rapids, MI: Eerdmans, 1997); and Richard Swinburne, *The Existence of God*, 2nd edn. (New York: Oxford University Press, 2004).

true way of things, is contingent. It could have been otherwise.... We have a contingent fact or state of affairs, how things happen to be in the actual world, for which we are entitled to ask the reason....

Any answer to that question – if there is one – would have to be a *necessary* being, a being about which it would make no sense to ask the question why *that* exists rather than not. For the theist God is the answer to this question, and God is needed as the ultimate explanation for existence at any time, keeping things in whatever existence things have....

For me the question 'Why is there something rather than nothing?' has become a bit like what Zen Buddhists call a *koan*. It is a constant niggling question that has worried and goaded me (often, I think, against my will) into a different level of understanding, a different vision, of the world and our place in it.[18]

In teasing out the implications of contingency – in turning Leibniz's question into a Zen koan – Williams captures nicely what is at the heart of classical cosmological arguments and applies it effectively in analysis of Buddhist metaphysics. The analogy to a Zen koan is intriguing, for just as the koan is used in Zen to prompt one to see reality from a radically new perspective, so too the question about contingency can stimulate reconsideration of basic Buddhist assumptions, prodding one to recognize the plausibility of Christian theism.

Jesus

In popular consciousness today Jesus and Gautama are often regarded as essentially similar religious figures who happen to have lived at different times and in different cultures. When stripped of the contingencies of time and place, however, the messages of Jesus and the Buddha are said to be almost interchangeable. D. T. Suzuki, for example, states that 'If the Buddha and the Christ changed their accidental places of birth, Gautama might have been a Christ rising against Jewish traditionalism, and Jesus a Buddha,

---

[18] Paul Williams, *The Unexpected Way*, pp. 27–30 (emphasis in the original).

perhaps propounding the doctrine of non-ego and Nirvana and Dharmakaya.'[19]

Just as many Christians have been attracted to the serene figure of the Buddha, so too many Buddhists have been fascinated by the New Testament portrait of Jesus. In particular, many have been impressed by the strong social ethics in Jesus' teachings. José Cabezón, for example, while acknowledging that both Gautama and Jesus challenged unjust social practices of their times, states that 'Nonetheless, as a program of social reform, Jesus' must be recognized as being the more radical and far-reaching, and this no doubt is why the Christian tradition to this day, even when impeded by its own institutional forms, has been at the forefront of social transformation.... We Buddhists have a great deal to learn from this aspect of the life of Jesus.'[20] The Japanese Buddhist Masao Abe observes that whereas justice is a central concept within Christianity, 'there is no Buddhist equivalent to the Christian notion of justice. Instead of justice, Buddhism talks about wisdom, *prajna.*' Abe acknowledges that 'Buddhist history shows indifference to social evil, with a few exceptions,' and he suggests that Buddhists need to 'learn from Christianity how to solve the problem of society and history at large and interpret this in terms of the Buddhist standpoint of wisdom and compassion.'[21]

In spite of such expressions of appreciation, however, Buddhists often reinterpret Jesus, understanding him in terms of Buddhist assumptions and categories. The Dalai Lama, for example, states, 'As a Buddhist, my attitude toward Jesus Christ is that he was either a fully enlightened being or a bodhisattva of a very high spiritual realization.'[22] While this is no doubt intended as a

---

[19] Daisetz Teitaro Suzuki, *Outlines of Mahayana Buddhism* (New York: Schocken Books, 1963), p. 29.

[20] José Cabezón, 'A God, But Not a Savior,' p. 20.

[21] Masao Abe, 'The Impact of Dialogue with Christianity on My Self-Understanding as a Buddhist,' in *Buddhism and Interfaith Dialogue,* ed. Steven Heine (Honolulu, HI: University of Hawaii Press, 1995), p. 58.

[22] His Holiness the Dalai Lama, *The Good Heart: A Buddhist Perspective on the Teachings of Jesus,* p. 83.

high compliment, it removes Jesus from his first-century Jewish monotheistic framework and turns him into a crypto-Buddhist. In similar fashion, Cabezón, reflecting as a Buddhist upon the significance of Jesus, readily acknowledges the historically factual nature of the New Testament accounts of Jesus' miracles, exorcisms, healings, and even his resurrection from the dead. But, he asserts, these facts do not indicate that Jesus was actually God incarnate.

> That Jesus had these powers – that he could cure the sick, manipulate matter, cast out demons, raise others (and himself be raised) from the dead – most certainly points to the fact that he was an extraordinary individual. None of these events are for Buddhists outside the realm of possibility. At the same time, they are not unique in history, nor is the person possessing these attributes unique. More important, they do not prove that such a person is God or that he or she is enlightened or worthy of worship.[23]

Cabezón accounts for such phenomena in terms of Buddhist understandings of 'magic.' But, while certainly novel, Cabezón's interpretation completely dehistoricizes Jesus, removing him from his own historical and religious context, and 'explains' Jesus' miracles without reference to the Jewish monotheistic context in which they occur. Any responsible comparison of Jesus and Gautama must locate each figure within the historical and religious context of his time. When Jesus and Gautama are considered on their own terms, within their own respective contexts, the differences between them become more apparent than the similarities. As the distinguished historian of religion Ninian Smart reminds us:

> The very lives of the great heroes and saviours, of the Buddha and Christ, are so different. The earthly career of the one was so brief and turbulent, ending in a criminal's death on the Cross and the subsequent brilliant light of the Resurrection. The Buddha left his home around the age of thirty, and after a few years of learning, austerity, meditation and thought reached a supreme insight under

---

23 José Cabezón, 'A God, But Not a Savior,' p. 21.

the Bodhi tree: subsequently he had forty-five years or so of moving round the cities and villages of northern India, until he died of a digestive complaint at the age of eighty. The one's life is storm, humiliation and triumph; the other's is disturbance, withdrawal, huge insight and active serenity. Both used parables and images, but Jesus' were often shot through with mystery and intimations of the God behind. The Buddha's similes were instructional in purpose, and his teachings were built on a highly analytic scaffolding. Moreover, the logic of salvation wrought by the two central figures differs. Jesus saved humanity through his deeds and death – he was a sacrifice which restored the breach between human beings and the Divine, and the way of the Cross, however unlooked for, was nevertheless the path that the salvific plan of action took. The Buddha saves through his teaching above all.[24]

Both Jesus and the Buddha must be understood within the context of their times and the broader religious worldviews each embraced.

Although a comprehensive discussion of the New Testament portrait of Jesus is impossible here, brief attention will be given to five ways in which, according to their respective traditions, Jesus and Gautama the Buddha are different.

1. The relation between Jesus and history is different from the relation between Gautama and history

Although both Christians and Buddhists point to actual historical figures as the founders of their respective religions, the relation between history and religious claims are different in the two religions. Several points are relevant here.

First, it is frequently noted that Christianity and Buddhism regard the past and the future in very different ways. The Christian faith sees history moving in a linear direction from a definite starting point in the past to a climactic consummation in the future whereas Buddhism adopts a more cyclical view which has no particular starting point or end. In Christianity, the universe,

---

[24] Ninian Smart, *Buddhism and Christianity: Rivals and Allies* (Honolulu, HI: University of Hawaii Press, 1993), pp. 12–13.

and the events marking history as we know it, began with the creative act of the everlasting God: 'In the beginning God created the heavens and the earth' (Gen. 1:1). The Scriptures conclude with a glorious vision of a new and restored creation – 'a new heaven and a new earth' – in which evil and death, which have ravaged God's creation since the introduction of sin and rebellion against God (Gen. 3), are conquered (Rev. 20–21). The Scriptures provide a glimpse of the blessed communion between God and his people in the new creation: '[God] will wipe every tear from their eyes. There will be no more death or mourning or crying or pain, for the old order of things has passed away' (Rev. 21:4). There is a definite direction – a *telos* or purpose – to human history as it moves progressively toward the great culmination. Moreover, since there is a singularity to history – individual lives and events are not repeated endlessly – history has significance. There is one life, followed by the judgment and either everlasting life in God's presence in a new creation or self-chosen everlasting existence apart from God's presence.

Buddhism, by contrast, denies that there is a definite beginning to our universe, or, more correctly, to the entire series of universes. Masao Abe states, 'Since there is no God in Buddhism, there is no creation or last judgment, but rather Emptiness. Thus, for Buddhism, history has neither beginning nor end.'[25] There is no beginning point, no purpose or direction to history, and no culmination to the historical process. 'Unlike so many other traditions, the Buddhist scriptures contain no classic account of an end time, an apocalypse, an eschaton.'[26] Rather, history is part of the ongoing processes of samsara, the beginningless and endless cycles of birth–death–rebirth.

Second, the historicity of the events and sayings attributed to Jesus carries an importance for Christian faith that is not paralleled in Buddhism. For Buddhists, the problem of the historicity of certain events and sayings attributed to the Buddha emerged

---

[25] Masao Abe, *Zen and Western Thought*, ed. William R. LaFleur (Honolulu, HI: University of Hawaii Press, 1985), p. 214.
[26] Donald S. Lopez, *The Story of Buddhism* (New York: HarperSanFrancisco, 2001), p. 33.

with the growth of the Mahayana canon and the proliferation of new schools and teachings which were at variance with the earlier Pali canon and teachings of the Theravada traditions. How could the Mahayanists' claims that Mahayana texts contained the teachings of the historical Gautama be justified in light of the fact that they were written so much later than the Pali texts? The issue became especially problematic for Japanese Buddhism in the late nineteenth century, as Japan was forced to grapple with not only modern liberal scholarship from the West but also the attacks from Christian missionaries who argued that the Mahayana did not represent the authentic teaching of the historical Gautama.[27] While many Buddhists continued to insist that Mahayana teachings are implicit in earlier Pali sutras, others followed the lead of the influential Buddhist scholar Sensho Murakami (1851–1929), who readily acknowledged that Mahayana was not the teaching of the historical Gautama. But in admitting this Murakami did not mean that Mahayana teachings were therefore illegitimate or false. To the contrary, he claimed that Mahayana teachings were timelessly true regardless whether Gautama actually spoke the words attributed to him in the Mahayana texts.[28] The dharma, the truth Mahayana teaches, is to be identified with the transcendental Buddha or Dharmakaya (hosshin-butsu) and is thus eternal and transcends any particular expression of it.

The same point emerged in a fascinating conversation between the Protestant theologian Paul Tillich and Japanese Buddhists in 1960. In a visit to Kyoto, Japan, Tillich put the following question to Buddhist scholars: 'If some historian should make it probable that a man of the name Gautama never lived, what would be the consequence for Buddhism?' After noting that the question of the historicity of Gautama Buddha has never been a central issue for Buddhism, one scholar responded by saying, 'According to the

---

[27] See Whalen Lai, 'The Search for the Historical Sakyamuni in Light of the Historical Jesus,' *Buddhist – Christian Studies*, vol. 2 (1982), pp. 77–91; and Notto R. Thelle, *Buddhism and Christianity in Japan: From Conflict to Dialogue, 1854–1899* (Honolulu, HI: University of Hawaii Press, 1987), chapter 5.

[28] Whalen Lai, 'The Search for the Historical Sakyamuni in Light of the Historical Jesus,' pp. 80–81.

doctrine of Buddhism, the *dharma kaya* [the body of truth] is eternal, and so it does not depend upon the historicity of Gautama.'[29]

This incident graphically illustrates a major difference between not only Christianity and Buddhism but also most other religions as well. In many religions the religious teachings can be considered independently of any particular historical person. The teachings of Hinduism, for example, are regarded as eternal truths that transcend the contingencies of history, and thus are not rooted in any particular historical individual or event. Islam is a religion which takes history very seriously, but even here we can distinguish the truths said to be revealed by Allah through the Qur'an from Muhammad as the human recipient of this revelation. There is no necessary connection between Muhammad and the Qur'an; had Muhammad never been born Allah could have revealed the Qur'an to someone else. Although most Buddhists would argue that the teachings of contemporary Buddhist movements are consistent with what the historical Gautama taught, they also would acknowledge that the truth of Buddhist teachings is distinct from and does not depend upon the particularities of Gautama the person.

Christian faith, by contrast, is inextricably rooted in the historical person of Jesus so that Christian teachings cannot be separated from his life, death and resurrection. The teachings of the Christian faith are not simply eternal truths which are unrelated to events in history; they grow out of and depend upon what Jesus of Nazareth actually said and did. In particular, Christian faith rests upon the event of the resurrection of Jesus Christ from the dead, a supernatural work of God which is understood in Scripture as God's stamp of approval upon the life and teachings of Jesus of Nazareth, the defeat of death and the powers of evil, and the inauguration of a qualitatively new form of life (Rom. 1:4; 1 Cor. 15:26, 50–58). The resurrection of Jesus Christ is more than just an inspiring idea. The Scriptures insist that it actually did occur and that the truth of Christian faith depends upon it actually having occurred. The apostle Paul, for example, writing in 55 AD to early

---

[29] 'Tillich Encounters Japan,' edited by Robert W. Wood, *Japanese Religions*, vol. 2 (May 1961), pp. 48–50.

Christians in Corinth, unambiguously states that if in fact Jesus was not raised from the dead then our faith is futile and useless.

> And if Christ has not been raised, our preaching is useless and so is your faith. More than that, we are then found to be false witnesses about God that he raised Christ from the dead.... And if Christ has not been raised your faith is futile; you are still in your sins. Then those also who have fallen asleep in Christ are lost. If only for this life we have hope in Christ, we are to be pitied more than all men (1 Cor. 15:14–15, 17–19).

Paul would have nothing to do with the pious sentimentality of some today which insists upon the 'resurrection hope' as an inspiration for living while simultaneously denying that Jesus Christ was actually resurrected bodily to a new form of life. Paul is clear: If Jesus Christ was not resurrected from the dead then there is no point to continuing in the Christian faith.[30] In this sense, Christian faith is in principle falsifiable. For if it could be demonstrated that Jesus Christ was not resurrected or that Jesus of Nazareth never even existed then the Christian faith would be falsified. This sets apart Jesus and the Christian faith from Gautama and Buddhism. Whereas it is possible to think of Buddhist teachings apart from the historical person of Gautama (it is possible that another individual at another time would have attained enlightenment and proclaimed the dharma) the Christian faith cannot be conceived apart from the actual life, teaching, death and resurrection of Jesus of Nazareth.

Given the importance of the life of the historical Jesus to Christian faith, the issue of faith and historicity naturally arises: can we have confidence that the New Testament writings are at all accurate in what they say about the life and teachings of Jesus? No other ancient texts have been as meticulously and thoroughly

---

[30] For helpful discussions of the resurrection of Jesus Christ, see N.T. Wright, *The Resurrection of the Son of God: Christian Origins and the Question of God*, vol. 3 (Minneapolis, MN: Fortress Press, 2003); Stephen T. Davis, *Risen Indeed: Making Sense of the Resurrection* (Grand Rapids, MI: Eerdmans, 1993); and Richard Swinburne, *The Resurrection of God Incarnate* (New York: Oxford University Press, 2003).

analyzed as the New Testament writings, and questions about their interpretation continue to be controversial. Interpreters of the New Testament writings generally fall into one of two broad categories: (1) those who, while fully aware of the critical issues involved, nevertheless accept the New Testament writings as authentic, historically reliable material describing what Jesus said and did; and (2) those who maintain that the documents are primarily the creative product of the Christian community some time after Jesus' death and that, although they inform us of the beliefs and experiences of the early church, trying to ascertain what Jesus of Nazareth actually said and did is at best highly problematic. The literature is extensive and the issues complex, but several brief comments should be made by way of contrasting the issues arising from New Testament studies from similar issues in the Buddhist context.[31]

We noted in chapter one that although there is little question about the fact of Gautama's existence, there is considerable dispute over when he lived and died. Dates for his death range from 480 BC to 386 BC. The earliest Buddhist scriptures were put into writing in Pali sometime in the first century BC; prior to that time they were transmitted orally. Thus, assuming the Buddha's death at 386 BC and the writing of the Pali texts around 80 BC (the

---

[31] For helpful introductions to the issues of history, the New Testament and Christian faith, see Colin Brown, 'Historical Jesus' in *Dictionary of Jesus and the Gospels*, ed. Joel B. Green, Scot McKnight, and I. Howard Marshall (Downers Grove, IL: InterVarsity Press, 1992), pp. 362–41; Paul Barnett, *Is the New Testament Reliable?* 2nd edn. (Downers Grove, IL: InterVarsity Press, 2003); Ben Witherington III, *The Jesus Quest: The Third Search for the Jew of Nazareth*, new edition (Downers Grove, IL: InterVarsity Press, 1997). More technical discussions include N. T. Wright, *The New Testament and the People of God: Christian Origins and the Question of God*, vol. 1 (Minneapolis, MN: Fortress Press, 1992), and *Jesus and the Victory of God: Christian Origins and the Question of God*, vol. 2 (Minneapolis, MN: Fortress, 1996); Richard Bauckham, *Jesus and the Eyewitnesses: The Gospels as Eyewitness Testimony* (Grand Rapids, MI: Eerdmans, 2006); and the essays in *The Encyclopedia of the Historical Jesus*, ed. Craig Evans (New York: Routledge, 2008). For a thoughtful treatment of biblical, historical and philosophical issues, see C. Stephen Evans, *The Historical Christ and the Jesus of Faith: The Incarnational Narrative as History* (New York: Oxford University Press, 1996).

actual time of writing is unknown and might well be later), that leaves a gap of 300 years between Gautama's death and the first Buddhist writings. If the 480 BC date is accepted, then we have a gap of over 400 years. While oral transmission can be remarkably accurate, especially over several generations, this is a significant time gap, raising questions about the reliability of reports of the Buddha's deeds and teachings. Moreover, the early Pali writings consisted largely of instructions for monastic life and sayings, stories and anecdotes of the Buddha and the early disciples. More complete 'biographies' of the Buddha came later.

By contrast, the temporal gap between the death of Jesus and the New Testament writings is much shorter. It is generally agreed that Jesus was crucified in either 30 or 33 AD.[32] The apostle Paul's writings took place between about AD 50 and the late 60s (1 Thessalonians, arguably the earliest of the New Testament writings, was probably written by Paul in 50 AD). Thus, we have a gap of only seventeen to twenty years between Jesus' death and the earliest New Testament writing, with all or most of Paul's writings falling within about thirty-five years of Jesus' death. The last of the New Testament writings was probably completed around 90 AD, leaving about sixty years separating these writings from the death of Jesus. This, combined with the abundance of manuscript evidence for the New Testament writings, provides grounds for much greater confidence in the reliability of the New Testament portraits of Jesus than is the case with early Buddhist writings and the historical Gautama.

2. Jesus was a strict monotheist, and Gautama was not a monotheist

Both the Buddha and Jesus must be understood within the religious contexts of their times. While accepting much of the contemporary religious framework, each rejected or modified aspects of prevailing views. The Buddha, for example, accepted many of the current assumptions about samsara, karma, and rebirth. But

---

[32] On issues relating to the year of Jesus' death, see J.B. Green, 'Death of Jesus,' in *Dictionary of Jesus and the Gospels*, pp. 148–49.

he clearly rejected Brahmanical teachings about the existence of Brahman, the supreme being. The teaching of the Buddha does not presuppose the existence of a supreme being and, as we have seen, some of the central tenets of Buddhism are incompatible with there being a creator God. Furthermore, the Buddha made no claim to special inspiration or revelation from God or any divine source. His insights into reality were the product of his own human self discipline, intelligence, and endeavor.

By contrast, Jesus of Nazareth was a first-century Jew who fully embraced the contemporary Jewish understanding of Yahweh as the one everlasting God, creator of the universe. Judaism at the time of Jesus was characterized by what Richard Bauckham calls a 'strict monotheism,' in that 'most Jews in this period were highly self-consciously monotheistic' and 'they drew the line of distinction between the one God and all other reality clearly.'[33] Only Yahweh, the God of Israel, is the true God, the creator of all that exists and the ruler of all things. The importance of monotheism is reflected in the Shema, which was central to Jewish liturgy: 'Hear, O Israel: The LORD our God, the LORD is one' (Deut. 6:4). When asked by a religious expert which is the greatest commandment, Jesus answered by quoting the Shema followed by the commands to love God and neighbor (Mk.12:28–31). When we locate Gautama the Buddha and Jesus the Christ within their own religious and historical contexts a striking difference becomes apparent: Jesus understood everything he said and did in light of the reality of God and his purposes; the Buddha not only did not acknowledge God's reality but his metaphysical claims rule out the possible existence of such a being.

3. For Jesus the root problem confronting humankind is sin; for Gautama it is ignorance

The Buddha diagnosed the root problem as one of ignorance – ignorance about the true nature of reality and the impermanence

---

[33] Richard Bauckham, *God Crucified: Monotheism and Christology in the New Testament* (Grand Rapids, MI: Eerdmans, 1998), p. 3.

of all things, resulting in craving and attachment. Walpola Rahula states, 'There is no "sin" in Buddhism, as sin is understood in some religions. The root of all evil is ignorance (avijja) and false views (micchaditthi).'[34] Although the Buddha has much to say about moral principles, there is nothing in his teaching resembling the Biblical understanding of sin. Nor is this surprising. For sin, according to Scripture, is always sin against a holy and righteous God, and with the Buddha we have no holy and righteous God against whom to sin. Thus, what is at the center of Christianity – God's being incarnate in Jesus Christ, dying for our sins, and rising the third day for our justification – has no role at all in Buddhism.

The difference here with Jesus is striking. According to Jesus our root problem is not ignorance but rather sin, the deliberate rejection of God's righteous ways. It is not ignorance of the true nature of reality or external forces acting upon us that result in our propensity to sin; evil is a matter of the corruption of the heart, our inner person with its desires, dispositions and inclinations (Mt. 15:10–20). Furthermore, although Jesus consistently called others to repentance he never repented for any sin. He challenged others to point out any sin in his own life. In a monotheistic culture in which it was axiomatic that God alone can forgive sin, Jesus audaciously assumed the authority to forgive individuals of their sin (Mk. 2:1–12). The contrast between Jesus and Gautama here is deep, and it does honor to neither religion to ignore or downplay it.

4. The one creator God became incarnate in Jesus of Nazareth; Gautama was a human being who is said to have been the human manifestation of the Buddha essence or Dharmakaya

What sets Christian faith apart from other religious traditions is the remarkable claim that in the historical Jesus of Nazareth the one creator God became man – Jesus the Messiah is also God incarnate. The Incarnation forms the apex of God's self-revelation

---

34 Walpola Rahula, *What the Buddha Taught*, p. 3.

to humankind.[35] The Letter to the Hebrews states, 'In the past God spoke to our forefathers through the prophets at many times and in various ways, but in these last days he has spoken to us by his Son, whom he appointed heir of all things and through whom he made the universe' (Heb. 1:1–2). The Gospel of John begins by affirming the preexistence of the Word (the Logos, who is identified with Jesus Christ) as deity and the Word's 'becoming flesh':

> In the beginning was the Word, and the Word was with God, and the Word was God. He was with God in the beginning. Through him all things were made; without him nothing was made that has been made. In him was life, and that life was the light of men... The Word became flesh and made his dwelling among us. We have seen his glory, the glory of the One and Only, who came from the Father, full of grace and truth (Jn. 1:1–4, 14).

Throughout the New Testament writings, sometimes explicitly and often implicitly, the human person Jesus is placed in an unprecedented relationship of identity with Yahweh, the everlasting creator God who had revealed himself to the patriarchs and prophets of the Hebrew scriptures. Jesus is presented as claiming the authority to do things that only God can do, such as forgive sins (Mk. 2:5–11); judge the world (Mt. 19:28; 25:31–46); give life, even to the dead (Jn. 5:21, 25–29; 11:17–44); and speak authoritatively for God in interpreting the purposes of the Sabbath (Mk. 2:23–27). Jesus states that anyone who has seen him has seen the Father (Jn. 14:9) – a remarkable claim in the context of Jewish monotheism. Jesus identifies himself with the I AM of Exodus 3:14 and in so doing is understood to be identifying himself with God (Jn. 8:58).

---

[35] There is a large literature on the Incarnation. For helpful discussions, see *The Incarnation*, eds. Stephen T. Davis, Daniel Kendall, and Gerald O'Collins (New York: Oxford University Press, 2002); Oliver D. Crisp, *Divinity and Humanity: The Incarnation Reconsidered* (Cambridge: Cambridge University Press, 2007); T.V. Morris, *The Logic of God Incarnate* (Ithaca, NY: Cornell University Press, 1986); Murray J. Harris, *Jesus as God: The New Testament Use of Theos in Reference to Jesus* (Grand Rapids, MI: Baker, 1992); Ben Witherington, *Christology of Jesus* (Minneapolis, MN: Fortress Press, 1990); Simon Gathercole, *The Preexistent Son: Recovering the Christologies of Matthew, Mark, and Luke* (Grand Rapids, MI: Eerdmans, 2006).

The apostle Paul asserts that all of the 'fullness' (pleroma) of God is present in the human person of Jesus; 'In Christ all the fullness of the Deity lives in bodily form' (Col. 1:19; 2:9).

Philippians 2:5–11 contains one of the more remarkable passages identifying Jesus with Yahweh, the one God of the Hebrew scriptures. In verses six through eight the preexistence of Jesus Christ and his essential equality with God are affirmed. Then verses ten and eleven ascribe to Jesus language used in the Old Testament book of Isaiah for God:

> At the name of Jesus every knee should bow
> in heaven and on earth and under the earth,
> and every tongue confess that Jesus Christ is Lord
> to the glory of God the Father (Phil. 2:10–11)

This is a partial quotation of Isaiah 45:21–23, where the words are spoken by Yahweh about himself. Old Testament scholar Chris Wright comments,

> This declaration by God comes in the most unambiguously monotheistic section of the whole Old Testament. The magnificent prophecies of Isaiah 40–55 assert again and again that Yahweh is utterly unique as the only living God in his sovereign power over all nations and all history, and in his ability to save. This early Christian hymn, therefore, by deliberately selecting a scripture from such a context and applying it to Jesus, is affirming that Jesus is as unique as Yahweh in those same respects.[36]

Understood within the context of first-century Jewish monotheism, the assertion that in Jesus of Nazareth the one eternal God has become man is unique in its audacity and is unparalleled in other religions. The Christian doctrine of the Incarnation pre-supposes both a robust monotheism and the reality of enduring persons, and it is this which separates it from anything remotely Buddhist.

---

[36] Christopher J.H. Wright, *What's So Unique About Jesus?* (Eastbourne, England: Monarch, 1990), p. 69.

It is sometimes said that the historical Jesus himself never taught anything like the orthodox Christian teaching on the Incarnation – Jesus Christ as fully God and fully man – and that this was a much later doctrinal innovation of the Christian church. Sometimes a parallel with developments in Buddhism is affirmed. Although Gautama was originally regarded merely as an extraordinary human being who attained enlightenment, over several centuries he gradually came to be understood within Mahayana as an almost deified figure, part of the Trikaya, or Three Bodies of the Buddha, the human manifestation of the Buddha essence, or Dharmakaya. So too, it is said, the human Jesus, originally understood by his followers as just a great teacher and perhaps even the Messiah, over time became revered as more than merely a man, resulting, under Greek influence, in the metaphysical conceptions of him as Son of God, God the Son and finally the sophisticated Trinitarian formula of the Second Person of the Holy Trinity. Consider, for example, the following statement by John Hick:

> Gautama was a human teacher, though one who had attained perfect enlightenment and who accordingly spoke with the authority of firsthand knowledge. After his death he was spoken about in the developing Buddhist literature in exalted terms, frequently as the Blessed One and the Exalted One. Stories of his many previous lives became popular, and legend attributed to him a supernatural conception, birth and childhood.... The later Mahayana doctrine of the Trikaya is comparable with the Johannine doctrine of the Logos and its development of the incarnation idea. As Jesus was the incarnation of the pre-existent Word / Son, who was of one substance with the Father in the eternal Trinity, so Gautama was the earthly manifestation of a heavenly Buddha, and all the Buddhas are one in the ultimate reality of the eternal Dharmakaya. Thus, the developed Buddhology of the Mahayana, some five centuries after the death of Gautama, parallels the developed Christology that reached its completion at the fifth-century Council of Chalcedon.[37]

---

[37] John Hick, *Disputed Questions in Theology and the Philosophy of Religion* (New Haven, CT: Yale University Press, 1993), p. 47.

According to Hick, then, the Christian teaching on the deity of Jesus Christ is the product of a long evolutionary process which is paralleled in Buddhism, resulting in the view of the exalted Buddha and Trikaya of Mahayana.

There is much that could be said by way of response, but we will confine ourselves to one major point distinguishing Jesus from Gautama. Given the significant time gap between the life of Gautama and the earliest Pali writings, and the time lapse again between the earlier Theravada traditions and the later Mahayana teachings on the Trikaya, it is plausible to think in terms of gradual progression or evolution within Buddhist traditions on the nature and significance of the historical Gautama, resulting in the 'high Buddhology' of the Trikaya. But this is not so easily done with Jesus and the New Testament. While some development within the New Testament writings themselves can be traced, the 'high Christology' which identifies Jesus with Yahweh, God the creator, is actually found in the earliest evidence we have of Christian belief and practice.

As noted above, all of the writings of the New Testament were completed by about 90 AD (many of them considerably earlier) so that at most there is a gap of some sixty years between the death of Jesus and the completion of the last New Testament writing. This is not sufficient time for a radical evolution from the view that Jesus is just an extraordinary man to that of him as in fact God the creator become man. Cambridge New Testament scholar C. F. D. Moule argues that the suggestion that such 'high' Christology evolved from a primitive 'low' Christology by a gradual process over time simply does not fit the data. To the contrary, he argues, the transition from invoking Jesus as revered Master to the acclamation of him as divine Lord is best understood as a development in understanding according to which 'the various estimates of Jesus reflected in the New Testament [are], in essence, only attempts to describe what was already there from the beginning. They are not successive additions of something new, but only the drawing out and articulating of what is there.' Moule claims that, 'Jesus was, *from the beginning,* such a one as appropriately to be described in the ways in which, sooner or later, he did come to be described in the New Testament period – for instance, as "Lord" and even, in some sense, as "God".'[38] Some of the most elevated Christology, and clearest affirmations of the deity of Christ, are in the Pauline epistles, widely accepted as the earliest documents in the New Testament (e.g. Rom. 9:5; Phil. 2:5–11; Col. 1:15–17, 19; 2:9).[39]

One way to determine early perspectives on Christology is to consider not merely the language in the New Testament used in reference to Jesus but to examine the devotional practices of the early Christians. In several seminal studies Larry Hurtado has demonstrated that worship of Jesus is presupposed by the earliest New Testament writings and thus that the practice of worshiping Jesus as divine by his early followers – most of whom were Jewish – is even earlier than these writings.[40] Hurtado claims that within the first couple of decades of the Christian movement, between roughly 30–50 AD, 'Jesus was treated as a recipient of religious devotion and was associated with God in striking ways.'[41] He emphasizes the fact that 'the origins of the worship of Jesus are so early that practically any evolutionary approach is rendered invalid as historical explanation. Our earliest Christian writings,

---

[38] C.F.D. Moule, *The Origin of Christology* (Cambridge: Cambridge University Press, 1977), pp. 2–4. Emphasis original.

[39] Similarly, Martin Hengel argues that the title Son of God is not a late accretion to Christology but rather was already applied to Jesus prior to 50 AD. Martin Hengel, *The Son of God: The Origin of Christology and the History of the Jewish-Hellenistic Religion* (Philadelphia, PA: Fortress, 1976), pp. 2, 10.

[40] Larry W. Hurtado, *One God, One Lord: Early Christian Devotion and Ancient Jewish Monotheism* (Philadelphia, PA: Fortress, 1988); *Lord Jesus Christ: Devotion to Jesus in Earliest Christianity* (Grand Rapids, MI: Eerdmans, 2003); *How on Earth Did Jesus Become a God? Historical Questions about Earliest Devotion to Jesus* (Grand Rapids, MI: Eerdmans, 2005).

[41] Larry Hurtado, *Lord Jesus Christ*, p. 2. As indicators of such worship, he points to the practices of calling upon the name of the Lord Jesus Christ when believers gathered together (1 Cor. 1:2); the use of hymns about or to Jesus as regular parts of Christian worship (Phil. 2:5–11); prayer to God 'through' Jesus (Rom. 1:8), and direct prayer to Jesus himself (Acts 7:59–60; 2 Cor. 12:8–9; 1 Thess. 3:11–13; 2 Thess. 2:16–17); use of the formula 'Marana tha!' ('O Lord, Come!') as a prayer in worship (1 Cor. 16:22); invoking Jesus' name in healing and exorcism (Acts 3:16; 16:18) as well as in baptism (Acts 2:38); and the celebration of the 'Lord's Supper' (1 Cor. 11:17–34).

from approximately 50–60 CE, already presuppose cultic devotion to Jesus as a familiar and defining feature of Christian circles wherever they were found (1 Cor. 1:2).'[42]

Not only was this devotion to Jesus very early, and thus not a product of extraneous influences in a secondary stage of gradual development, but it 'was exhibited in an unparalleled intensity and diversity of expression, for which we have no true analogy in the religious environment of the time.' Furthermore, Hurtado maintains that, 'This intense devotion to Jesus, which includes reverencing him as divine, was offered and articulated characteristically within a firm stance of exclusivist monotheism, particularly in the circles of early Christians that anticipated and helped to establish what became mainstream (and subsequently, familiar) Christianity.'[43] Significantly, the ascription of deity to Jesus did not include a modification of Jewish monotheism. As Richard Bauckham argues, it involved 'identifying Jesus directly with the one God of Israel, including Jesus in the unique identity of this one God.'[44]

5. Whereas Gautama presents teachings and practices leading to enlightenment, Jesus does not merely teach the way to reconciliation with God – he himself is the Way to salvation

As we have seen, there is within the early teachings attributed to the Buddha a strong sense of the individual being responsible for his or her own liberation. True, the Buddha proclaimed the dharma, the teaching leading to liberation, and in this way he can be said to assist all sentient beings. But it is up to the individual to grasp the dharma, to appropriate it, and thereby to attain nirvana.

Although later Buddhism did develop the idea of the bodhisattva who assists others on the way to nirvana, the Buddha

---

[42] Larry Hurtado, *How on Earth Did Jesus Become a God?*, p. 25.
[43] Ibid., pp. 2–3.
[44] Richard Bauckham, *God Crucified: Monotheism and Christology in the New Testament*, p. 4.

himself seems to have regarded each person as responsible for his or her own destiny. At his death, the Buddha's parting words to his followers were: 'So, Ananda, you must be your own lamps, be your own refuges. Take refuge in nothing outside yourselves. Hold firm to the truth as a lamp and a refuge, and do not look for refuge to anything besides yourselves ... All composite things must pass away. Strive onward vigilantly.'[45] Rahula puts it this way: 'If the Buddha is to be called a "saviour" at all, it is only in the sense that he discovered and showed the Path to Liberation, *Nirvana*. But we must tread the Path ourselves.'[46]

The difference with Jesus is unmistakeable. According to the Christian Scriptures, human beings cannot save themselves; we are utterly helpless and hopeless apart from the grace of God and the atoning work of Jesus Christ on the cross for us (Eph. 2:1–10; Rom. 3:9–28). The New Testament consistently presents Jesus as the one Savior for all people in all cultures (Jn. 3:16; Acts 2:37–39; 4:12; Rom. 3:21–25; 1 Tim. 2:5–6). Jesus called upon others to believe in him and to find salvation only in him (Jn. 5:24; 6:35–58). Jesus does not merely teach the way – He claims to *be* the Way (Jn 14:6). It is not simply that Jesus has discovered the way and the truth, and that if we follow his teachings we too can find the way for ourselves. In effect the Buddha says, 'Follow my teachings, follow the dharma and you too can experience the way leading to enlightenment.' But Jesus says much more than simply that he has discovered the way to the father and that if we follow him and his teachings we too can find the way. He puts himself forward as the embodiment of the Way, and the Truth and the Life. It is because of who he is and what he has done for us on the cross and in the resurrection that he is himself the Way, the Truth, and the Life. Thus the truth of Jesus' teachings cannot be separated from the ontological grounding of this truth in the person of Christ as the incarnate Word of God. In a thoughtful essay in which she reflects

---

[45] Digha Nikaya 2.99f, 156; as cited in *Sources of Indian Tradition*, vol. 1, ed. William Theodore de Bary (New York: Columbia University Press, 1958), pp. 110–11.
[46] Walpola Rahula, *What the Buddha Taught*, pp. 1–2.

as a Christian on the significance of Gautama the Buddha, Bonnie
Thurston offers the following comparison:

> While I admire the confidence in the human being that asserts that
> everyone who strives for emancipation and enlightenment can find it
> by personal effort, that, alas, does not square with my experience....
> My experience is less that of the Dhammapada, which notes, 'by
> Oneself indeed is evil done and by oneself is one defiled. By oneself
> is evil left undone and by oneself indeed is one purified. Purity
> and impurity depend upon oneself,' and more that of St. Paul, who
> lamented, 'I do not understand my own actions. For I do not do
> what I want but I do the very thing I hate' (Rom. 7:15) and 'For I do
> not do the good I want but the evil I do not want is what I do' (Rom.
> 7:19). The darkness is so great. My candle is so small. Strive as I may,
> I can't illuminate myself.... In the struggle to be a lamp to myself, I
> am brought face to face with Jesus Christ.... The Buddha says, 'Be
> lamps unto yourselves' and 'one is one's own refuge.'... The Christ
> says, 'Come to me, all you that are weary and are carrying heavy
> burdens and I will give you rest' (Mt. 11:28) and 'I am the light of
> the world. Whoever follows me will never walk in darkness but
> will have the light of life' (Jn. 8:12) and 'I am the way, and the truth,
> and the life' (Jn. 14:6). The Buddha directs me away from himself.
> The Christ invites me to himself. In the Four Reliances, the Buddha
> teaches, 'Rely on the teaching not the teacher.' In Christianity, the
> teaching is the Teacher.[47]

Conclusion

The question that prompted Gautama in his search was that of
the causes of suffering, and he set out to uncover the causes for
suffering and the way to their elimination. His answer is contained
in the Four Noble Truths and the Noble Eightfold Path, as well
as the metaphysical assumptions underlying these principles. In
the preceding chapters we have explored some of the implications
of the Buddha's teachings, and have raised questions about the
coherence and plausibility of aspects of Buddhist metaphysics.

---

[47] Bonnie Thurston, 'The Buddha Offered Me a Raft,' in *Buddhists Talk About
Jesus, Christians Talk About the Buddha*, p. 124.

Jesus too was deeply concerned with human suffering. But the Christian Scriptures take a very different approach to suffering, locating suffering within the context of sin and God's redemptive purposes for humankind, culminating in the defeat of evil and a restored creation (Rev. 20–21). Jesus' death on the cross and resurrection provide the Christian answer to the question that haunted the Buddha.

The Buddha or the Christ? The dharma or the gospel? These are not simply variations on a common theme, or different ways of expressing the same spiritual insight. The choice here is between two radically different perspectives on reality, on the nature of the human predicament, and the way to overcome it.

Bibliography

Abe, Masao, 'The Meaning of Life in Buddhism,' in *The Meaning of Life in the World Religions*, eds. Joseph Runzo and Nancy M. Martin (Oxford: Oneworld, 2000), pp. 153–61.

——, 'Ethics and Social Responsibility in Buddhism,' *Eastern Buddhist* 30:2 (1997), pp. 161–72.

——, *Zen and Comparative Studies*, ed. Steven Heine (Honolulu, HI: University of Hawaii Press, 1997).

——, *Buddhism and Interfaith Dialogue*, ed. Steven Heine (Honolulu, HI: University of Hawaii Press, 1995).

——, 'Kenotic God and Dynamic Sunyata,' in *The Emptying God: A Buddhist-Jewish-Christian Conversation*, eds. John B. Cobb, Jr. and Christopher Ives (Maryknoll, NY: Orbis Books, 1990), pp. 3–65.

——, 'The Impact of Dialogue with Christianity on My Self-Understanding as a Buddhist,' *Buddhist–Christian Studies* 9 (1989), pp. 63–70.

——, 'The Problem of Evil in Christianity and Buddhism,' in *Buddhist–Christian Dialogue: Mutual Renewal and Transformation*, eds. Paul Ingram and Frederick J. Streng (Honolulu, HI: University of Hawaii Press, 1986), pp. 139–54.

——, ed., *A Zen Life: D.T. Suzuki Remembered* (New York: Weatherhill, 1986).

——, *Zen and Western Thought*, ed. William R. LaFleur (Honolulu, HI: University of Hawaii Press, 1985).

Almond, Philip C., *The British Discovery of Buddhism* (Cambridge: Cambridge University Press, 1988).

Amstutz, Galen, *Interpreting Amida: History and Orientalism in the Study of Pure Land Buddhism* (Albany, NY: State University of New York Press, 1997).

Andreasen, Esben, *Popular Buddhism in Japan: Shin Buddhist Religion and Culture* (Honolulu, HI: University of Hawaii Press, 1998).

Arnold, Edwin, *The Light of Asia, or The Great Renunciation* (New York: A.L. Burt, 1879).

Batchelor, Stephen, 'Life As a Question, Not a Fact,' in *Why Buddhism? Westerners in Search of Wisdom*, ed. Vickie Mackenzie (London: Element, 2002), pp. 142–62.

——, *Buddhism Without Beliefs: A Contemporary Guide to Awakening* (New York: Riverhead Books, 1997).

Bauckham, Richard, *God Crucified: Monotheism and Christology in the New Testament* (Grand Rapids, MI: Eerdmans, 1998).

Baumann, Martin, 'Buddhism in Europe: Past, Present, Prospects,' in *Westward Dharma: Buddhism Beyond Asia*, ed. Charles S. Prebish (Berkeley, CA: University of California Press, 2002), pp. 85–105.

Bentley, Jerry H., *Old World Encounters: Cross-Cultural Encounters and Exchanges in Pre-Modern Times* (New York: Oxford University Press, 1993).

Bloom, Alfred, *Shinran's Gospel of Pure Grace* (Tucson, AZ: University of Arizona Press, 1965).

Cabezón, José, 'A God, But Not a Savior,' in *Buddhists Talk About Jesus, Christians Talk About the Buddha*, eds. Rita Gross and Terry C. Muck (New York: Continuum, 2000), pp. 17–31.

Carrithers, Michael, *The Buddha* (New York: Oxford University Press, 1983).

Ch'en, Kenneth K.S., *The Chinese Transformation of Buddhism* (Princeton, NJ: Princeton University Press, 1973).

——, *Buddhism in China: A Historical Survey* (Princeton, NJ: Princeton University Press, 1964).

Christian, William A. Sr., *Doctrines of Religious Communities: A Philosophical Study* (New Haven, CT: Yale University Press, 1987).

Clarke, J.J., *Oriental Enlightenment: The Encounter Between Asian and Western Thought* (London: Routledge, 1997).

Cobb, John B. Jr., *Beyond Dialogue: Toward a Mutual Transformation of Christianity and Buddhism* (Philadelphia, PA: Fortress Press, 1982).

———, 'Can a Christian Be a Buddhist, Too?' *Japanese Religions* 10 (December 1978), pp. 1–20.

Cobb, John B. and Christopher Ives, eds., *The Emptying God: A Buddhist-Jewish-Christian Conversation* (Maryknoll, NY: Orbis Books, 1990).

Coleman, James William, *The New Buddhism: The Western Transformation of an Ancient Tradition* (New York: Oxford University Press, 2001).

Collins, Steven, *Selfless Persons: Imagery and Thought in Theravada Buddhism* (Cambridge: Cambridge University Press, 1982).

Conze, Edward, ed. and trans., *Buddhist Scriptures* (New York: Penguin Books, 1959).

———, I.B. Horner, David Snellgrove, and Arthur Waley, eds., *Buddhist Texts Through the Ages* (Oxford: Oneworld, 1995).

Cox, Harvey, 'Christianity,' in *Global Religions: An Introduction*, ed. Mark Juergensmeyer (New York: Oxford University Press, 2003), pp. 17–27.

Dallmayr, Fred, *Beyond Orientalism: Essays on Cross-Cultural Encounter* (Albany, NY: State University of New York Press, 1996).

De Bary, William Theodore, ed., *The Buddhist Tradition* (New York: Random House, 1969).

———, ed., *Sources of Indian Tradition*, vol. 1 (New York: Columbia University Press, 1958).

Dharmasiri, Gunapala, *A Buddhist Critique of the Christian Concept of God* (Antioch, CA: Golden Leaves Publishing Company, 1988).

Dumoulin, Heinrich, *Zen Buddhism in the 20th Century*, trans. Joseph S. O'Leary (New York: Weatherhill, 1992).
——, *Zen Buddhism: A History. Volume 2: Japan*, trans. James W. Heisig and Paul Knitter (New York: Macmillan, 1990).
——, *Zen Buddhism: A History. Volume 1: India and China*, trans. James W. Heisig and Paul Knitter (New York: Macmillan, 1988).
——, *Zen Enlightenment: Origins and Meaning*, trans. Joseph C. Maraldo (New York: Weatherhill, 1979).

Ellwood, Robert S., *The Sixties Spiritual Awakening: American Religion Moving From Modern to Postmodern* (New Brunswick, NJ: Rutgers University Press, 1994).
——, *Alternative Altars: Unconventional and Eastern Spirituality in America* (Chicago, IL: University of Chicago Press, 1979).

Faure, Bernard, *Chan Insights and Oversights: An Epistemological Critique of the Chan Tradition* (Princeton, NJ: Princeton University Press, 1993).
Fields, Rick, *How the Swans Came to the Lake: A Narrative History of Buddhism in America*, 3rd edn. (Boston, MA: Shamhala, 1992).

Gomez, Luis O., 'Buddhism in India,' in *The Religious Traditions of Asia*, ed. Joseph M. Kitagawa (New York: Macmillan, 1989), pp. 41–95.
Griffiths, Paul J., *On Being Buddha: The Classical Doctrine of Buddhahood* (Albany, NY: State University of New York Press, 1994).
——, *An Apology for Apologetics: A Study in the Logic of Interreligious Dialogue* (Maryknoll, NY: Orbis Books, 1991).
——, 'Why Buddhas Can't Remember Their Previous Lives,' *Philosophy East and West* 39:4 (October 1989), pp. 449–51.
——, *On Being Mindless* (LaSalle, IL: Open Court, 1986).
——, 'Notes Towards A Critique of Buddhist Karmic Theory,' *Religious Studies* 18 (1982), pp. 277–91.

Harvey, Peter, *An Introduction to Buddhist Ethics* (Cambridge: Cambridge University Press, 2000).

Heelas, Paul and Linda Woodhead, et al., *The Spiritual Revolution: Why Religion is Giving Way to Spirituality* (Oxford: Blackwell, 2005).

Heine, Steven and Charles S. Prebish, eds., *Buddhism in the Modern World: Adaptations of an Ancient Tradition* (New York: Oxford University Press, 2003).

Heisig, James W. and John C. Maraldo, eds., *Rude Awakenings: Zen, the Kyoto School and the Question of Nationalism* (Honolulu, HI: University of Hawaii Press, 1994).

Herman, A.L., 'Religions as Failed Theodicies: Atheism in Hinduism and Buddhism,' in *Indian Philosophy of Religion*, ed. Roy W. Perrett (Dordrecht, The Netherlands: Kluwer Academic Publishers, 1989), pp. 35–60.

Hick, John, *Disputed Questions in Theology and the Philosophy of Religion* (New Haven, CT: Yale University Press, 1993).

Hirakawa, Akira, *A History of Indian Buddhism: From Sakyamuni to Early Mahayana*, trans. and ed. Paul Groner (Honolulu, HI: University of Hawaii Press, 1990).

Hopkins, Thomas J., *The Hindu Tradition* (Belmont, CA: Dickenson Publishing Company, 1971).

Hubbard, Jamie and Paul L. Swanson, eds., *Pruning the Bodhi Tree: The Storm Over Critical Buddhism* (Honolulu, HI: University of Hawaii Press, 1997).

Humphreys, Christmas, *Sixty Years of Buddhism in England: A History and Survey* (London: The Buddhist Society, 1968).

Hurtado, Larry W., *How on Earth Did Jesus Become a God? Historical Questions about Earliest Devotion to Jesus* (Grand Rapids, MI: Eerdmans, 2005).

——, *Lord Jesus Christ: Devotion to Jesus in Earliest Christianity* (Grand Rapids, MI: Eerdmans, 2003).

Ingram, Paul O. and Frederick J. Streng, eds., *Buddhist-Christian Dialogue: Mutual Renewal and Transformation* (Honolulu, HI: University of Hawaii Press, 1986).

Ishihara, John, 'Luther and Shinran: SIMUL IUSTUS ET PECCATOR and NISHY JINSHIN,' *Japanese Religions*, 14 (July 1987), pp. 31–54.

Ives, Christopher, 'Ethical Pitfalls in Imperial Zen and Nishida Philosophy,' in *Rude Awakenings: Zen, the Kyoto School and the Question of Nationalism*, eds. James W. Heisig and John C. Maraldo (Honolulu, HI: University of Hawaii Press, 1994), pp. 16–39.

Jackson, Carl T., *The Oriental Religions and American Thought: Nineteenth Century Explorations* (Westport, CT: Greenwood Press, 1981).

Jayatilleke, K.N., *The Buddhist Attitude to Other Religions* (Kandy, Sri Lanka: Buddhist Publication Society, 1975).

——, *The Message of the Buddha*, ed. Ninian Smart (New York: The Free Press, 1974).

Jenkins, Philip, *The Next Christendom: The Coming of Global Christianity* (New York: Oxford University Press, 2002).

Juergensmeyer, Mark, 'Thinking Globally About Religion,' in *Global Religions: An Introduction*, ed. Mark Juergensmeyer (New York: Oxford University Press, 2003), pp. 3–13.

Kalupahana, David J., *Ethics in Early Buddhism* (Honolulu, HI: University of Hawaii Press, 1995).

——, *A History of Buddhist Philosophy: Continuities and Discontinuities* (Honolulu, HI: University of Hawaii Press, 1992).

——, *Nagarjuna: The Philosophy of the Middle Way* (Albany, NY: State University of New York Press, 1986).

——, *Buddhist Philosophy: A Historical Analysis* (Honolulu, HI: University of Hawaii Press, 1976).

Kasulis, Thomas, 'Nirvana,' in *The Encyclopedia of Religion*, vol. 10, ed. Mircea Eliade (New York: Macmillan, 1987), pp. 448–56.

Kiblinger, Kristin Beise, *Buddhist Inclusivism: Attitudes Towards Religious Others* (Burlington, VT: Ashgate Publishing, 2005).

King, Richard. *Indian Philosophy: An Introduction to Hindu and Buddhist Thought* (Washington, DC: Georgetown University Press, 1999).

——, *Orientalism and Religion: Postcolonial Theory, India and 'The Mystic East'* (London: Routledge, 1999).

King, Sallie, *Being Benevolence: The Social Ethics of Engaged Buddhism* (Honolulu, HI: University of Hawaii Press, 2005).

Kitagawa, Joseph M., *On Understanding Japanese Religion* (Princeton, NJ: Princeton University Press, 1987).

——, 'The 1893 World's Parliament of Religions and Its Legacy,' in *The History of Religions: Understanding Human Experience* (Atlanta, GA: Scholars Press, 1987), pp. 353–68.

——, *Religion in Japanese History* (New York: Columbia University Press, 1966).

Kitagawa, Joseph M., ed., *The Religious Traditions of Asia* (New York: Macmillan, 1989).

Koller, John M. and Patricia Koller, eds., *A Sourcebook in Asian Philosophy* (New York: Macmillan, 1991).

Kvaerne, Per, 'The Religions of Tibet,' in *The Religious Traditions of Asia*, ed. J. Kitagawa, pp. 195–206.

Lau, D. C., trans., *Lao Tzu: Tao Te Ching* (Hammondsworth: Penguin Books, 1963).

Lai, Whalen, 'The Search for the Historical Sakyamuni in Light of the Historical Jesus,' in *Buddhist–Christian Studies* 2 (1982), pp. 77–91.

Learman, Linda, ed., *Buddhist Missionaries in the Era of Globalization* (Honolulu, HI: University of Hawaii Press, 2005).

Lopez, Donald S. Jr., *The Story of Buddhism: A Concise Guide to Its History and Teachings* (New York: HarperCollins, 2001).

——, ed., *Curators of the Buddha: The Study of Buddhism Under Colonialism* (Chicago, IL: University of Chicago Press, 1995).

McMahan, David L., 'Repackaging Zen for the West,' in *Westward Dharma*, pp. 218–29.

Mitchell, Donald W., *Buddhism: Introducing the Buddhist Experience*, 2nd edn. (New York: Oxford University Press, 2008).

——, ed., *Masao Abe: A Zen Life of Dialogue* (Boston, MA: Charles E. Tuttle, 1998).

Moule, C.F.D., *The Origin of Christology* (Cambridge: Cambridge University Press, 1977).

Nagarjuna, *The Fundamental Wisdom of the Middle Way: Nagarjuna's Mulamadhyamakakarika*, trans. and commentary by Jay L. Garfield (New York: Oxford University Press, 1995).

Nakamura, Hajime, *Gotama Buddha: A Biography Based on the Most Reliable Texts*, vol. 1, trans. Gaynor Sekimori (Tokyo: Kosei Publishing, 2000).

——, *Gotama Buddha* (Tokyo: Buddhist Books International, 1977).

——, *Ways of Thinking of Eastern Peoples*, rev. edn., trans. Philip P. Wiener (Honolulu, HI: University of Hawaii Press, 1964).

——, 'Unity and Diversity in Buddhism,' in *The Path of the Buddha: Buddhism Interpreted by Buddhists*, ed. Kenneth W. Morgan (New York: Ronald Press Company, 1956), pp. 364–400.

Neill, Stephen, *The Supremacy of Jesus* (Downers Grove, IL: InterVarsity Press, 1984).

——, *Christian Faith and Other Faiths* (London: Oxford University Press, 1961).

Netland, Harold, *Encountering Religious Pluralism* (Downers Grove, IL: InterVarsity Press, 2001).

Nishida, Kitaro, *An Inquiry into the Good*, trans. Masao Abe and Christopher Ives (New Haven, CT: Yale University Press, 1987 [1927]).

O'Flaherty, Wendy Doniger, ed. and trans., *The Rig Veda: An Anthology* (Hammondsworth: Penguin Books, 1981).

——, 'The Origin of Heresy in Hindu Mythology,' *History of Religions*, 10:4 (1971), pp. 271–333.

Overmyer, Daniel L., 'Chinese Religion,' in *The Religious Traditions of Asia*, pp. 257–304.

Payne, Richard K. and Kenneth K. Tanaka, eds., *Approaching the Land of Bliss: Religious Praxis in the Cult of Amitabha* (Honolulu, HI: University of Hawaii Press, 2004).

Perrett, Roy W., ed., *Indian Philosophy of Religion* (Dordrecht, The Netherlands: Kluwer Academic Publishers, 1989).

Plantinga, Cornelius, *Not the Way It's Supposed to Be: A Breviary of Sin* (Grand Rapids, MI: Eerdmans, 1995).

Porterfield, Amanda, *The Transformation of American Religion* (New York: Oxford University Press, 2001).

Prebish, Charles S., *Luminous Passage: The Practice and Study of Buddhism in America* (Berkeley, CA: University of California Press, 1999).

——, and Martin Baumann, eds., *Westward Dharma: Buddhism Beyond Asia* (Berkeley, CA: University of California Press, 2002).

——, and Kenneth Tanaka, eds., *The Faces of Buddhism in America* (Berkeley, CA: University of California Press, 1998).

Queen, Christopher S. and Sallie B. King, eds., *Engaged Buddhism: Buddhist Liberation Movements in Asia* (Albany, NY: State University of New York Press, 1996).

Radhakrishnan, Sarvepalli and Charles A. Moore, eds., *A Source Book in Indian Philosophy* (Princeton, NJ: Princeton University Press, 1957).

Rahula, Walpola, *What the Buddha Taught*, 2nd edn. (New York: Grove Press, 1974).

Reader, Ian, *Religion in Contemporary Japan* (New York: Macmillan, 1991).

Reat, Noble Ross, 'Karma and Rebirth in the Upanishads and Buddhism,' in *Numen* 24 (December 1977), pp. 163–85.

Reichenbach, Bruce R., *The Law of Karma: A Philosophical Study* (Honolulu, HI: University of Hawaii Press, 1990).

Robinson, Richard H. and Willard L. Johnson, *The Buddhist Religion: A Historical Introduction*, 4th edn. (Belmont, CA: Wadsworth Publishing Company, 1997).

Rhys Davids, T.W., trans., *Buddhist Suttas* (New York: Dover Publications, 1969).

Said, Edward, *Orientalism* (New York: Vintage, 1978).

Saunders, E. Dale, *Buddhism in Japan* (Tokyo: Charles E. Tuttle, 1964).

Schell, Orville, *Virtual Tibet: Searching for Shangri-La From the Himalayas to Hollywood* (New York: Metropolitan Books, 2000).

Schepers, Gerhard, 'Shinran's View of the Human Predicament and the Christian Concept of Sin,' *Japanese Religions*, 15 (July 1988), pp. 1–17.

Seager, Richard Hughes, *Buddhism in America* (New York: Columbia University Press, 1999).

——, Richard Hughes, ed., *The Dawn of Religious Pluralism: Voices From the World's Parliament of Religions, 1893* (La Salle, IL: Open Court, 1993).

Shaner, David Edward, 'Biographies of the Buddha,' *Philosophy East and West*, vol. XXXVII, no. 3 (July 1987), pp. 306–22.

Sharf, Robert H., 'The Zen of Japanese Nationalism,' in *Curators of the Buddha: The Study of Buddhism Under Colonialism*, ed. Donald S. Lopez (Chicago, IL: University of Chicago Press, 1995), pp. 107–60.

——, 'Whose Zen? Zen Nationalism Revisited,' *Rude Awakenings: Zen, the Kyoto School and the Question of Nationalism*, eds. James Heisig and John Maraldo (Honolulu, HI: University of Hawaii Press, 1994), pp. 40–51.

Sharma, Arvind, *The Philosophy of Religion: A Buddhist Perspective* (Delhi: Oxford University Press, 1995).

Siderits, Mark, *Buddhism as Philosophy: An Introduction* (Indianapolis, IN: Hackett Publishing Company, 2007).

Smart, Ninian, *Worldviews: Crosscultural Explorations of Human Beliefs*, 2nd edn. (Englewood Cliffs, NJ: Prentice Hall, 1995).

——, *Buddhism and Christianity: Rivals and Allies* (Honolulu, HI: University of Hawaii Press, 1993).

Snellgrove, David, 'The Schools of Tibetan Buddhism,' in *The Religious Traditions of Asia*, pp. 207–15.

Snodgrass, Judith, *Presenting Japanese Buddhism to the West: Orientalism, Occidentalism and the Columbian Exposition* (Chapel Hill, NC: University of North Carolina Press, 2003).

Streng, Frederick, *Emptiness: A Study in Religious Meaning* (Nashville, TN: Abingdon Press, 1967).

Strong, John S., *The Buddha: A Short Biography* (Oxford: Oneworld, 2001).

——, ed., *The Experience of Buddhism: Sources and Interpretations* (Belmont, CA: Wadsworth, 1995).

Suzuki, D.T., *The Essentials of Zen Buddhism: Selected from the Writings of Daisetz T. Suzuki*, ed. Bernard Phillips (Westport, CT: Greenwood Press, 1962).

——, *Essays in Zen: First Series* (New York: Weidenfeld, 1961 [1949]).

——, *Zen and Japanese Culture* (Princeton, NJ: Princeton University Press, 1959).

Swanson, Paul L., 'Why They Say Zen Is Not Buddhism,' in *Pruning the Bodhi Tree: The Storm Over Critical Buddhism*, pp. 3–29.

The Dalai Lama, Tenzin Gyatso, *The Good Heart: A Buddhist Perspective on the Teachings of Jesus*, trans. Geshe Thupten Jinpa, ed. Robert Kiely (Boston, MA: Wisdom Publications, 1996).

——, *Freedom in Exile: The Autobiography of the Dalai Lama* (New York: HarperCollins, 1990).

——, '"Religious Harmony" and Extracts From *The Bodhgaya Interviews*,' in *Christianity Through Non-Christian Eyes*, ed. Paul J. Griffiths (Maryknoll, NY: Orbis Books, 1990), pp. 162–70.

Thelle, Notto, *Buddhism and Christianity in Japan: From Conflict to Dialogue, 1854–1899* (Honolulu, HI: University of Hawaii Press, 1987).

Thittila, U., 'The Fundamental Principles of Theravada Buddhism,' in *The Path of the Buddha: Buddhism Interpreted by Buddhists*, ed. Kenneth W. Morgan (New York: Ronald Press Company, 1956), pp. 67–112.

Thurston, Bonnie, 'The Buddha Offered Me a Raft,' in *Buddhists Talk About Jesus, Christians Talk About the Buddha*, pp. 118–28.

Tweed, Thomas A., 'American Occultism and Japanese Buddhism: Albert J. Edmunds, D.T. Suzuki and Translocative History,' *Japanese Journal of Religious Studies* 32:2 (2005), pp. 249–81.

Tweed, Thomas A., 'Who Is a Buddhist? Nightstand Buddhists and Other Creatures' in *Westward Dharma*, ed. C. Prebish and M. Baumann, pp. 17–33.

—— and Stephen Prothero, eds., *Asian Religions in America: A Documentary History* (New York: Oxford University Press, 1999).

Van Bragt, Jan, 'Reflections on Zen and Ethics,' *Studies in Interreligious Dialogue*, 12 (2002), pp. 133–47.

——, 'Buddhism – Jodo Shinshu – Christianity: Does Jodo Shinshu Form a Bridge Between Buddhism and Christianity?,' *Japanese Religions* 18 (January 1993), pp. 47–75.

Verhoeven, Martin J., 'Americanizing the Buddha: Paul Carus and the Transformation of Asian Thought,' in *The Faces of Buddhism in America*, eds. Charles S. Prebish and Kenneth K. Tanaka (Berkeley, CA: University of California Press, 1998), pp. 207–27.

Watts, Alan, *The Way of Zen* (New York: Pantheon Books, 1957).

Williams, Paul, 'Aquinas Meets the Buddhists: Prolegomenon to an Authentically Thomas-ist Basis for Dialogue,' in *Aquinas in Dialogue: Thomas for the Twenty-First Century*, eds. Jim Fodor and Christian Bauerschmidt (Oxford: Blackwell Publishing, 2004), pp. 87–117.

——, *The Unexpected Way: On Converting From Buddhism to Catholicism* (Edinburgh: T&T Clark, 2002).

——, *Mahayana Buddhism: The Doctrinal Foundations* (London: Routledge, 1989).

Wood, Robert W., ed., 'Tillich Encounters Japan,' *Japanese Religions*, 2 (May 1961), pp. 48–71.

Wright, Christopher J.H., *What's So Unique About Jesus?* (Eastbourne, England: Monarch, 1990).

Wuthnow, Robert and Wendy Cage, 'Buddhists and Buddhism in the United States: The Scope of Influence,' in *Journal for the Scientific Study of Religion* 43:3 (2004), pp. 363–80.

Yandell, Keith, 'How to Sink in Cognitive Quicksand: Nuancing Religious Pluralism,' in *Contemporary Debates in Philosophy of Religion*, eds. Michael L. Peterson and Raymond J. VanArragon (Oxford: Blackwell Publishing, 2004), pp. 191–200.

——, *Philosophy of Religion: A Contemporary Introduction* (London: Routledge, 1999).

——, 'Some Varieties of Indian Theological Dualism,' in *Indian Philosophy of Religion*, ed. R. Perrett, pp. 5–34.

——, *The Epistemology of Religious Experience* (Cambridge: Cambridge University Press, 1993).

Yusa, Michiko, *Zen and Philosophy: An Intellectual Biography of Nishida Kitaro* (Honolulu, HI: University of Hawaii Press, 2002).

Index

Abe, Masao 70, 79, 86 n., 90 n., 95–103, 193, 196
Almond, Philip C. 71 n.
Amstutz, Galen 49, 82 n.
Andreasen, Esben 49 n., 54 n.
Arnold, Sir Edwin 72

Barnett, Paul 200 n.
Barth, Karl 55 n.
Batchelor, Stephen xiv, 111 n.
Bauckham, Richard 200 n., 202, 209 n.
Baumann, Martin x n., 70, 71 n., 75
Bentley, Jerry H. 33
Bloom, Alfred 49, 50 n., 53, 54
Borowitz, Eugene 102
Brown, Colin 200 n.
Buddhaghosa 29
Buddhism
    And reason 17–18, 61–2
    Appearance/reality 128–31, 166–74
    Arahat 29, 40–41
    Bodhisattva 40–42, 160
    Buddha nature 47–9
    Dependent co-origination 44, 99–100, 116, 124–9, 131–6, 152
    Emptiness 42–6, 96, 99, 196
    Enlightenment 12–13, 18, 56, 58, 61–2, 89–92, 110, 115, 119, 136, 141–4, 145, 153–7, 209–10
    Four Noble Truths 15–17, 28, 57, 117, 161–3
    Impermanence 18–19, 116, 121–8
    In the West x–xii, 69–103
    Karma 18–22, 117–21, 131–4, 148–52

Buddhism (cont.)
    Madhyamaka 145, 157–66
    Mahayana 31, 33–62, 112, 157, 159
    Nirvana 13, 22–6, 40, 45, 57, 115, 141–4, 158, 159–60, 173, 179
    No-Self xiii, 18–22, 120–28, 136–40, 148–57, 172
    Pudgalavadins (Personalists) 130–31, 145, 147–7
    Pure Land 49–56
    Rebirth 18–22, 117–21, 148–53
    Reductionism 166–74
    Theravada 26–32, 34, 40–41
    Tibetan 64–7
    Two levels of truth 45–6, 171
    Vajrayana 62–4
    Zen 56–62, 77, 79, 82, 83–103
Buruma, Ian 83 n.

Cabezón, José 184, 193–4
Cage, Wendy x n., 75
Carrithers, Michael 15 n., 16
Carter, Robert E. 90 n.
Carus, Paul 86, 87, 92
Ch'en, Kenneth K.S. 36 n., 51 n., 58, 59 n.
Christian, William A. xv
Clarke, J.J. 71 n.
Cobb, John B., Jr. xii n., 101 n.
Coleman, James William x n., 70 n.
Collins, Steven 120 n.
Confuciansim xviii, 35–6
Conze, Edward 11 n., 24 n., 41 n., 124 n., 148 n.

Cox, Harvey ix, x n., 77 n.
Christian gospel 177–81
Crisp, Oliver 204

Dallmayr, Fred 81 n.
Daoism xviii, 35–7, 59
Davis, Stephen T. 191 n. , 199 n., 204 n.
DeBary, William Theodore 41 n., 210 n.
Denny, Frederick 28 n.
Dharmasiri, Gunapala 183 n.
Dobbins, James C. 49 n.
Dumoulin, Heinrich 56 n., 57 n., 58 n.,
   59, 60 n., 61 n., 88 n., 89 n., 91

Eck, Diana xi n.
Ellwood, Robert S. 77 n.
Evans, C. Stephen 200 n.
Evans, Craig 200 n.

Fader, Larry A. 88 n.
Faure, Bernard 86 n., 90 n., 91 n., 92 n.,
   95 n.
Fields, Rick 70 n.
Fox, Richard G. 81 n.
Franck, Frederick 90 n.
Frykenberg, Robert Eric 82 n.

Gathercole, Simon 204 n.
Garfield, Jay L. 43 n., 46
Gautama, the Buddha xii, 1, 9–14, 28,
   31–2, 40, 47, 56–7,175–6, 192–212
Gimello, Robert 116
God
   Buddhism and xii-xiii, 29–30, 99–100,
      127–8, 139, 181–90, 196
   Christianity and xiii, 181, 191–2, 202,
      203–9
Gomez, Luis 2 n.
Green, J. B. 201 n.
Griffiths, Paul J. xvii n., 47 n., 107 n., 109
   n., 135, 140 n., 174

Harris, Murray J. 204 n.
Harvey, Peter 99
Heelas, Paul xi n.
Hiebert, Paul G. xiv
Heine, Steven x n.
Heisig, James W. 86 n.

Hengel, Martin 208 n.
Herman, A.L. 183 n., 186 n.
Hick, John 206–7
Hinduism xviii, 2–9, 34, 81–2, 108, 127,
   146–7, 149, 157, 161
   Brahman 3–4
   Karma 4–8, 119
   Reincarnation 4–8, 119, 146–7
   Moksha 7
Hirakawa, Akira 5, 10, 21 n., 26 n., 28 n.
Hisamatsu, Shin'ichi 92
Holocaust 101–3
Honen 52–4
Hopkins, Thomas J. 4 n.
Hori, G. Victor Sogen 79
Howard-Snyder, Daniel 186 n.
Hubbard, Jamie 48 n., 88 n., 91 n.
Hurtado, Larry 208–9

Ineffability 142–3, 161–6
Ingram, Paul O. xii n., 99 n.
Ishihara, John 56 n.
Ives, Christopher 90 n., 97 n., 101 n.

Jackson, Carl T. 72
Jainism xviii, 5, 7, 82, 108, 119, 127, 146,
   149, 157, 173
Jayatilleke, K.N. 2, 9, 17, 18 n., 30, 32,
   107 n., 116, 117, 183, 185 n.
Jenkins, Philip x
Jesus Christ xii-xiii, 107, 110, 175–8,
   192–212
Johnson, Willard L. 10, 15 n., 23 n., 27 n.,
   34 n., 38 n., 130 n., 147 n., 167 n.
Johnston, William xii n.
Jones, Elving 109 n.
Juergensmeyer, Mark x, 69

Kalupahana, David 2 n., 9, 43 n., 92 n.,
   99, 142 n.
Kärkkäinen, Veli-Matti 107 n.
Kasulis, Thomas 36 n., 90 n.
Katz, Steven T. 116 n.
Keown, Damien 99 n.
Kiblinger, Kristin Beise 107 n.
King, Richard 2 n., 18, 19, 43 n., 80 n.,
   108 n., 112 n.
King, Sallie B. 78 n.

Kitagawa, Joseph M. 2, 38, 72 n.
Kirita, Kiyohide 97 n., 98
Knitter, Paul 107 n.
Koller, John M. 42 n., 115 n., 125 n., 160 n.
Koller, Patricia 42 n., 115 n., 125 n., 160 n.
Kopf, David 81 n.
Kvaerne, Per 64 n.

LaFleur, William R. 96 n.
Lai, Whalen 39 n., 197 n.
Lancaster, Lewis R. 28 n.
Lavine, Amy 78 n.
Learman, Linda 33, 70 n.
Lopez, Donald S. 15 n., 20 n., 21 n., 24, 63 n., 85 n., 196 n.

Mackenzie, Vicki xi, 111 n.
Mahoney, William K. 4 n.
Maraldo, John C. 86 n., 97 n.
Margolit, Arvid 83 n.
Martin, Nancy M. 100
McMahan, David 83, 84, 86 n., 92, 93 n.
Mellor, Philip A. 81 n.
Mitchell, Donald W. 7, 10 n., 13 n., 14, 15 n., 19, 23 n., 24 n., 26 n., 29 n., 39 n., 45, 46 n., 47 n., 48 n., 50 n., 63, 66 n., 67 n., 96 n., 124 n., 166 n., 167 n.
Moore, Charles A. 3, 159 n.
Morris, T.V. 204 n.
Moule, C.F.D. 207, 208 n.
Müller, Max 71, 108 n.
Murakami, Sensho 197

Nagarjuna 42–6, 98, 157, 188, 190
Nakamura, Hajime 10, 11 n., 17, 22 n., 69, 70 n., 81 n.
Neill, Stephen 176
Netland, Harold 107 n.
Niebuhr, Reinhold 96
Nishida, Kitaro 86, 90, 96, 97

O'Flaherty, Wendy Doniger 3, 9
Orientalism 80–83
Overmyer, Daniel L. 35 n. 37

Parrinder, Geoffrey 147 n.
Payne, Richard K. 49 n.
Peterson, Michael L. xvi
Plantinga, Alvin 186 n.
Plantinga, Cornelius 180 n.
Prebish, Charles S. x n., 70 n.
Porterfield, Amanda x n., 77 n.
Prothero, Stephen 77 n.

Queen, Christopher S. 78 n.

Radhakrishnan, Sarvepalli 3, 146, 159 n.
Rahula, Walpola 15 n., 16 n., 17, 20 n., 25, 30, 31, 32, 114, 142 n., 184, 203 n., 210
Ray, Reginald A. 28 n., 39 n.
Reader, Ian 38 n.
Reat, Noble Ross 8
Reichenbach, Bruce R. 118 n.
Religion
   Religious exclusivism 106–11
   Dimensions of xiv-xv
   Interreligious polemics xvii-xviii
   Religious beliefs xiii-xvi, 109–17, 131, 161–3
   Truth 111–17, 162
Rhys Davids, Thomas W. 14 n., 71
Robbins, Bruce 81 n.
Robinson, Richard H. 10, 15 n., 23 n., 27 n., 34 n., 38 n., 130 n., 147 n., 167 n.
Roof, Wade Clark xi n.
Runzo, Joseph 100

Said, Edward 80, 81
Schell, Orville 78 n.
Schepers, Gerhard 56 n.
Seager, Richard Hughes x n., xi, 70 n., 72 n., 73, 74 n., 75, 76, 78
Seiko, Hirata 97 n.
Sharma, Arvind 183 n.
Shaner, David Edward 10 n.
Shankara xviii, 108
Sharf, Robert H. 85 n., 86 n., 90 n., 92 n., 93, 94 n., 95
Shaw, R. Daniel xiv
Shinran 52–5

Shintoism xviii, 37–8
Siderits, Mark 167 n.
Smart, Ninian xiv, xv, 2, 195 n.
Smith, David 81 n., 82 n.
Snellgrove, David 65 n.
Snodgrass, Judith 73 n.
Soen, Shaku 73, 74 n., 86, 87
Sopa, Geshe 109 n.
Stackhouse, John Jr. 186 n.
Streng, Frederick J. xii n., 43 n., 99 n.
Strong, John S. 23 n., 24 n.
Suzuki, D.T. 57, 60 n., 61, 62, 70, 73, 74,
    79, 83–97, 192, 193 n.
Swanson, Paul L. 48 n., 88 n., 91 n.
Swinburne, Richard 186 n., 191 n., 199 n.

Tachibana, Shundo 99
Tanaka, Kenneth K. 49 n.
Taylor, Rodney L. 28 n., 70 n.
The Dalai Lama (Tenzin Gyatso) 66–7,
    78, 109, 183, 184 n., 193
Thelle, Notto 74, 197 n.
Thittila, U. 27 n., 29 n., 30, 31
Thurston, Bonnie 211
Tiénou, Tite xiv
Tillich, Paul 96, 102, 197
Tweed, Thomas 75, 77 n., 88 n.

Ui, Hakuju 10

VanArragon, Raymond xvi
Van Bragt, Jan 50 n., 55 n., 97 n.
Vasubandhu 148, 166 n.
Verhoeven, Martin J. 86 n., 87 n.
Viswanathan, Gauri 81 n.

Watts, Alan 77 n.
Williams, Paul 27 n., 34 n., 39 n., 42, 43
    n., 44, 47, 50 n., 51 n., 52 n., 55 n., 64
    n., 112 n., 128 n., 181, 183, 184 n., 188
    n., 191, 192
Witherington, Ben 200 n., 204 n.
Wood, Robert W. 103 n., 198 n.
Wood, Thomas E. 141 n.
Woodhead, Linda xi n.
World's Parliament of Religions 72–5
Wright Christopher J. H. 205
Wright, N.T. 199 n. , 200 n.
Wuthnow, Robert x n., 75

Yandell, Keith xvi, 191 n
Young, Richard Fox xviii, 186 n.
Yusa, Michiko 90 n.

Ziolkowski, Eric J. 72 n.,